D1603804

Ancient Symbology
in Fantasy Literature

ALSO BY WILLIAM INDICK

The Psychology of the Western: How the American Psyche Plays Out on Screen (McFarland, 2008)

Psycho Thrillers: Cinematic Explorations of the Mysteries of the Mind (McFarland, 2006)

Movies and the Mind: Theories of the Great Psychoanalysts Applied to Film (McFarland, 2004)

Ancient Symbology in Fantasy Literature

A Psychological Study

WILLIAM INDICK

McFarland & Company, Inc., Publishers

Jefferson, North Carolina, and London

Library of Congress Cataloguing-in-Publication Data

Indick, William, 1971–
    Ancient symbology in fantasy literature : a psychological
study / William Indick.
        p.   cm.
    Includes bibliographical references and index.

    ISBN 978-0-7864-6039-7
    softcover : acid free paper ♾

    1. Fantasy literature — Psychological aspects.   2. Symbolism
in literature.   3 Literature and myth.   4. Fantastic, The, in
literature.   I. Title.
    PN56.F34I49 2012
    809'.915 — dc23   2012016186

British Library cataloguing data are available

Front cover image: *The Lord of the Rings: The Fellowship of the Ring*,
2001 (New Line Cinema/Photofest).

Manufactured in the United States of America

*McFarland & Company, Inc., Publishers
    Box 611, Jefferson, North Carolina 28640
    www.mcfarlandpub.com*

For Casey

Table of Contents

Acknowledgments

I would like to thank the faculty, students, and administration of Dowling College in Oakdale, New York, for their continued support of my research and writing projects.

Preface

What do we think about when we think about fantasy? Magic and magical creatures, wizards and witches, giants and monsters, haunted forests and mythical worlds ... all of these archetypal figures and themes give shape to the world of fantasy, but what, if anything, do they mean? Psychology, in its eternal search for deeper meaning within all forms of human behavior, has maintained a long and enduring fascination in the common symbols found throughout fantasy literature. Marie von Franz, the famous Jungian psychologist and scholar, asserted that "fantasy is not just whimsical ego-nonsense, but comes really from the depths; it constellates symbolic situations which give life a deeper meaning and a deeper realization."[1] Jungian psychology understands dreams as unconscious fantasies that shed light on the inner world of the dreamer. Similarly, fantasy is a sort of dream — an expression of a parallel reality, an alternative consciousness — which can be explored and interpreted in much the same way that both nighttime dreams and conscious daydreams are studied by psychoanalysts.

The symbols seen throughout fantasy literature were not born independently. All fantasy has its roots in ancient mythology. J.R.R. Tolkien, for example, created a unique mythology for the English. His inspiration for "Middle Earth" was taken from the themes and figures of the ancient Norse, Celtic, Finnish, and German mythologies. Similarly, C.S. Lewis created the fantasy realm of "Narnia" with the legendary creatures of classical Greek mythology in mind, while also infusing the chivalry and gallantry of the Arthurian romances into his human characters, and overarching all of it with the faith-and-virtue symbolism of the Judeo-Christian tradition. Lloyd Alexander's "Prydain," on the other hand, is derived rather directly from the ancient Welsh mythological tales recorded in the *Mabinogion*. And the wizarding world of J.K. Rowling's *Harry Potter* books are filled from cover to cover with magical beings and mythical creatures gleaned from millennia of European mythology,

1

folk legend, and fairytale. Ancient myths are the blueprints of modern fantasy. The symbols of the genre cannot be properly understood without reference to the archetypes established in ancient mythology.

In turn, the folktales, nursery tales, and fairytales of the European Middle Ages that, to a large degree, serve as a bridge between classical mythology and contemporary fantasy, not only conveyed the ancient symbols into modern times, but also added to and embellished them. While psychologists such as Freud, Jung, and Rank (to name a few) have long mined the treasuries of classical mythology and fairytales for psychologically relevant symbols, few have taken the time to explore the modern myths — contemporary fantasy literature — nor has there been much effort to understand the psychological symbolism of modern fantasy in reference to the myths and fairytales that informed them. Furthermore, while psychologists such as Erich Fromm, Marie-Louise von Franz, and Bruno Bettelheim have analyzed fairytales for deeper psychological meaning, few psychologists have made equivalent studies of the fairytale elements found in contemporary fantasy literature.

The purpose of this book is to explore the modern dreamscape of contemporary fantasy, using the maps of ancient myths and traditional fairytales as guides, and shedding the light of psychological insight onto every symbolic figure and theme that we pass along the way. Chapters are dedicated to all of the significant archetypes that inhabit the world of modern fantasy. Heroes and princesses, fairy godmothers and evil witches, wizards and dark lords, magic and magical beasts are all explored in reference to the myths and fairytales that gave birth to them. The analyses and interpretations are informed by the classic psychoanalytic studies of scholars such as Sigmund Freud, Carl Jung, Otto Rank, Marie-Louise von Frank, Bruno Bettelheim, and others. The fantasy literature studied in this book include the most popular and influential works in the genre — the novels of J.R.R. Tolkien, C.S. Lewis, J.K. Rowling, Lloyd Alexander, and others — will all be explored.

In his seminal psychoanalytic study of fairytales, Bruno Bettelheim noted that "in Hindu medicine ... the mentally deranged person is told a fairy story, contemplation of which will help him overcome his emotional disturbance."[2] Mythmakers, fairytale tellers, and fantasists are essentially the same, all weaving worlds of wonder and glory that inspire their audiences with tales of heroic deeds and mystical encounters. The reason why their stories, all filled with somewhat similar narratives and analogous figures, have endured for as long as human history can recall, is that they serve a common function. There is a psychologically curative power of myth that has been sustained in fairytales and fantasy. They communicate on a deep unconscious level, revealing eternal truths that often evade the conscious mind, expressing the anguish of inner conflict in symbolic form. When we peer into the primal imagery of fantasy, we uncover the realities before our eyes that we too often fail to see. We see the things that we always knew, but somehow forgot long ago. We reflect upon sides of ourselves that have been hidden away since the adult forsook the child and grew up, foolishly throwing away his childhood dreams.

Introduction

"Deeper meaning resides in the fairy tales told me in my childhood than in any truth that is taught in life."

Johann Schiller

Carl Jung believed that the mind is always seeking balance. When an imbalance is formed in the mind by anxiety or neurotic conflict, the mind will either consciously or unconsciously try to regain a sense of equilibrium by creating a counterforce to this source of the imbalance. This concept, referred to by Jung as "enantiodromia," is a foundational principle in his theory of archetypes.[1] For example, an individual so wrapped up in his public "persona" that he completely represses all his wishes, desires, and fears, will be haunted in his dreams and fantasies by his own "shadow," an unconscious archetype that symbolically represents the hidden and unexpressed elements of the self. If we apply the same mode of analysis to fantasy literature, we immediately observe an abundance of enantiodromic dualities in the archetypal figures of the genre. Every meek and passive princess is eventually rescued by a strong and forceful prince. If the princess is held captive by a menacing evil stepmother, she is frequently aided by a nurturing fairy godmother. If the prince is thwarted by a dark lord, he is invariably mentored by a kind and sagely wizard. In fantasy, each dark force is countered unerringly by a parallel force of light. Each weak thing meets its source of power, and each primal fear encountered is met by a rejuvenating promise of faith and hope.

When we explore the esoteric realms of fairytale, myth, and fantasy, we analyze the archetypal dualities within the unconscious mind. Just as fantasy literature tends to appeal to the young reader, the dualities within fantasy are particularly relevant to the young person's struggles in life. Real mothers, for instance, are seldom purely evil, nor are they unconditionally good. Mother figures in fantasy, however, are typically either wholly wicked or entirely good. The

5

psychological process of dividing one's associations with a real attachment figure into two fantasy figures is known as "splitting." The real parent, who is at once good and bad, can be more easily dealt with in the child's fantasies by splitting the parent into two contrasting figures. As Bettelheim noted: "The fantasy of the wicked stepmother not only preserves the good mother intact, it also prevents having to feel guilty about one's angry thoughts and wishes about her — a guilt which would seriously interfere with the good relation to Mother."[2]

Each chapter in this book addresses the psychological functions associated with common symbols found in fantasy literature. The first two chapters review the psychological approaches to myth and fairytale. The middle chapters focus on the archetypal dualities: feminine and masculine representations of the self, good and evil mother figures, good and evil father figures, and the dualistic nature of Man itself (i.e., civilized man and savage beast). Chapter Eight studies the representation of magic in fantasy literature, and the last chapter employs Julian Jaynes' theory of bicameralism as an alternate approach to psychoanalysis in the psychological study of fantasy literature.

In Chapter One, "Myth and Fantasy," the significance of myth and ritual in the formation of cultural and individual identity is examined. A discussion of the historical origins of myth leads into the notion that myths fulfill specific psychological functions in the individual and within society, such as imparting a sense of personal identity, transmitting moral and cultural values, as well as affording a collective sense of community to a culture or nation.[3] The archetypal themes of myth, whether absorbed passively as a reader/listener or engaged in actively as a participant in a ritual, function almost entirely at a symbolic level. The ancient symbols found within myth and ritual contain the essence of the myth's transcendent power, and it is these symbols that have been retained in medieval fairytale and contemporary fantasy. Consequently, the significance of an archetypal theme remains constant, regardless of whether it is experienced as a ritual reenactment of a living myth (such as reading from the Torah at a Bar Mitzvah ceremony), or as a tale within a mythological legend (such as Arthur drawing Excalibur from the stone), or as a chapter in a modern fantasy novel (such as Harry Potter's experience of wearing the Sorting Hat at the Hogwarts School of Witchcraft and Wizardry). In each instance, a young man experiences a transforming rite of passage, elevating him from a state of childhood and initiating him into a new and more mature status within the community. The transcendent power of myth is maintained within its symbols. This power, experienced directly as a transforming force in traditional rites of passage, is also experienced vicariously by the modern fantasy reader, who identifies with the hero as he is initiated into the realm of adventure.

The ethereal imagery of the fairytale setting is investigated in Chapter Two, "The Realm of Faërie." Fairytales typically take place in dark primeval forests, mysterious unnamed kingdoms, and cryptic underworlds. Time is equally vague in fairytales. All we know is that the tale occurred a long time ago. Bettelheim explained that the deliberate vagueness of the fairytale setting imparts the sense that we are leaving the realm of ordinary reality and entering the realm of fantasy, where anything can happen. We are descending from the conscious to the unconscious parts of the mind. The vague setting "Once upon a time" gives us the sense that we are dealing with "the most archaic events," issues that are as old as humanity itself, and issues that recall our earliest memories and fears.[4] It is also clear that the symbols and themes in fairytales are remnants of the pagan belief systems that preceded the ascent of Judeo-Christianity in Near Eastern and European cultures.[5] The preponderance of enchantments, witches, ogres, spirits, and giants in fairytales reveals a contemporary desire to reconnect with the fabled marvels of the primeval world; just as the mythical themes in fantasy literature reveal a contemporary desire to escape the modern world of logic and reason in favor of a world filled with magic and wonder. The realm of Faërie represents a desire to experience the world when it was still as young and innocent as a little child. When the fantasy reader enters this world, he reacquaints himself with his own inner child, and once again believes in the transformative power of magic.

Chapters Three and Four, "The Hero" and "The Princess," respectively, focus on the essential dualities of budding masculinity and femininity as represented in the most typical protagonists in myth, fairytale, and fantasy literature. The hero and princess symbolize, respectively, the boy becoming the man and the girl becoming the woman. Their particular journeys through adolescent maturation and cultural initiation express issues that are relevant to every young person. The hero's adventure requires the accomplishment of certain ritualistic tasks that demonstrate his worthiness and merit. This hero is innately greater than other humans, but he uses his super powers to help his community, and ultimately sacrifices himself for the greater good of his society. Heroes represent the very best in humanity, the part of our selves that transcends our mortality and links us with the divine.

Princesses in myth, such as the infamous Helen of Troy, are oftentimes the incarnation of temptation and desire, impulses that the hero must either yield to or overcome. In fairytale and fantasy, the princess or heroine is all too often a victim of temptation herself. The salacious wolf in "Little Red Riding Hood," the forbidden room in "Bluebeard," the solicitous frog in "The Frog King," all represent prohibitive taboos that the girl must foreswear. If she gives in to her temptation, she falls victim to the primal beastly forces that are released. In this sense, the princess in fairytales is facing a fear of sexual maturation, a process that has much more visceral implications than it does for boys. Only girls must await with dread the first monthly appearance of menstrual blood, accompanied by aches and pains and repulsion. Only girls foresee the first experience of coitus as a painful act, also accompanied by blood and, if committed hastily or unwillingly, fear and guilt. And only girls envisage with dubious anticipation the fruition of sexual maturation — pregnancy and childbirth — which of course are accompanied by what might seem to a young girl to be rivers of blood and mountains of agonizing pain. The symbols of temptation and "menses anxiety," established in myth and fairytale, reappear in modern fantasy as abstract images and artifacts. The moment at which the pubescent girl's biological clock reaches the critical hour of menarche is often represented in fairytale and fantasy as either a threat of death or a curse resulting in a "sleeping death." The hourglass in the film version of *The Wizard of Oz*, for instance, is filled with red sand. The wicked witch's curse decrees that when the final grain of sand falls, Dorothy will die. The girl's fear of passing time represents the anxiety she has over getting older, as the death of childhood is feared by the child as much as real death, while the hope of rebirth into a new and mature form is also simultaneously anticipated, though with much apprehension. The mortally cursed hourglass filled with blood colored sand is a particularly apt symbol for menses anxiety, for as Rollo May pointed out, "Menstruation, indeed, is named time, *menses* being the Latin word for 'months.' In our vernacular we refer to menstruation also in terms of time, one's period."[6]

Chapter Five, "The Goddess and the Witch," focuses on the mother archetype, split in two. Her positive image represents the caring aspect of mother, the mother who gives birth, nurtures, loves, and heals. In myth she is the Earth Goddess, the spirit of fertility, Mother Nature. In fairytales she is the fairy godmother, oftentimes only present in spirit and represented symbolically as a bird or a tree. In fantasy, the mother is often an absent figure, such as the mother of the Pevensie children in *The Lion, the Witch, and the Wardrobe*. Harry Potter's mother, Lilith, is dead. Nevertheless, these mothers are still present in spirit, and as such play important roles in the adventures of their children. Little is mentioned of Frodo's mother in *The Lord of the Rings*. However, at a time of great need, he encounters an elven queen who epitomizes the mythological archetype of the wise and powerful Earth Goddess, Galadriel, the Lady of the Wood.

The shadow mother in myth is represented as a sorceress of death and destruction. Like Medea from Greek mythology, she is jealous, vain, and possessive. When scorned she becomes wrathful, ferocious, and sadistic. In contrast to the good mother, she curses rather than blesses, destroys rather than creates. Instead of healing, she wounds. Instead of nurturing she thwarts. And instead of nourishing, she devours. Wicked witches and evil stepmothers in fairytale and fantasy depart very little from the mythological model. Queen Jadis, the White Witch of Narnia, is a prototypical example of this archetype. In defeating the witch, the child hero overcomes the negative aspect of mother, achieving an epic victory in the fantasy world, while also allowing the young reader to conquer an inner demon in the real world.

In Chapter Six, "The Wizard and the Dark Lord," the opposing aspects of the father archetype are analyzed. Joseph Campbell notes of the mythological hero: "the first encounter of the hero-journey is with a protective figure (often a little old crone or old man) who provides the adventurer with amulets against the dragon forces he is about to pass."[7] Significantly, the wizard character who plays this paternal role to the hero is *not* his father. The hero's real father is typically deceased. The wizard's charge is to fill for a time this vacant role of father, and to instruct and empower the hero in the ways of magic. As he does so, he often teaches the hero about his real father, the knowledge of whom is crucial, as it is the key to the hero's true identity. Dumbledore, for example, the sage old wizard in the Harry Potter series, plays the roles of mentor, teacher, protector, and guide to young Harry. He is Harry's father in every sense of the word — except for the biological one. Furthermore, he represents the ideal image of what any young wizard would want in a father figure. Professor Dumbledore is kind, gentle, patient, and he is the wisest and most powerful of all wizards. Of course, Harry needs the greatest wizard on his side, as his enemy is none other than the darkest and most evil wizard in the world, the Dark Lord, Voldemort.

Images of the shadow element of the father archetype are ubiquitous in fantasy literature. Lord Voldemort in *Harry Potter*, The Dark Lord, Sauron, in *The Lord of the Rings*, the Death Lord, Arawn, in *The Chronicles of Prydain*, are just a few examples. Like his female counterpart, the Death Witch, the Shadow Lord is the object of all of the hostile and aggressive impulses projected towards the father. He embodies every negative and unacceptable emotion within the hero, and also within the reader who identifies with the hero. Sometimes the Shadow Lord is the hero's actual father, such as in the *Star Wars* films and books; but even when the plot is not so directly evocative of the underlying symbolism, the quest of the fantasy hero always involves the task of encountering the Shadow Lord and in some way integrating him into his consciousness. Just as the external quest of the hero is not complete until the forces of darkness are destroyed, so too is the internal quest of the reader not complete until all of the unconscious fears, unfulfilled wishes, and repressed impulses — no matter how dark — are somehow acknowledged.

The focus of Chapter Seven, "Man and Beast," is on how the dual nature of humankind is represented by animalistic figures in myth, fairytale, and fantasy. Beginning with Freud's interpretation of the seminal influence of totemism on the archaic human psyche,[8] we see that the practice of worshipping and identifying with animal spirits that was typical of primitive human societies is still alive today in the world of fantasy. For example, in *Harry Potter*, each house in the Hogwarts school has its own totem animal — a snake for Slytherin, a lion for Gryffindor, etc. Each animal embodies the spirit and character of its respective house. Furthermore, every witch and wizard has his own particular animal spirit called a "Patronus." In times of distress, the wizard can call on and even materialize his inner Patronus and use it in battle. In Pullman's *His Dark Materials* trilogy, every main character has an animal spirit called a "dæmon," which is an outward projection of his or her internal identity. The dæmon is a physical being. It stays close to its human host at all times, and changes in form as the character grows and develops.

Fantasy literature is rife with miraculous beasts and mythical creatures of infinite variety and form. The archetype of the man-beast, creatures that are half human and half animal, arose from the ancient rituals and beliefs of totemism, as Campbell explains:

> For the primitive hunting peoples of those remotest human millennia when the sabertooth tiger, the mammoth, and the lesser presences of the animal kingdom were the primary manifestations of what was alien — the source at once of danger, and of sustenance — the great human problem was to be linked psychologically to the task of sharing the wilderness with these beings. An unconscious identification took place, and this was finally rendered conscious in the half-human, half-animal figures of the mythological totem-ancestors.[9]

From here comes the root of mythical creatures such as the centaur, minotaur, and satyr, which reappear in modern fantasy literature such as the Narnia books and the Harry Potter series. While the man-beast is sometimes representative of the atavistic traits of primitive man, he is also a link to the esoteric lost wisdom of the ancients. On the other hand, the figure of the therianthrope — the being that transfigures from a human into a savage animal — is more directly symbolic of the gossamer boundary between civilized humans and wild beast. Werewolves and other shapeshifters are ubiquitous figures in modern fantasy, as is the common theme of transfiguration, which represents both the regenerative quality of the human spirit, and the tendency to regress to our more primal natures.

Another archetype, the "Man of Nature," embodies the post-modern age desire to reconnect with nature and lead a more eco-friendly existence. Based in equal parts on the Biblical figure of Noah and the Greek god/hero, Deucalion, he is depicted as the character of Medwyn in Lloyd Alexander's *The Book of Three*, as the Hermit of the Southern March in C.S. Lewis' *The Horse and His Boy*, and as Beorn, the bear-man, in Tolkien's *The Hobbit*. In each instance, the Man of Nature represents a state of unity with nature and therefore a status of unity within the self. In a mythological sense, he suggests a state of atonement with the primal or natural state of order which man (Adam) enjoyed briefly in his primary state (Eden) before the Fall. As an archetype, he can be considered a male counterpart to the female Earth Goddess or Mother Nature.

Fantasy and fairytales exist in what psychologists refer to as an "animistic" mode of perception, a viewpoint in which everything around us is alive and has a spirit or life force. Animals, plants, and even inanimate objects all have a sense of consciousness. For this reason, it is quite unsurprising when a bear, a bird, or even a tree or a hat speaks. This form of perception exists as a primary mode in early childhood, and many anthropologists and psychologists believe that it was also a primary mode of perception in primitive peoples and cultures. Hence, in fantasy, we have a world where animals often have the same traits and abilities as humans. Tolkien noted that "this marvel derives from one of the primal 'desires' that lie near the heart of Faërie: the desire of men to hold communion with other living things."[10] Talking animals in fantasy usually have some generalized qualities. Bears, for instance, in C.S. Lewis' Narnia and Pullman's Svalbard, are a bit slow; but typically, they are kind and gentle, unless provoked, at which times they become ferocious and fearsome — much like a sleepy father. Frogs, in their ability to completely metamorphosize, represent the biological changes of life at puberty, which often appear gross and repugnant to the developing youngster. Dogs, wolves, giant birds, horses, apes, and other animals all represent different aspects of humanity in fantasy literature.

Dwarves and giants, omnipresent in fairytale and fantasy, respectively represent the child's favorable reflection upon himself and his unfavorable projection of childish qualities onto adults. This is why dwarves, though small, tend to be wiser and more robust than their taller companions, while giants, though huge, tend to be foolish and more vulnerable than the smaller folk. "Fell" creatures also abound in fantasy, embodying the corrupt and vile aspects of humanity. Dragons, who demand the sacrifice of virgins and a bounty of gold, despite the fact that they have no use for either, represent the all-too-human vice of greed, which drives men to desire, as dragons devour much more than what they actually need. Orcs and goblins, in their drive to create machines that plunder the earth, represent the ironically self-defeating will to power. In search of power, they build machines to enslave the earth; but in their blind and single-minded toil, they succeed only in enslaving themselves, and become the unthinking servants of the Dark Lord. Monsters, giant spiders, and serpents evoke both the primeval fears of archaic man and the nightmarish terrors of early childhood. And ghosts, demons, and undead spirits represent the gone but not forgotten figures of our past, the memories and repressed conflicts of childhood that we must reencounter before we can move forward freely into the future.

Chapter Eight is devoted to the analysis of Magic, the definitive literary device within the fantasy genre. On a psychological level, Magic — as opposed to Logic — signifies a psychic duality. In fantasy, the protagonist's reliance on magic represents an opposing function to the principles of reality in the real world, which operate primarily according to the standards of reason and logic. As such, the predominance of magic in fantasy signifies a host of significant issues in the young reader's mind. On a simple level, the child longs to escape or avoid the adult's world of reality in favor of the child's world of fantasy. There is also the conflict between faith and reason, as well as the conflicting pressures of maturation and the desire to maintain one's childish innocence.

The archetypal magical beliefs and practices, descended from the rituals and myths of primitive societies, are recapitulated in fairytale and fantasy in ways that naturally resonate in the imagination of the child's mind, which is guided by the more "primitive" animistic mode of perception. So, the powers of magic exist in the fantasy world without question, as long as the rules of magic (as they are defined in the fantasy world itself) are not betrayed. The principle of "sympathetic magic," according to Frazer's explanation of primitive magical beliefs, assumes that "things act on each other at a distance through a secret sympathy, the impulse being transmitted from one to the other by means of what we may conceive as a kind of invisible ether."[11] This "invisible ether" is later referred to by Frazer as "mana," which is a primal essence — a universal source of magical power that can be tapped into. In fantasy, magical beings such as fairies and elves are organically connected with this magical force, just as the spirits and demons in primitive belief systems are preternaturally infused with "mana." Humanlike figures such as wizards, witches, sorcerers, and the like are in touch with the forces of magic, but more indirectly. They must either conjure the spirits to perform magic for them, or use spells, curses, charms, enchantments, or magical objects to elicit the desired magical result. In the category of magical objects, there are many to be explored — magic swords, wands, rings, crystal balls, flying brooms, and precious gems all have their own legacy in myth, ritual, fairytale, and fantasy.

In addition, the practitioner of magic has many other tools at his command, such as the brewing of magical potions, the playing of magical music, the invocation of magical names, and the configuration of magical numbers. All of these elements of magic in fantasy literature are explored in Chapter Eight.

Chapter Nine will digress somewhat from the psychoanalytic/psycho-mythological perspective of this book, in which figures and themes in fantasy literature are interpreted as symbols of unconscious issues. Julian Jaynes' theory of bicameralism will be introduced as an alternative lens through which to understand the origin of the archetypes discussed in this book. In his theory, Jaynes posited that prior to the advent of formal conscious thought in humans, the cognitive functions of abstract reasoning and self reflection were unconscious processes.[12] In times of stress or distress, especially when an important decision needed to be made, the unconscious mind would communicate its abstract messages in the form of a voice or vision, which would take the form of an auditory or visual hallucination. Is it possible that these "bicameral" hallucinatory images and ideas, which emerged in the primitive mentalities of Stone Age humans, may be the origin of the archetypal figures and themes that have been with us through the ages? Chapter Nine will explore this possibility, focusing especially on the area of dream imagery — a state of unconsciousness marked by abstract reflection and image creation — not unlike the "bicameral" mentality suggested by Jaynes.

The Conclusion of this book will address the dangers of "mythoclasm" — what happens to a culture when it becomes dissociated from its mythological heritage — and the challenges of mythopoeic fantasy — the endeavor of creating a fantasy world based on its own mythology. Jerome Bruner asserted that "when the prevailing myths fail to fit the varieties of man's plight, frustration expresses itself first in mythoclasm and then in the lonely search for internal identity."[13] Ancient myths, legends, folktales, and stories are forgotten because they no longer fulfill the same psychological function that they used to. Mythopoeic fantasy fills this gap by reinventing the old myths. It revives the ancient archetypes and conjures the primal magic in ways that are relevant to the modern reader. Modern fantasy, therefore, performs the same psychological functions of identity formation, cultural identification, and personal catharsis, that are as necessary today as they were in the days when the archetypal images were first dreamed of.

Tolkien used the term "sub-creation" to refer to art in general and to the art of mythopoeic fantasy writing in particular. While the Earth and everything in it was made by the "Creator," we, his creations, were made in his image. Therefore we are creators as well, or "sub-creators," in Tolkien's words. "Fantasy," Tolkien declared, "remains a human right: we make in our measure and in our derivative mode, because we are made: and not only made, but made in the image and likeness of a Maker."[14] So, in essence, the act of mythopoeic fantasy writing is an act of world creation, similar in every way except proportion to the divine act of world creating, in which the "Creator" breathed life into the void through the power of words ... through the power of imagination.

ONE

Myth and Fantasy

"Dream is the personalized myth, myth the depersonalized dream ... in the dream the forms are quirked by the peculiar troubles of the dreamer, whereas in myth the problems and solutions shown are directly valid for all mankind."[1]

While the specific origins of mythology, in all its various forms and cultural manifestations, is a broad and highly debated subject that is well beyond the scope of this chapter, a brief discussion of the topic is necessary prior to a discussion of the psychological function of the archetypes and motifs commonly found in myth. Thomas Bulfinch, who did so much to introduce the figures and themes of classical mythology to American readers, provides an adequate outline of the primary theories of the origins of myth.

The "Scriptural Theory" contends that all mythological legends are derived from narratives of the biblical scriptures, "thus Deucalion is only another name for Noah, Hercules for Samson, Arion for Jonah, etc." Even Bulfinch, as conservative as any other 19th century Christian gentleman, admitted that "the theory cannot without extravagance be pushed so far as to account for any great proportion of the stories." The "Historical Theory," on the other hand, contends that persons mentioned in mythology were once real human beings. Though there may be some accuracy in this assumption, relating to the notion that there is a kernel of truth in every story, no matter how fictitious the story may be, this theory offers no real plausible explanation for the supernatural quality of myth, which is ubiquitous. What of the gods and goddesses, monsters and man-beasts, magic and magical objects, and superhuman feats of the heroes? History cannot fully account for these figures and themes, which are without a doubt some of the most appealing aspects of the myth.

A third approach, the "Physical Theory," is based on the notion that "the elements of air, fire, and water were originally the objects of religious adoration, and the principal deities were personifications of the powers of nature." This theory, indeed, may well explain many of the genesis myths, which seem to be related to the creation and maintenance of the natural universe; but it does nothing to explain the origin of the hero myths, which in frequency of appearance outnumber the genesis myths. Finally, the "Allegorical Theory" contends that the myths contain allegories or symbols that are psychologically relevant to the cultures that created them. Bulfinch diplomatically concluded: "All the theories which have been mentioned are true to a certain extent. It would therefore be more correct to say that the mythology of a nation has sprung from all these sources combined than from any one in particular."[2] For the purposes of this discussion, the Allegorical Theory will be the primary mode of interpretation. The myths provide us with profound symbols that are both culturally relevant and psychologically significant. In attempting to understand the allegorical symbols in myths, we are attempting to understand the minds of the men and women who created and transmitted them, and in a broader sense, we are attempting to understand ourselves.[3]

Rollo May, the renowned psychoanalyst who descried great existential meaning in myth, suggested four primary psychological functions of mythology. First, "myths give us our *sense of personal identity*."[4] In particular, the mythological hero, through the execution of his quest, provides an identification figure for the individual reader. Regardless of the details of his external quest — be it dragon slaying, princess rescuing, grail finding, etc. — the deeds and encounters always represent an internal quest for the identifying reader, who experiences the quest vicariously through the hero. This singular quest, the internal quest, is the search for personal identity.

Secondly, "myths make possible our *sense of community*."[5] The myth, especially when it is believed in religiously and associated with a cultural ritual, provides a common ground within which the people of a shared ancestry or cultural mindset can commune. "Myths are our self-interpretation of our inner selves in relation to the outside world. They are narrations by which our society is unified."[6] And on another level, "*myths undergrid our moral values*."[7] Occasionally, mythological texts actually state moral dictates, such as the chapter in the Bible where the Ten Commandments are enumerated; but more typically, the myth provides a hero who is either rewarded or punished for his behaviors. "We hunger for heroes as role models, as standards of action, as ethics in flesh and bones like our own. *A hero is a myth in action*."[8]

And finally, "mythology is our way of dealing with the inscrutable *mystery of creation*."[9] While historical research can address the questions of when and where we came from, and scientific inquiry can address the questions of how we developed on a physical level and what, theoretically, we are developing into, only mythological thought can address the metaphysical question "Why?" Why do we exist? Why are we here? What happens to us after death? What is the meaning of life? These questions cannot be answered unequivocally because they don't necessarily have answers. And even if answers are provided, they cannot necessarily be proven to be objectively or empirically correct, nor can they be assumed to be acceptable answers for everyone. Nevertheless, they are important questions. Some would assert that they are the most important questions in the world. Only myths aspire to address the ultimate questions of our existence. They provide meaning in an ostensibly meaningless universe, and give substance and form to our deepest doubts and fears. In attempting to answer the seemingly unanswerable questions, myths succeed where science and logic fall short. That is why the myths are eternal.

Myth and Faërie

Though the myth, fairytale, and fantasy story differ in frame and form, they remain similar in function. They are all overflowing with archetypes. As Carl Jung stated:

> Whoever speaks in primordial images speaks with a thousand voices; he enthralls and overpowers, while at the same time he lifts the idea he is seeking into the realm of the ever-enduring... That is the secret of great art, and of its effect upon us. The creative process, so far as we are able to follow it at all, consists in the unconscious activation of an archetypal image, and in elaborating and shaping this image into the finished work. By giving it shape, the artist translates it into the language of the present, and so makes it possible for us to find our way back to the deepest springs of life.[10]

J.R.R. Tolkien, a scholar of myth and folktale in addition to being a universally acknowledged master of modern fantasy, believed that the "nature-myths" and their direct descendants, the hero epics, legends, and sagas, became "localized" in real places and "humanized" by association with ancestral heroes and legendary figures. Thus the basic elements of the "Higher mythology" became, over time, diluted into the "Lower mythology." The folk-tales, fairy-tales, and nursery-tales were derived from the "dwindling down" of the more ancient legends and myths.[11] However, while Tolkien does delineate between a "Higher" and "Lower" mythology, he does not separate them into entirely different traditions. "Speaking of the history of stories and especially fairy-stories we may say that the Pot of Soup, the Cauldron of Story, has always been boiling, and to it have continually been added new bits, dainty and undainty."[12]

Bettelheim, the renowned psychoanalyst, was less definitive in his view of the origin of folktales and fairytales. "In most cultures, there is no clear line separating myth from folk or fairy tale; all these together form the literature of preliterate societies. The Nordic languages have only one word for both: *saga*."[13] Bettelheim also notes that the most significant transformative process in the transmission of archetypal symbols is not the transition from myth to fairytale, but the transition from an oral tradition to a written tradition.

> Myths and fairy tales alike attain a definite form only when they are committed to writing and are no longer subject to continuous change. Before being written down, these stories were either condensed or vastly elaborated in the retelling over the centuries; some stories merged with others. All became modified by what the teller thought was of greatest interest to his listeners, by what his concerns of the moment or the special problems of his era were.[14]

Rollo May contends that the distinction between fairytales and myths is existential.

> *Fairy tales are our myths before we become conscious of ourselves.* Only fairy tales were present in the Garden of Eden before the mythic "fall" of Adam and Eve. The myth, then, adds the existential dimensions to the fairy tale. Myths challenge us to confront our destiny, our death, our love, our joy.[15]

In May's view, the archetypes in fairytale and myth are the same, only the interpretations differ. But how did the archetypal themes found in both myth and fairytales spread from culture to culture? For Tolkien, "the debate between *independent evolution* (or rather *invention*) of the similar; *inheritance* from a common ancestry; and *diffusion* at various times from one or more centuries," is more or less irrelevant.[16] A true understanding of "Faërie" (Tolkien's preferred term for the subject of myth, folktales, and fairytales) is beyond the scope of the literary historian or cultural anthropologist, as the various theories tend to dissect and deconstruct the stories in order to analyze specific themes and artifacts. This method, for Tolkien, is akin to losing sight of the forest for the trees, as the stories need to be appreciated as they are as a whole, rather than in relation to their various parts. "Faërie cannot be caught in a net of words; for it is one of its qualities to be indescribable, though not imperceptible. It has many ingredients, but analysis will not necessarily discover the secret of the whole."[17]

Nevertheless, Tolkien admits that Faërie does offer some specific psychological functions for its readers, similar in scope to May's model of the psychological functions of myth. For Tolkien, "fairy-stories offer also, in a peculiar degree or mode, these things: Fantasy, Recovery, Escape, Consolation, all things of which children have, as a rule, less need than older people."[18] "Fantasy," the primary function of Faërie, offers the reader an entryway into a different world. The real world, so full of unanswerable questions and irresolvable problems, is abandoned for the fantasy world, in which the mysteries of creation are beheld, and the underlying forces of nature are revealed. "Escape" offers the reader relief from a preexisting state of despair, the world of sorrows is left behind in favor of a fantasy world of limitless potential and eternal hope. The escape from reality expresses

> the desire to visit, free as a fish, the deep sea; or the longing for the noiseless, gracious, economical flight of a bird, that longing which the aeroplane cheats... the desire to converse with other living things. On this desire, as ancient as the Fall, is largely founded the talking of beasts and creatures in fairy-tales, and especially the magical understanding of their proper speech... Other creatures are like other realms with which Man has broken off relations, and sees now only from the outside at a distance, being at war with them, or on the terms of an uneasy armistice.[19]

The ultimate mystery of creation, the true nature of mortality, is also addressed in the "Escape." "And lastly there is the oldest and deepest desire, the Great Escape: the Escape from Death."[20]

In Faërie, the reader vicariously experiences the "Recovery" of a simpler time and place, a dimension replete with the more basic truths, "a re-gaining — regaining of a clear view."[21] In that treasured place, "we should meet the centaur and the dragon, and then perhaps suddenly behold, like the ancient shepherds, sheep, and dogs, and horses — and wolves. This recovery fairystories help us to make. In that sense only a taste for them may make us, or keep us, childish."[22]

Wordsworth, in his famous sonnet "The World Is Too Much with Us," expresses a similar yearning for "Recovery":

> Great God, I'd rather be
> A Pagan, suckled in a creed outworn,
> So might I, standing on this pleasant lea,
> Have glimpses that would make me less forlorn;
> Have sight of Proteus rising from the sea,
> And hear old Triton blow his wreathed horn.[23]

"Consolation" offers justice in the form of a reward for the hero, and a comeuppance for the villain. True resolution, which is rarely-if-ever achieved in the real world, is almost always achieved in Faërie, within "the Consolation of the Happy Ending."[24] Bettelheim agrees that the fairytale offers consolation as a happy ending, as opposed to myth, which is typically more tragic and "pessimistic" in nature.[25]

Myth and Archetype

In Joseph Campbell's view, it simply does not matter whether certain literary figures and motifs, which the psychoanalyst refers to as "archetypes," arose from invention, inheritance, or diffusion. The archetypes fulfill a psychological function for both the storyteller and his audience, which is why they were invented, passed down, and dispersed. If they did not serve a function, they would have been abandoned or forgotten long ago.[26] Furthermore, Campbell insists that the primary function of the myth and fairytale is a psychological function.[27]

> Mythology, in other words, is psychology misread as biography, history, and cosmology. The modern psychologist can translate it back to its proper denotations and thus rescue for the contemporary world a rich and eloquent document of the profoundest depths of human character.[28]

Ursula Le Guin, essayist and author of the extremely popular *Earthsea* fantasy novels, contends: "The great fantasies, myths and tales ... speak *from* the unconscious *to* the unconscious, in the *language* of the unconscious — symbol and archetype."[29] The psychoanalytic view posits that the archetypes and motifs spring naturally from the unconscious mind in the form of dream — "the individual myth" — and in the form of myth — "the collective dream".[30] Thus, there is a cyclical nature to the archetypes. They arise in dreams as expressions of individual anxieties and psychological conflicts, and reside in the phantasmagoric part of the psyche called the imagination. They are then expressed by the dreamer through the gateway of imagination in the form of stories and art. This is why, Jung believed, many artists and writers experience the art of creation as a form of catharsis — an outflowing of pre-existing images and ideas from the unconscious — rather than a deliberate or conscious act of invention. The artist doesn't produce an image from scratch, he reproduces an image that emerges spontaneously, preformed, from the recesses of his imagination. Inspiration, like Athena bursting forth, fully formed, from the forehead of Zeus, is the intuitive revelation of an archetype from the unconscious mind. If the revelations of the individual find collective acceptance within that individual's culture, they then become part of the basic elements of that culture's myth and folklore. The images and themes from myth and folktale are then consumed by the children of the culture who created them, becoming archetypes within their own unconscious minds. These same archetypes, molded somewhat by time and culture, are reborn in the dreams and imaginations of the next generation, and are thus transmitted from generation to generation and culture to culture in a never-ending cycle of dreaming and storytelling. Though immaterial, the archetypes themselves are the relics and artifacts of each successive generation of humanity, accompanying the storytellers as they dream up new and more relevant means of expressing the same ideas and images that have been with us forever. The archetypes, perpetually changing yet eternally the same, drive the progression of our imagination into the future while simultaneously linking us to the distant past, retaining in their essence the original dream of the primordial human, who first journeyed into the depths of his own psyche and emerged from the abyss with the symbols of insight and wisdom that have been with us since the dawn of humankind, carried forward by his descendants in an unending chain of fantasy and imagination.

Ritual and Myth

There exists a contrasting though not necessarily conflicting view of the origin of archetypes in myth and folklore. According to this view, elements of prehistoric primitive ritual, passed down through countless generations, became absorbed in the ritual narrative, which is otherwise known as "myth." According to Lord Raglan, myths are narratives associated with specific rites. The myth explains the symbolic significance of the ritual it is associated with, according to the historical, religious, and/or psychological matters that are being addressed. "Living myths" are those narratives that are still linked with their associated rituals, such as the Catholic Communion or the Jewish Passover Seder. "Dead myths" are those narratives that are no longer connected with their associated rituals, such as the myths of Ancient Greece, which Raglan believed were all associated with specific sacrificial polytheistic rites.[31]

By process of dispersion, these essential ideas spread out into a wide panoply of mythological systems. When the ancient rituals died out or were replaced, the myths that were created to accompany them either survived as relics, such as with the Greco-Roman mythology; or in the case of less literate cultures, the essential ideas became recycled as plot elements in folk tales, which are the building blocks of fairytales and fantasy stories. In this way, the reoccurring patterns and ubiquitous figures in ancient myths, folktales, fairytales, and fantasy stories, can be seen as the product of the combined forces of primitive ritual and cultural dispersion. In contrast with psychoanalytic interpretations, the archetypes do not represent universal psychological functions. Rather, they represent primitive beliefs regarding the power of magic and Nature, humanity's relationship with these powers, and the interrelation of humankind and Nature through acts of ritual and sacrifice.

Raglan's narrow view of the origin of myth—that it is nothing more than a narrative associated with a ritual—is highly debatable. Most scholars adopt a more fluid approach to the origin of myth, though the place of ritual in its connection with myth is universally accepted. Rollo May's simple statement, "Myth gives birth to rituals, rituals give birth to myths,"[32] seems to explain the relationship between the two traditions in a way that is suitable enough for a psychologist, if not for a cultural anthropologist. But while Raglan's model and the psychological model diverge on the subject of the origin of the archetypes in myth, the two viewpoints, however, become complementary when they focus on the subject of the hero. The figure of the young person who is forced to leave his or her home, overcome obstacles, and eventually achieve some sort of transformative victory, is by far the most common archetype in both myth and folktale. Raglan asserts that the incidents within the pattern of the hero cycle "fall definitely into three groups: those connected with the hero's birth, those connected with his accession to the throne, and those connected with his death. They thus correspond to the three principal rites de passage—that is to say, the rites at birth, at initiation, and at death."[33]

The advocates of the psychoanalytic model agree with Raglan's main point. The hero myth (and the hero archetype) symbolize the rites of passage that all humans must undergo at different times in life. The hero, specifically, and his story, represent the rites of passage undergone by the adolescent as a process of emerging out of childhood and becoming initiated into the fold of adult society. Campbell states:

> The tribal ceremonies of birth, initiation, marriage, burial, installation, and so forth, serve to translate the individual's life-crises and life-deeds into classic, impersonal forms. They disclose him to himself, not as this personality or that, but as the warrior, the bride, the widow, the priest, the chieftain; at the same time rehearsing for the rest of the community the old lesson of the archetypal stages... Rites of initiation and installation, then, teach the lesson of the essential oneness of the individual and the group....[34]

Campbell believed that the function of the ritual—to unify the individual with the collective—is so important that, if it is not experienced through ritual, the individual will display the neurotic need for initiatory transformation in other ways.

> Apparently, there is something in these initiatory images so necessary to the psyche that if they are not supplied from without, through myth and ritual, they will have to be announced again, through dream, from within—lest our energies should remain locked in a banal, long-outmoded toy-room, at the bottom of the sea.[35]

Bettelheim, in reference to fairytales, reiterates the important link between archetypes and ritual.

> What happens to the heroes and heroines in fairy tales can be likened — and has been compared — to initiation rites which the novice enters naïve and unformed, and which dismiss him at their end on a higher level of existence undreamed of at the start of this sacred voyage through which he gains his reward or salvation.[36]

Bettelehim quotes Mircea Eliade, who described fairytales as "models for human behavior ... that give meaning and value to life."[37] Rituals bond the individual on physical, spiritual, emotional, and psychological levels to the collective myth of his respective group, thus connecting the individual being to the whole. In the absence of truly meaningful rituals, in a modern age bereft of culturally significant mythology,[38] contemporary fantasy emerges as a replacement myth, providing young people with culturally relevant heroes with whom they could identify, whose journeys provide vicarious catharsis and initiation into the realm of adulthood.

The motif of the initiation of the hero archetype can be seen in countless incidences throughout myth, folklore, and fantasy. The initiation usually involves the inheritance or discovery of a magical object, which informs the hero of his identity, typically by identifying the initiate with his same-sex biological parent, who is usually deceased. For the purpose of illustration, one example from myth, fairytale, and modern fantasy will suffice, though the topic of the initiatory transformations of the hero and princess will be examined in more depth in subsequent chapters. In the legends of the mythical King of the Britons, Arthur, there is a ritual involving the drawing of a sacred sword from a stone. It is said that the only man who can draw and wield Excalibur is the true king, the heir of Uther Pendragon, who is destined to bring back peace and prosperity to the land. The hero, while still a boy, encounters the sword in the stone. In drawing the sword, Arthur initiates himself into the world of men and warriors, while also establishing his own heritage and identity, identifying himself through ownership of Excalibur as the son and heir of the fallen king, Uther Pendragon.

In fairytale, where the hero is more often a girl than a boy, the rite of passage from maidenhood to motherhood via the marriage ceremony is the most typical culmination of the heroine's tale. In the Cinderella story, possibly the most widespread folktale motif in the world, a girl who is abused and debased by her wicked stepmother has only one chance of improving her lot and escaping her horrid situation. She must marry well. Through the intervention of her fairy godmother (the spirit of her deceased real mother), Cinderella wins the love of a prince; but she must depart before their relationship is consummated, leaving her true identity a mystery to the prince. But the slipper she left behind (made of glass or gold or some other precious material, depending on which variation of the story is being told) is the key to her identity and her destiny. When she fits her dainty foot into the slipper, Cinderella verifies her identity, proving that she is worthy of her initiation into the role of bride and princess. She achieves this as a reward for her faith and constancy, and also as a vindication for her mistreatment at the hand of her stepmother, who treated her as a scullery maid, denying her the proper station of life that she was born into. The foot in the slipper, in this sense, is like the sword in the stone. They are both symbols of identity — magical objects inherited from a deceased parent — which verify the identity of the owner, designate a true heritage, and facilitate initiatory passage from childhood obscurity into the fold of a regal adulthood.

In the first book of the Harry Potter series, young Harry's first experience in his new school, Hogwarts, is the Sorting Ceremony. The ceremony is an initiation ritual that informs the initiate of his identity, his place in the society of Hogwarts, and to a larger extent, his place in the "wizarding world." All of these social structures are indicated by the house one is placed in, Gryffindor, Slytherin, Hufflepuff, or Ravenclaw. The placement decision is made by the "Sorting Hat," an ancient mystical wizard's hat that looks into the mind of the child who is wearing it, and descries the basic elements of his identity. When Harry places the Sorting Hat on his head and is placed in Gryffindor, he is immediately initiated into the same fraternity that both his father and mother belonged to. For the next seven years, Harry's position as a member of Gryffindor will define his status and alliances within the wizarding world.

Myths and fairytales provide an essential existential function in the lives of people young and old.[39] Myths and fairytales do not tell us how to live; rather, they provide symbols for ideas to live by. In the end, we have to interpret the symbols ourselves, just as we have to interpret the meaning of our own lives by ourselves. The ancient wisdom in the tales is not found in the stories they tell, but in the way that the stories affect our understanding of our own lives.

TWO

The Realm of Faërie

"Toyland! Toyland! Little girl and boy land.
While you dwell within it, you are ever happy then.
Childhood's joy land, mystic merry joy land.
Once you pass its borders, you can never return again...."
— Victor Herbert & Glen Macdonough,
from the musical *Babes in Toyland*

The world of the fairytale, with its eternal landscape and fanciful panoply of characters derived from the "ageless tale" of myth, provides the basic psychological elements of the fantasy story. At an archetypal level, "myth, fairytale, and fantasy can and ought to be understood as different aspects of the same category: what Tolkien calls *Faërie*."[1] The imaginary realm of Faërie is the homeland of the creatures that provide us with the "picture-language of the soul,"[2] the images and ideas that are projected in some way or form in every fantasy story. The wisdom revealed through this "picture language" is the wisdom of self-knowledge, "fairy tales reveal truths about mankind and oneself."[3] The magic of this wisdom is that it does not need to be studied or learned, only experienced. Furthermore, one need not be a sage or scholar to decipher and comprehend this wisdom, any child can understand it at the intuitive, unconscious level, because it is written in a language that everyone, especially children, can understand — the language of symbols. Additionally, Faërie is a secret, hidden place, a place where children can retreat from their real lives in order to privately confront their psychological conflicts and issues within the safe confines of a symbolic, imaginary arena. "The fairy tale is a verification of the interior life of the child."[4]

In his book *The Forgotten Language* (1951), Erich Fromm contends that symbols represent a primal mode of comprehension, a preliterate form of communication that existed as a primary language in humankind for hundreds

25

of centuries before the advent of a formal written language.[5] These potent symbols are retained, like artifacts from an earlier stage of human development, in fairytale and myth. In this way, the symbols of Faërie are more deeply embedded in the psyche than the words of modern language. "In fairy tales, the hero escapes the tiresome clichés of reality by entering a world where the figurative or metaphorical dimension of language takes on literal meaning. Ideas become matter. The mother or stepmother who is like an ogress at the beginning of a tale becomes an actual witch."[6] Fantasy overcomes reality in Faërie by invoking a more primitive system of consciousness, a system that is preexistent to rational, sophisticated language.

Fromm insists that the symbolic language of Faërie and the symbolic language of dreams are one in the same. The fairytale is like a dream world, where the reader's most basic anxieties are given form and voice through the story and its characters. This perspective is similar to the views of other psychoanalytic theorists such as Freud, Jung, Rank, Bettelheim, Von Franz, Tatar, and others. In the psychoanalytic interpretation, symbols in myth, fairytale, and fantasy can be interpreted in the same way that symbols in dreams are interpreted in the process of psychoanalytic dream analysis. The main difference is that the associations between a symbol and the dreamer in the interpretation of a dream are unique to the individual (except for instances when the symbol in the dream is interpreted as an archetype ... i.e. a universal symbol); while the association between a symbol and the reader in the interpretation of a fairytale are thought to be collective.[7] As Freud observed, "Folklore in general takes advantage of symbols that have universal validity. Kings and queens as a rule represent parents; a prince or princess signifies the self. A deep, impenetrable forest symbolizes the dark, hidden depths of the soul. A body of water is often associated with the process of birth."[8] In a word, symbols in the realm of Faërie are both timeless and universal. The symbols can be understood by the smallest child, because, in the mind, the comprehension of symbolic figures predates the comprehension of words and logic.

The Fairytale Setting

"*Once upon a time* is a magical incantation that recalls us to that spot where time is and is not, where as one wag put it, "things never were and always are." The timelessness of the fantasy world begins for all of us with that opening line."[9] The realm of Faërie is usually not set in a specific time or place, but rather, in a timeless era, in a place that is open to the imagination. Tolkien refers to this "mythical" place as "Other Time," a place where "we stand outside our own time, outside Time itself."[10] This temporal and geographical ambiguity provides the vagueness that is necessary for the seeds of imagination to take root. If the setting was specific to time and place, then the logical aspect of consciousness would lead the foray into the fantasy world. But since time and place are left unspecific, the aspects of consciousness dominated by symbolic thinking — the areas of imagination and dreams — become the reader's primary mode of perception. As Bettelheim noted:

> "Once upon a time," "In a certain country," "A thousand years ago, or longer," "At a time when animals still talked," "Once in an old castle in the midst of a large and dense forest" — such beginnings suggest that what follows does not pertain to the here and now that we know. This deliberate vagueness in the beginnings of fairy tales symbolizes that we are leaving the concrete world of ordinary reality. The old castles, dark caves, locked rooms one is forbidden to enter, impenetrable woods all suggest that something normally hidden will be revealed, while the "long ago" implies that we are going to learn about the most archaic events.[11]

Because the realm of Faërie is not dated on a calendar or charted on a map, the embarking explorers are blissfully unaware that their journey through this realm will not take them somewhere else; rather, it will lead them cunningly within, into the secret recesses of their own minds, and the carefully hidden memories of their childhoods.

The concept of "Dream Time" in "primitive" societies such as that of the Australian aborigines is a connecting principle between the ritualistic, mythic, and psychoanalytic concepts of non-sequential time. Dream Time for the aborigines refers to the mythical time before the world as it exists now was created. In concept, it is similar to the infinite, eternal state of nothingness, the chaotic void, which preceded the first words of the Old Testament — "In the Beginning." The time before the beginning refers to a time before the creation of time, a notion that seems incomprehensible, at least on a conscious or rational level, which is why it can only be truly understood or experienced on an unconscious level. For the Australian aborigines, the Dream Time was the era before humankind, when the Supernatural Beings wandered across the vast emptiness of what would eventually become the World, creating animals and plants and objects as they went along. The Dream Time was the mythical time, because it was the time when the gods of creation invented and inhabited both the time and the space that would become the universe. This sacred time is accessible to humans in two ways ... in sleep, via the descending passageway of dreams; and in spirit, via the ascending ladder of ritual. Both routes perform the same function, as they reestablish contact with the Supernatural Beings by reenacting a sacred event that once took place in the Dream Time. And, of course, since Dream Time is non-sequential, everything that happened then is still happening now, and will always be happening.

The ritualistic understanding of Sacred Time refers to the notion that when a sacred ritual is being performed, time itself is transformed from mortal time to immortal time, a time that is governed by the gods. As Campbell explains: "Time collapses in 'ceremonial time,' and what was 'then' becomes 'now' — the world-fashioning events of the 'time of the beginning of the world.'"[12] The participants of a primitive ritual, (if they are performing their roles properly), truly believe that they are re-enacting a sacred event that took place during the mythical time. Hence, the ritual itself allows the participants to transcend the earthly plane and enter Sacred Time. This is why phenomena which could normally never take place on the earthly plane — communion or communication with spirits or with a god, seeing visions, speaking in tongues, the performance of magic or miracles, out-of-body experiences, etc. — can take place while the participants are under the mystical influence of the primal ritual. Since myth and fairytale, according to some interpretations, are narratives that were once associated with rites, the sense of time in Faërie is the same as the sense of time in the ritual. It is not earthly time, but Sacred Time.

The psychoanalytic concept of "Primordial Time" refers to the time in an individual's life before the rational understanding of time and space existed. This is the time of early childhood and toddlerhood, the magical age before the world was governed by logic and reason; and the time of infancy, when the goddess of creation gave forth life and nourishment from the fecundity of her own body; and even back to the prenatal period, before the beginning of birth, when the universe itself was a living goddess, and the notion that anything existed outside of that nurturing womb was incomprehensible. The primordial events of those archaic times, especially the traumatic events, are not consciously remembered by the older child or the adult because they never truly came into consciousness in the first place. The primordial traumas occurred either at a time when perception was primarily unconscious (i.e. the "birth trauma," according to Rank), or in a place that was primarily unconscious (the oedipal fantasies and nightmares of the infant, toddler, and young child). In either case, the primordial trauma was always the same — an unwanted and unexpected separation from Mother — who is still perceived in Primordial Time as both the Earth Goddess, and as the Earth or Universe itself. This primordial trauma is perceived as a rejection, expulsion, or abandonment, an experience of being cast away by Life itself, a pain so acute that it is worth than death. As Bettelheim explained:

There is no greater threat in life than that we will be deserted, left all alone. Psychoanalysis has named this — man's greatest fear — separation anxiety; and the younger we are, the more excruciating is our anxiety when we feel deserted, for the young child actually perishes when not adequately protected and taken care of...[13]

Though the primordial trauma occurred long ago in the personal past, it remains lodged in the psyche of the individual, an unresolved conflict repressed in the unconscious. Like events of the mythical Dream Time, repressed memories are timeless. They happened, but they are still happening, and they will always be happening. They live forever in the unconscious. They reemerge like specters, primarily in our dreams and nightmares, as dreams also exist in Primordial Time. Normal sequential time has no bearing in dreams. When we dream, we can suddenly become a small child again, or even a babe in our mother's arms. In dreams we can have experiences that seem to go on for years, even though our bodies back on the earthly plane have only been sleeping for a few hours.

The only way to cope with the primordial trauma is to relive it, to go back into Primordial Time, and in doing so, to somehow mend the unity of the symbiotic relationship that was torn apart. There are two ways to go back into Primordial Time: through the intra-psychic realm of dreams; and through the inter-psychic realm of Faërie. The purpose of this *"descensus ad inferus"* is the same purpose as the primitive ritual, to reconnect with the Supernatural Beings, the Creators. To go back to the time when the physical Mother and the archetypal Mother — the goddess of Life, Life itself — were one in the same. "Therefore, the ultimate consolation is that we shall never be deserted.... This, then, is the ultimate consolation, the one that is implied in the common fairy-tale ending, "And they lived happily ever after.'"[14]

Thus, the quintessential fairytale ending, "and they lived happily ever after," is a timeless state of paradise, a fantasy of returning to the Primordial Time, which is represented in Myth as the epoch of Genesis, the era of Eden, when gods and goddesses created and still inhabited the world. The motif represents an unconscious yearning to return to the Eden from whence we came, to somehow pass through the flaming sword that turns every way, and to eat from the Tree of Life. In psychoanalysis, this is represented as either the return to the physical mother of infancy, to the archetypal goddess of Life, or to the blissful unity of the womb. In this way, the "Happily Ever After" of Faërie is one-in-the-same with the "Happily Ever After" promised by religion, as Heaven is perceived as nothing other than a communion with the Creator. This may explain why the experience of death is so often visualized as a passage through a tunnel — a reliving of the primordial birth experience — and this may also explain why the passage to Hell, in medieval texts, has been occasionally depicted as the "Vagina Dentata," a vaginal open-ing lined with razor sharp teeth. For the initiated soul, the ascent to Heaven is a return to the Goddess who embraces and unifies; a re-entry and re-merging with the womb, from which we will re-emerge, re-born into a new life. For the uninitiated soul, the descent to Hell is a reliving of the primordial trauma, the moment in which the infant was cut off from the infinite by the severance of his umbilical cord; or, in a more Freudian vein, the moment in which the "Hieros Gamos" or sacred copulation between Heavenly Mother and Divine Child was cut off in castration, abandonment, and eternal exile.

For Tolkien, the "Conciliation" of the happy ending marks an end to the hero's suffering, though it must be noted that it usually comes with the fringe benefit of retaliation against the villain, who is usually a parent or sym-bolic parental figure. Dramatic justice is meted out in the end with all its ferocity, as the longtime suffering of the hero is paid back with compound interest, only all at once. Indeed, the villain's comeuppance in fairytales is typically primeval in its wantonness of pain and suffering. The witch in *Hansel and Gretel* is burned alive. The queen in *Snow White* is forced to wear red hot iron shoes, compelling her to dance to her death. The stepsisters in the Broth-ers Grimm version of Cinderella have their eyes pecked out by birds. This primal need for violent vengeance in Faërie may be interpreted as a long repressed sadistic desire in the child, felt towards the parent, especially the mother. (Freud called this desire "oral sadism.") If the process of weaning or even the event of birth is construed by the infant-child as a deliberate act of abandonment on the part of the mother, then deep-seated feelings of hatred and resentment, harbored in the unconscious for years, could be expressed in fantasy via the torturous acts of retribution directed towards the symbolic evil parent figure, i.e. the wicked stepmother. The tortures that consummate the typical fairytale can be seen as a catharsis, in which the child's inappropriate feelings of aggression towards the parent, born out of unresolved separation anxiety, are safely discharged.

The revenge fantasy may also be interpreted as the natural response of an individual who often perceives himself as being a powerless victim in the hands of a ruthless tyrant. As Tatar noted:

A sense of forlorn weakness in the face of all-powerful guardians and adversaries replicates perfectly the feelings of young children towards adults. The fairy tale's movement from victimization to retaliation gives vivid but disguised shape to the dreams of revenge that inevitably drift into the mind of every child beset by a sense of powerlessness. That the hero's initial state of misery is exaggerated and inflated beyond the limits of realism makes the fantasy all the more satisfying. Both the hero's reward and his oppressor's sufferings are richly deserved.[15]

Into the Woods

In the beginning of *The Divine Comedy,* Dante evokes the symbolism of the forest: "In the middle of the journey of our life, I found myself alone in a dark wood, where the straight way was lost." The impenetrable woods, the dark forest, the deepest jungles ... these settings are a universal symbol of the physically unknown and the psychologically repressed. As such, they serve as the archetypal entryways into the realm of Faërie.

In *The Magician's Nephew,* the sixth book in C.S. Lewis' Narnia series, the characters venture into a timeless void called "The Woods between the Worlds." The "Woods" is not a real place, but rather a portal station through which one can enter into any number of imaginary worlds. It is not a literal place that exists in space and time — it is a place in the mind — enterable only through imagination. When the characters are in these woods, just as when they are in Narnia, earthly time stands still. Similarly, the "Forbidden Forest" surrounding the Hogwarts school in J.K. Rowling's *Harry Potter* series seems to be a place that is unaffected by the passing of time. It is an oasis of Faërie, never intruded upon by the real world, a sanctuary for mythical creatures such as unicorns and centaurs, as well as a labyrinth replete with monstrous creatures such as werewolves and giant spiders. The immense forest of Mirkwood, which lies at the heart of Tolkien's Middle Earth, fulfills an identical function. Like the unconscious itself, the dark forest is a place of wonder and magic, a place that exists in Primordial Time, unaffected by the worldly events that go on outside of it. But the dark forest is also a haunted place, where reside the ghosts of the past and the embodied fears of infantile anxieties and traumas.

Technology and industry are notably absent from the woods of Faërie. Although there are people in the woods, the woods are not dominated by people. In essence, the woods of Faërie represent a primeval age, a figurative Garden of Eden, in which humankind is at one with Nature, having not yet learned to dominate Nature through technology and industry. If this biblical metaphor is taken one step further, the woods of Faërie can be seen as a representation of the state of humanity before the Fall, a stage of childhood-like innocence in line with the more earthy existence of primitive humankind.

For Tolkien, the ascent of modern humankind was always associated with the destruction of Nature. For instance, towards the conclusion of *The Return of the King,* upon returning to the Shire at the end of their very long journey, the hobbit heroes experience a direct encounter with humankind subsequent to his Fall:

It was one of the saddest hours in their lives. The great chimney rose up before them; and as they drew near the old village across the Water, through rows of new mean houses along each side of the road, they saw the new mill in all its frowning and dirty ugliness: a great brick building straddling the stream, which it fouled with a streaming and stinking outflow. All along the Bywater Road every tree had been felled.[16]

Hence, the felling of trees for the vile purposes of industry is an act of Fell men, men who are no longer in touch with Nature. A similar "green" sentiment runs through the Narnia books. In *Prince Caspian*, the victory against the corrupt monarch is achieved through the magical "awakening" of the trees, in which the "living Wood" wreaks vengeance upon the Fell men who have subdued her.[17] The exact same motif can be seen in Tolkien's *The Two Towers*. In the chapter entitled "The Last March of the Ents," the Ents of Fangorn Forest (walking, talking trees) siege and destroy the fortress of the evil wizard who had been chopping down multitudes of trees in order to feed the engines of war. At last, we see Trees chopping down Man!

On a broader level, evil in Faërie is characterized as that which destroys Nature, or that which goes against the natural order. Nature, in turn, will wreak its vengeance. Hence the theme of animals and trees and even inanimate forces of nature such as rivers and seas all rallying together to defeat the dark lord. This is a ubiquitous theme in Faërie, especially in the *Narnia* books.

The Netherworld

"Going down into the darkness of the earth is a descent into the netherworld ... [a] voyage into the interior."[18] As an entrance into the realm of Faërie, the "*descensus ad inferus,*" the descent beneath the earth, is equally as common as the entrance though the wood.[19] Tolkien's "Middle Earth" was derived both linguistically and conceptually from the realm of "Midgard" in Norse mythology, which means "the middle space." The notion that there are layers of Earth, one atop the other, is a common theme in many mythologies. Sometimes the realms beneath the surface of the Earth are infernal, such as the Greek Hades or the Christian Hell. Other times the netherworlds are places of fantasy and wonder, such as the Judaic Neshiah or the Welsh Annwyn. In any case, the downward descent into the netherworld represents a psychological regression down to the intra-psychic realm of the unconscious, the domain of fantasy, imagination, and dreams.

Just as deeper strata of Earth represent earlier generations and civilizations to archaeologists and anthropologists, so too does the Netherworld represent earlier stages of culture and psychology. When we delve into the realm of

Faërie, we encounter the demons, spirits, and monsters of earlier belief systems. Though they have been banished from the surface of the earth by the Church and Science and all of their accomplices, the spirits and monsters still exist. They're right there, beneath the surface. One needs only to descend into the Netherworld to see them. The gods and goddesses as well as the witches and demons and all the spirits of nature in the pagan and polytheistic belief systems did not vanish. The primitive beliefs were syncretically assimilated into modern culture, retained as symbols in Faërie.

Bettelheim provides a particularly good example of the syncretism of pagan figures into fairytales in his analysis of *The Seven Ravens*:

> In the Brothers Grimm's story "The Seven Ravens," seven brothers disappear and become ravens as their sister enters life. Water has to be fetched from the well in a jug for the girl's baptism, and the loss of the jug is the fateful event which sets the stage for the story. The ceremony of baptism also heralds the beginning of a Christian experience. It is possible to view the seven brothers as representing that which had to disappear for Christianity to come into being. If so, they represent the pre–Christian, pagan world in which the seven planets stood for the sky gods of antiquity. The newborn girl is then the new religion, which can succeed only if the old creed does not interfere with its development. With Christianity, the brothers who represent paganism become relegated to darkness. But as ravens, they dwell in a mountain at the end of the world, and this suggests their continued existence in a subterranean, subconscious world.[20]

It is interesting to note that while some fundamentalist Christian groups have railed against the Harry Potter books for being anti–Christian, because the characters practice witchcraft and the stories are filled with creatures from ancient pagan mythologies; the same groups fail to recognize that all of the themes and figures from Rowling's books have been an accepted part of children's literature for centuries. Fairytales and fantasy stories have always been filled with magic and magical creatures, they are the bridges that link us to the pagan myths that preceded our current Judeo-Christian and Islamic belief systems, but still dominate our imaginations on a more primary level.

Childhood's End

Childhood is regarded as the developmental age appropriate for Fantasy, as it is the age that precedes adulthood, when thinking is governed by logic and reason. The fantasy material within this stage, in turn, is filled with figures and themes from the cultural-religious belief systems that preceded the predominance of Judeo-Christian monotheism in the Western world ... paganism, polytheism, and pantheism. Hence, the age that preceded the other, and everything associated with it, is romanticized as a lost wonder world, a magical, timeless, mythical era in which the fantastic and supernatural reigns supreme over the rational and mundane. Peter Pan (as his last name portends) is a perfect example of how childhood and pantheism elicit similar associations in the reader. Childhood is an age when the belief in fairies and spirits (i.e. the tooth-fairy and Santa Claus) is tolerated and even encouraged. It is an age of magic and wonder, all too briefly experienced before Church and Science as well as Logic and Reason proscribe the belief in all non-religious and pre-monotheistic supernatural figures. This sentiment, and the resulting yearning to return to that magical age, is expressed quite poetically in the song, *Never Never Land*, written for the stage musical version of *Peter Pan* (1954).

> I have a place where dreams are born,
> And time is never planned.
> It's not on any chart,
> You must find it with your heart.
> Never Never Land.
>
> It might be miles beyond the moon,
> Or right there where you stand.
> Just keep an open mind,
> And then suddenly you'll find
> Never Never Land.
>
> You'll have a treasure if you stay there,
> More precious far than gold.
> For once you have found your way there,
> You can never, never grow old....[21]

While one stays in "Never Never Land," the land where time does not exist, one can never grow old. However, like Eden, once you leave this magical place in time, you can never return. As Peter warns Wendy in the Disney movie *Peter Pan* (1953), "Once you grow up, you can never come back!"[22] This is true, except for the secret passageway, through the realm of Faërie.

A similar yearning for an earlier state of being is expressed by Wordsworth in his timeless poem "The World Is Too Much with Us" (1807):

> The world is too much with us; late and soon,
> Getting and spending, we lay waste our powers;
> Little we see in Nature that is ours;
> We have given our hearts away, a sordid boon!
> This Sea that bares her bosom to the moon,
> The winds that will be howling at all hours,
> And are up-gathered now like sleeping flowers,
> For this, for everything, we are out of tune;
> It moves us not. — Great God! I'd rather be
> A Pagan suckled in a creed outworn;

> So might I, standing on this pleasant lea,
> Have glimpses that would make me less forlorn;
> Have sight of Proteus rising from the sea;
> Or hear old Triton blow his wreathed horn.

The analogous desires to return to childhood and to return to a more natural and fanciful perception of the world, embodied by the pagan and polytheistic belief systems, are both satisfied simultaneously via the entrance to Faërie.

While the typical fairytale ends with the consolation of the villain's comeuppance and the heroes' timeless happiness, the denouement of the contemporary fantasy novel usually involves the heroes' voyage away from the fantasy world. At the conclusion of Lloyd Alexander's *Prydain Chronicles*, "The Sons of Don" board golden ships and set sail for the "Summer Country."[23] Similarly, in the last chapter of Tolkien's *Lord of the Rings* trilogy, and in Lewis' last *Narnia* book, the end of the fantasy requires the departure of the mythical beings and legendary figures. The end of the Age of Magic hearkens the beginning of the Age of Men — representing the end of childhood and the passage into adulthood.

The ending of C.S. Lewis' third Chronicle of Narnia, *The Voyage of the Dawn Treader* (1952), suggests a direct link between childhood and polytheistic beliefs. At the end of the last chapter of *The Voyage of the Dawn Treader*, when Lucy and Edmund must take that portentous step out of childhood fantasy and into adult reality, the passage is facilitated by Aslan the lion, a symbol that is at once a pagan anthropomorphic creature and the embodiment of Christ:

> "Please, Aslan," said Lucy. "Before we go, will you tell us when we can come back to Narnia again? Please. And oh, do, do, do make it soon."
> "Dearest," said Aslan very gently, "you and your brother will never come back to Narnia."
> "Oh, *Aslan!!*" said Edmund and Lucy both together in despairing voices.
> "You are too old, children," said Aslan, "and you must begin to come close to your own world now."
> "It isn't Narnia, you know," sobbed Lucy. "It's you. We shan't meet you there. And how can we live, never meeting you?"
> "But you shall meet me, dear one," said Aslan.
> "Are — are you there too, Sir?" said Edmund.
> "I am," said Aslan. "But there I have another name. You must learn to know me by that name. This was the very reason why you were brought to Narnia, that by knowing me here for a little, you may know me better there."[24]

In keeping with his deeply held Christian faith, Lewis thought it necessary to connect the theme of childhood's end, in which the child must grow up and leave behind the primordial realm of Faërie, to the more "mature" faith in Christ, who can be found in the "real world."

The tendency for children to believe that animals such as lions can talk and that magical creatures such as unicorns and fairies actually exist is seen by cognitive psychologists as examples of "preoperational thinking," in which the child's perception of the world is ruled by imagination rather than logic. Jean Piaget, the father of Cognitive Developmental psychology, asserted that the thinking of young children is neither logical nor scientific, making it "magical"—meaning that the causal link between observable events are not made according to reason. Hence, in the small child's mind, coincidental events are linked in meaningful ways, and the child may even believe that his own thoughts can cause physical changes in the world. Gradually, magical thinking is replaced by operational thinking, which is categorical, logical, and based on experience and observation. But this is not to say that adults do not occasionally engage in magical thinking as well ... superstition, belief in ghosts and supernatural phenomenon, and faith-based religion — i.e. belief without reason — could by the same definition be considered examples of pre-operational or magical thinking.[25]

One significant aspect of magical thinking is "animism"— the tendency to project humanlike qualities onto animals and objects. Bettelheim quoted Piaget in explaining the significance of animistic thinking in the child's understanding of the fairytale:

> His [the child's] thinking is animistic. Like all preliterate and many literate people, "the child assumes that his relations to the inanimate world are of one pattern with those to the animate world of people: he fondles as he would his mother the pretty thing that pleased him; he strikes the door that has slammed on him." It should be added that he does the first because he is convinced that this pretty thing loves to be petted as much as he does; and he punishes the door because he is certain that the door slammed deliberately, out of evil intention.... To the eight-year-old (to quote Piaget's examples), the sun is alive because it gives light (and, one may add, it does that because it wants to). To the animistic child's mind, the stone is alive because it can move, as it rolls down a hill. Even a twelve-and-a-half-year-old is convinced that a stream is alive and has a will, because its water is flowing. The sun, stone, and the water are believed to be inhabited by spirits very much like people, so they feel and act like people.[26]

Upon reading Piaget's and Bettelheim's explanation of animistic thinking in the preoperational child, one is tempted to apply the theory of recapitulation, in which ontogeny recapitulates phylogeny, onto the historical development of religious thought in culture. In this sense, earlier preliterate cultures who were practiced in animistic belief systems can be associated with the early stage of cognitive development in the child — the stage in which preoperational thinking is dominant — hence the tendency towards animistic thinking, in which animals can think and talk like humans, and streams and trees are imbued with humanlike spirits; as well as the tendency towards magical thinking. If so, then monotheistic belief systems can be associated with the middle stage of cognitive development in the child — concrete operational thinking — in which thinking is much more logical and reason-based. Thinking at this stage, however, is limited, because abstract concepts cannot be fully grasped, resulting in a "heteronymous" approach to moral and existential problems, in which the child simply believes what he is told to believe, as the logical assumption is that older figures of authority are correct, because they are wiser and more mature. Piaget called the most advanced level of cognitive development the "formal operational stage." At this stage, thinking is governed by a more sophisticated level of logic, so that even abstract concepts such as moral and existential problems are considered from a logical and reason-based position. Moral and existential thinking becomes more autonomous and less heteronymous, as adolescents and adults begin to question the rules and traditions handed down to them by older authority figures. And, as every assumption about life is questioned through a process of hypothetical deductive reasoning, beliefs about life become more reliant on objective science rather than subjective faith. [27] However, as science has proven itself more or less impotent at the task of providing significant insight into the meaning of life, the scientific mind retreats intermittently to the sanctuary of Faërie, where cold logic is no match for the flaming embers of magic.

Returning to Narnia, in the final chapters of the seventh and concluding Chronicle of Narnia, *The Last Battle* (1956), the end of the Narnian world seems to recapitulate the Genesis and pre–Genesis stages of Earth's ontogeny. In the chapter, *Night Falls on Narnia*, as the fantasy world descends into darkness, it seems to regress into a prehistoric age of dinosaurs:

> The Dragons and Giant Lizards now had Narnia to themselves. They went to and fro tearing up the trees by the roots and crunching them up...[28]

But then, almost as suddenly, as they emerge (or re-emerge), the dinosaurs become extinct:

> The monsters themselves grew old and lay down and died. Their flesh shriveled up and the bones appeared: soon they were only huge skeletons that lay here and there on the dead rock, looking as if they had died thousands of years ago. For a long time everything was still.[29]

After that, the land of Narnia is swept over by the sea in a cataclysmic flood, recapitulating in theme the great deluge of Noah in Genesis, except in this case there is no ark, just a host of refugees delivered from Narnia by Aslan through a mystical doorway. The antediluvian age (the age before the biblical flood), has often been imagined as an age of fantasy and wonder, a place much like the magical age described in ancient mythologies, filled with magical creatures and semi-divine heroes. The Bible itself alludes to these figures:

> "The sons of God saw the daughters of men that they were fair; and they took them wives, whomsoever they chose ... and they bore children to them; the same were the mighty men that were of old, the men of renown [Genesis 6: 22: 2–4].

These "men of renown" are commonly interpreted to refer to the demi-god heroes of antiquity, the sons of gods and mortal women. The Bible also mentions the Gibborim and Nephilim, vague references to figures who are commonly interpreted as ancient races of giants, such as the Titans in Greek mythology. Finally, the Bible also explains that "all flesh had corrupted their way upon the earth" (Genesis 6: 22: 12). This passage is commonly interpreted to mean that not only had the Sons of God corrupted themselves by interbreeding with mortal women, but humans and animals also corrupted each other through bestiality, resulting in the birth of impure hybrid creatures, such as minotaurs and centaurs, as well as magical creatures such as unicorns and dragons. God's decision to eradicate all flesh on earth, save Noah and his family and a breeding pair of every pure, uncorrupted animal species, resulted in the mass extinction of all semi-divine, magical, and anthropomorphic beings; hence the antediluvian age can, in a sense, be considered the Age of Faërie. Colorful visual depictions of this age can be seen in Disney's *Fantasia* (1940), in *The Pastoral Symphony* sequence, which features centaurs, unicorns, fauns, gods, and other anthropomorphic and divine figures from Greek mythology. Also, in Disney's *Fantasia 2000* (1999), in the *Pomp and Circumstance* sequence, which retells the Noah story starring Donald Duck in the title role, a group of antediluvian magical creatures, including a dragon, a unicorn, and a griffon, laugh at Donald/Noah as he loads the ark, blissfully unaware of their imminent extinction.

Returning to Narnia once again, at the very end of *The Last Battle*, Aslan escorts the children into the ultimate realm of Faërie — the magical kingdom promised at the end of all fairytales — where happiness is eternal, the place at the end of the rainbow, the fantasy world that exists in every mythology, and is called by a thousand names, the mythical country where you are reunited with all of your dead loved ones, and every day is just one extended moment of bliss.

> Lucy said, "We're so afraid of being sent away, Aslan. And you have sent us back into our own world so often."
> "No fear of that," said Aslan. "Have you not guessed?"
> Their hearts leapt, and a wild hope rose within them.

"There *was* a real railway accident," said Aslan softly. "Your father and mother and all of you are — as you used to call it in the Shadowlands — dead. The term is over: the holidays have begun. The dream is ended: this is the morning."

And as He spoke, He no longer looked to them like a lion; but the things that began to happen after that were so great and beautiful that I cannot write them. And for us this is the end of all the stories, and we can most truly say that they all lived happily ever after..."[30]

THREE

The Hero

> "For the mythological hero is the champion not of things become but of things becoming; the dragon to be slain by him is precisely the monster of the status quo: Holdfast, the keeper of the past."[1]

So much has been written about the hero figure in popular culture, from the ancient myths through modern literature and media, that even a summation of all the theories would be beyond the scope and purpose of this chapter. Rather, what will be presented is an interpretation of the hero figure in Faërie as a depiction of the collective male ego-ideal, which is to say, the image of the ideal male as perceived by the particular cultures that created the hero figure. The hero's story is invariably a symbolic tale of initiation. The hero's adventure is a metaphor for the rites of passage that every male adolescent must undergo, either physically or psychologically, in order to prove his masculinity, his male identity, and his worthiness of being accepted and initiated into the community of adult men.

"The hero is an archetypal figure which presents a model of ego functioning in accord with the Self."[2] In the Jungian perspective, the hero archetype provides a working model within the collective and personal unconscious of the ego-ideal — not the man that you are — but the man that you want to become. Bettelheim suggested that there is an essential difference in the hero as depicted in the different subgenres of Faërie: "Myths project an ideal personality acting on the basis of superego demands, while fairy tales depict an ego integration which allows for appropriate satisfaction of id desires. This difference accounts for the contrast between the pervasive pessimism of myths and the essential optimism of fairy tales."[3] As the primary audience for myths were adults and the primary audience for fairytales were children, we could see why the former would focus on the adult issues of living up to the expectations of family and community, while the latter would focus on the child's necessity of learning how to satisfy desires in a socially appropriate fashion. Fantasy, as a medium primarily targeted towards "young adults"—i.e. older children and young adolescents — seems to play the middle ground, providing heroes who are primarily dealing with the initiatory issues of self-identification and identity realization.

Raglan's Hero

"Myth is ritual projected back into the past, not a historical past of time, but a ritual past of eternity. It is a description of what should be done by a king (priest, chief, or magician) in order to secure and maintain the prosperity of his people, told in the form of a narrative of what a hero — that is, an ideal king, etc.— once did."[4] In Lord Raglan's perspective, the myth of the hero is a narrative that is or once was associated with a specific ritual. An example of a "living myth" would be the story of the Last Supper, in which Jesus is the hero and the Eucharist is the associated rite. A similar and associated example would be the biblical story of the Exodus, in which Moses is the hero and the Passover Seder is the associated rite. These are "living myths," because the heroes are still worshipped or adored by devoted followers, and their respective myths are still linked with the associated rituals. A "dead myth" is one that is no longer linked with its associated rite, usually because the religion or belief system connected to the myth and its hero has become defunct. Lord Raglan argued that all of the heroes of Classical mythology were worshipped according to specific rituals; hence, all of the Greco-Roman myths were once narratives associated with specific rites. Since these rituals have been forgotten through many centuries of non-practice, all of the associated myths — that is to say, all of Classical mythology — can therefore be considered "dead."

Though Raglan's case seems vastly overstated, his point is significant on a broader level. The psychological and sociological function of a ritual is similar to the function of an actual hero figure such as a king, a valiant warrior, a prophet, or a revered religious personage. The function of the hero, and by descent the function of the associated ritual and myth, is to bring the community together, to bind them as one, to provide a common identification figure, thereby forging a communal identity. The myth and rites associated with the hero figure serve the same social function, providing significant and meaningful rites of passage for new initiates, so that these young members may feel a sense of importance and belongingness within the community. In this sense, the hero's adventure, whether told in myth, fairytale, or fantasy, plays a vital role, as the young person identifies with the cultural hero, who is seen as the collective ideal. The young person, through this process of identification, vicariously experiences the rite of passage that binds him to the community, just by making this psychological connection with the hero figure.

In the case of the living myth, when, for example, the young Christian receives Holy Communion by eating the Eucharist, the symbolism is quite clear — he has become one with the hero — he *is* Jesus, as the body of Jesus is now within him. In the case of a dead myth, such as the Legends of Arthur, a young man may find great inspiration by reading the story of how Arthur drew Excalibur from the Stone, because on a psychological level, since the young man has identified with the hero, he has become one with Arthur — he *is* Arthur — because the image of Arthur as his own ego-ideal is now a part of his psyche. And finally, in the case of the modern fantasy story, such as the Harry Potter novels, the young person identifies with the fantasy hero in the exact same way that former generations of young people may have identified with Arthur or Jesus. The fact that Harry Potter is not real and was never assumed to be real is completely irrelevant in the mind of the young person, as fantasy is unencumbered by the constraints of reality, since its power is experienced in the unconscious realm of archetype, symbol, and dreams. In all three instances, the psychological rite of passage has been achieved, though only in the case of the "living myth" did the young man undergo an actual sociological rite of passage. It should be noted, however, that in the modern era, especially in secularized cultures, when traditional rites of passage such as the Communion and Bar Mitzvah hold less psychological and sociological significance for the typical adolescent, the identification with a hero figure from a fantasy medium — whether it be literature, film, television, comic books, video games, or an internet based fantasy world — holds much greater significance for the modern youth seeking an image for his personal ego-ideal.

Raglan summarized the pattern of the mythological hero as follows:

> The hero's mother is a royal virgin; his father is a king, and often a near relative of his mother, but the circumstance of his conception are unusual, and he is also reputed to be the son of a god. At birth, an attempt is made, usually by his father or his maternal grandfather, to kill him, but he is spirited away, and reared by foster-parents in a far country. We are told nothing of his childhood, but on reaching manhood he returns or goes to his future kingdom. After a victory over the king and/or a giant, dragon, or wild beast, he marries a princess, often the daughter of his predecessor, and becomes king. For a time he reigns uneventfully, and prescribes laws, but later he loses favor with the gods and/or his subjects, and is driven from the throne and city, after which he meets with a mysterious death, often at the top of a hill. His children, if any, do not succeed him. His body is not buried, but nevertheless he has one or more holy sepulchers.[5]

Raglan argues that the hero pattern is aligned with the major rites of passage in a man's life:

> the incidents fall definitely into three groups: those connected with the hero's birth, those connected with his accession to the throne, and those connected with his death. Thus they correspond to the three principal rites de passage — that is to say, the rites at birth, initiation, and at death.[6]

Hence, the mythological hero provides a role model or guiding image for the male's ego-ideal at every stage of life: whether it is childhood, when the task is to identify the self as part of a family and larger community; or adolescence, when the task is to initiate oneself into the adult society by taking on adult social roles; or adulthood, when the task is to meet the expectations of family and community through the ongoing commitment to social and occupational responsibilities and obligations. The hero's adventure, experienced vicariously by the listener as a de facto rite of passage, provides structure and guidance for those who identify with him. Furthermore, the hero's adventure provides insight into the basic existential problems of life: whether it is the question of birth — "Why am I here?"; the question of midlife — "What is the purpose or meaning of my life?"; or the question of death — "What happens to my soul after I die?" The hero's adventure, as part of a mythological system, deals explicitly with these existential problems in a way that is exemplary of the cultural ideals that the hero embodies:

> The god is the hero as he appears in ritual, and the hero is the god as he appears in myth; in other words, the hero and the god are two different aspects of the same superhuman being. The myth describes the victories that the hero won over the forces inimical to the people, the laws and customs which he instituted for their benefit and finally the apotheosis that enables him still to be their guardian and guide. When recited in full it embraces all his attributes, as god, as divine man, as idol, and as animal, and thus explains and justifies the whole of the ritual with which he is worshipped.[7]

For Raglan, the hero's adventure is the tale of how a mortal man becomes divine via selfless acts of sacrifice and extraordinary heroism. In a very real sense, this is the tale of every mortal man. Though the average man does not get the opportunity to draw a mystical sword from a stone or split the sea with a shepherd's staff, these symbolic acts give inspiration and guidance to the average man, whose heroism can be seen in smaller doses. The average man may take the bus everyday to work, where he sits at a desk for eight hours watching a screen, then he gets back on the bus and comes home, where he helps make dinner for his children and then bathes them and dresses them and puts them to bed. Then he wakes up the next morning and does the exact same thing. This he does five thousand times. That is the true heroism, the true sacrifice. This is not the sacrifice of Jesus on the cross or Moses on the mountaintop, but in order for this everyday sacrifice to take place, the average man must think of Jesus on the cross or Moses on the mountaintop or even Sisyphus in Tartarus, in order to inspire himself to go up onto the subway every morning, and descend from the bus every evening. And it is these small acts of heroism, these billions of daily hero sacrifices, that make the world go round. It is these acts of heroism that make the average man immortal, and even divine, in the sense that he gives life to the children who live on after him, and in the fact that his ceaseless labors give life to the world.

Rank's Hero

In his book *The Myth of the Birth of the Hero* (1914), Otto Rank delineated the hero pattern as depicted in the myths of dozens of prominent heroes, such as Jesus, Moses, Gilgamesh, Cyrus, Perseus, Hercules, Telephus, Oedipus, Romulus, Paris, Siegfried, Lohengrin, Tristan, Sargon, Karna, etc.

> The hero is the child of most distinguished parents, usually the son of a king.... During or before the pregnancy, there is a prophecy in the form of a dream or oracle, cautioning against his birth, and usually threatening danger to the father ... he is surrendered to the water.... He is then saved by animals, or by lowly people.... After he has grown up, he finds his distinguished parents, in a highly versatile fashion. He takes his revenge on his father, on the one hand, and is acknowledged, on the other. Finally he achieves rank and honors.[8]

As the name of Rank's theory portends, the focus is on the birth of the hero, placing emphasis on his conflicted relationship with his father. In his psychoanalytic interpretation of the hero figure, Rank contends that the pattern of the hero provides a wish fulfillment fantasy common to all children, in which the child fantasizes that his own parents are not really his own. For the male child, the real father, who is likely to be a mundane, ordinary man, is replaced with a fantasy father figure of his own imaginative creation.

> The entire endeavor to replace the real father by a more distinguished one is merely the expression of the child's longing for the vanished happy time, when his father still appeared to be the strongest and greatest man, and the mother seemed the dearest and most beautiful woman.[9]

Bettelheim made a similar interpretation of this archetypal theme, applying it to the ubiquitous stepmother figure in fairytales.

> The universality of such fantasies is suggested by what, in psychoanalysis, is known as the pubertal child's "family romance." These are fantasies or daydreams which the normal youngster partly recognizes as such, but nonetheless

also partly believes. They center on the idea that one's parents are not really one's parents, but that one is the child of some exalted personage, and that, due to unfortunate circumstances, one has been reduced to living with these people, who *claim* to be one's parents. These daydreams take various forms: often only one parent is thought to be a false one — which parallels a frequent situation in fairy tales, when one parent is the real one, the other a step-parent. The child's hopeful expectation is that one day, by chance or design, the real parent will appear and the child will be elevated into his rightful exalted state and live happily ever after.[10]

This fantasy provides an element of escapism for the child, a means of escaping his own reality, while also offering a boost to his own ego. In the case of the demi-god hero myth, the divine father provides the ultimate identification figure for the boy listener, as well as an extremely grandiose self-esteem boost for himself, as a divine father would mean that the son is at least half a god as well. The myth of the virgin birth (which is widespread among world mythologies) demonstrates a complete "repudiation of the father" by the boy-hero, as the real father is completely drawn out of the picture.[11]

Rank also places a lot of emphasis on the oedipal themes in the hero pattern:

> The true hero is, therefore, the ego, which finds itself in the hero, by reverting to the time when the ego was itself a hero, through its first heroic act, i.e. the revolt against the father.

In the final stage of the myth, the son avenges himself against the father, usurping his rank and position and inheriting everything that the father once possessed, symbolizing (or on occasion, including) the mother figure, as in the case of Oedipus himself. We see in Rank's explanation a very conflicted relationship between the hero and his father. On the one hand, the hero must rebel against the father figure and overthrow him; but through this act, he himself becomes his father, thus sowing the seed of future conflict with his own son. In this way, the hero saga is a cycle that never ends, each boy becoming a hero through defeating a father/tyrant, and then that hero in turn becoming a father/tyrant, who must eventually be overthrown by his own son.

The myth in Rank's interpretation depicts in melodramatic form the challenge of the average young man, who sees his father as both a role model and as a rival, as both a mentor and a nemesis. On the one hand, the boy identifies with the father, he wants to become like his father. On the other hand, the boy does not want to be limited or constrained by the achievements of the father either. He wants to venture out on his own, beat his own path, and outdo his father in the field of accomplishment. Thus, the father who guides with a firm hand on one day can easily be perceived on the next day as the tyrant who forces a direction and restricts free development. Father, in the mind of the son, becomes a conflicted dual presence. He is a figure that must be assimilated and absorbed into the Self, but at the same time, a figure that must be conquered and vanquished.

Campbell's Hero

Joseph Campbell's explanation of the hero archetype is the most comprehensive, as it absorbs both the ritualistic and psychoanalytic perspectives on the hero while adding elements of theology, mysticism, and philosophy as well. Campbell broke down the structure of the hero saga into its three most basic components:

> The standard path of the mythological adventure of the hero is a magnification of the formula represented in the rites of passage: *separation — initiation — return:* which might be named the nuclear unit of the monomyth.... A hero ventures forth from the world of common day into a region of supernatural wonder ... fabulous forces are there encountered and a decisive victory is won ... the hero comes back from this mysterious adventure with the power to bestow boons on his fellow man.[12]

The "monomyth" is a term that Campbell borrowed from James Joyce's *Finnegan's Wake* (1939). He uses the term to refer to the notion that all hero myths seem to follow the same pattern, hence the myths of the world are singular in their function and meaning. In the same sense, all heroes are singular in terms of their archetypal function and meaning, hence the title of Campbell's seminal book on the topic, *The Hero with a Thousand Faces* (1949). In his book, Campbell expands upon the "nuclear unit of the monomyth" by delineating seventeen stages of the hero's journey. While Campbell's stages of the hero's adventure was derived from hero myths, epics, sagas, and legends — the stages can clearly be seen in the tales of heroes in modern day fantasy stories. The structure is as follows:

I. Departure
    Stage 1: The Call to Adventure
    Stage 2: Refusal of the Call
    Stage 3: Supernatural Aid
    Stage 4: The Crossing of the First Threshold
    Stage 5: The Belly of the Whale

II. Initiation
    Stage 6: The Road of Trials
    Stage 7: The Meeting with the Goddess

Stage 8: Woman as the Temptress
Stage 9: Atonement with the Father
Stage 10: Apotheosis
Stage 11: The Ultimate Boon

III. Return
Stage 12: Refusal of the Return
Stage 13: The Magic Flight
Stage 14: Rescue from Without
Stage 15: The Crossing of the Return Threshold
Stage 16: Master of the Two Worlds
Stage 17: Freedom to Live

The Call to Adventure represents the initiating force that draws the boy out of his inert state of childhood and into the transitory phase of adolescence. The hero's adventure is a metaphor for the transformation of a boy into a man, and is therefore a symbolic story of the struggles of adolescence. If we imagine, as does Rank, that the hero myth is a narrative associated with a rite, then the primary rites associated with the hero myth are the puberty rituals, which mark the crossing from childhood into adolescence or adulthood. Harry Potter receives his Call to Adventure from an owl (or a series of owls) who deliver his invitation to the Hogwarts School of Witchcraft and Wizardry. The invitation is delivered on Harry's eleventh birthday, the perfect moment for a boy to take his first steps out of childhood and towards manhood.

The owl itself is a Herald figure, a common archetype in hero myths. The Herald is a figure from the outside world, from the realm of adventure, the realm of heroism and manhood. The role of the Herald is to draw the boy out of the static "world of the common day" and into the mutable world of physical and psychological transformation. Campbell noted that in hunting cultures such as those of the Native Americans who lived on the Great Plains, the Herald in their legends was often a deer or buffalo. The typical legend often begins with a boy out on the hunt (a narrative possibly associated with the "vision quest" puberty rite). The boy sees a deer or buffalo and chases it into the wilderness. The Herald animal continues to flee, and the boy continues his pursuit, until he finds himself in a land that he's never seen before. He has now, quite unwittingly, entered the realm of the animal spirits, and as Campbell put it, he has found himself "in full career of an adventure."

A famous Herald figure from fantasy literature is the white rabbit from Alice in Wonderland. Alice's experience with the rabbit is similar to that of the Native American boy's with the deer — the fleeing animal is pursued by the pubescent youth, and thus lured into the realm of adventure. The white rabbit, in Alice's case, may be interpreted as both a symbol of virginity (the color white), and a concurrent symbol of fertility (the rabbit), an indication of the girl's impending menarche. One more famous Herald figure is the robot droid, R2-D2, from the film *Star Wars* (1977). In this instance, we see a sci-fi take on a classic mythological theme. The young damsel in distress is being held captive by an evil tyrant. Her plea for rescue is received by the emergent hero via a holographic message saved onto R2-D2's hard-drive.

The Refusal of the Call represents the initial reluctance of the boy to take on adult roles, as it requires great sacrifice and the acceptance of great responsibility. The boy's first challenge is to overcome his own self-doubt and believe in himself. Frodo, the hobbit hero of *The Lord of the Rings* trilogy, is a reluctant hero. He refuses the call to adventure — the task of bearing the ring of power to Mordor — several times; and even after he accepts the task, he constantly doubts his own ability to live up to the responsibility of being the Ringbearer.

The legends of King Arthur tell a story of the boy Arthur, just 15 years old, who, while serving as squire to his older brother, Sir Kay, loses his brother's sword. In desperation, the boy pulls at the hilt of Excalibur, the legendary sword of kings, whose blade miraculously withdraws from the stone it was imbedded in with ease. Though just a boy, Arthur knows very well that only the true heir of Uther Pendragon — only the one true king of the Britons — could draw the sword from the stone. Nevertheless, young Arthur initially refuses this call to adventure. He brings the sword to his brother and gives it to him. However, the other knights demand that the sword be replaced into the stone and redrawn publicly. Only after Kay is unable to draw out Excalibur is it revealed that it was Arthur who drew the sword from the stone, and only after much prodding does Arthur perform this feat for a second time, proving to everyone, even himself, that he is the true and rightful heir to the throne.[13]

Moses is a similarly reluctant hero. In the biblical book of Exodus, when God's voice commands Moses from the burning bush —

> "So now, go. I am sending you to Pharaoh to bring my people the Israelites out of Egypt."[14]

Moses doubts his ability to complete the task, and in doing so, he even doubts God's decision to choose him as the Israelite messiah.

> But Moses said to God, "Who am I that I should go to Pharaoh and bring the Israelites out of Egypt?"[15]

God bolsters Moses' self-confidence by assuring him that he will support him in his task.

And God said, "I will be with you. And this will be the sign to you that it is I who have sent you: When you have brought the people out of Egypt, you will worship God on this mountain."[16]

But even after that encouragement, Moses is still reluctant and doubtful of his own abilities.

> And Moses answered and said: "But, behold, they will not believe me, nor hearken unto my voice; for they will say: The lord hath not appeared unto thee."[17]

God then bestows magic upon Moses' shepherd's staff and demonstrates three separate miracles that Moses can perform before the Pharaoh, to prove that he has been sent by God himself to redeem the Israelites. But even then, Moses *still* refuses the call.

> Moses said to the Lord, "Pardon your servant, Lord. I have never been eloquent, neither in the past nor since you have spoken to your servant. I am slow of speech and tongue."[18]

God, ever persistent, bolsters Moses once again with the promise that he will be with him the whole way.

> The Lord said to him, "Who gave human beings their mouths? Who makes them deaf or mute? Who gives them sight or makes them blind? Is it not I, the Lord? Now go; I will help you speak and will teach you what to say."[19]

Almost unbelievably, Moses still refuses the call of God to do his bidding

> But Moses said, "Pardon your servant, Lord. Please send someone else."[20]

Now the Bible reports that "the anger of God was kindled against Moses" for being so irritatingly reluctant. Only after God allows Moses to take his brother Aaron along with him as his spokesman, does the self-doubting Moses finally acquiesce to being the Israelite savior. In the history of myth, Moses is perhaps the most reluctant of the great religious heroes.

Supernatural Aid is an archetypal theme in myths, in which the hero finds or is given an important article, usually a weapon, that retains both magical and psychological power. The magical power is a link to the boy's true supernatural identity as a divine or semi-divine hero. The psychological power of the article is that it links the hero, typically an orphan, to his true, biological father. In this way, the Supernatural Aid is a physical reminder to the hero of both his heritage and his destiny, as the relationship with the father is usually at the heart of the mythological hero's adventure. Excalibur is probably the most famous mythological example of Supernatural Aid. By drawing the mystical sword from the stone, Arthur not only shows that he is the son and heir of the deceased king, Uther Pendragon; he affirms that he himself is destined to be the one true king, who will unite the fractured factions of England. Luke Skywalker's light-saber plays a similar role, as it is actually his father, Anakin's, light-saber. Hence, it links Luke to his dark father, Darth Vader, and it also becomes the weapon that defines Luke as a Jedi knight, the hero-warrior he was born to become. Moses' shepherd staff, especially after it is empowered with the spirit of God, represents not only Moses' personal identity as the man hand-chosen by God himself to redeem the Israelites; it also represents his public identity as a shepherd of men, a leader of the Israelite nation, who from Abraham through David, has always been identified as a shepherding people.

Harry Potter's Supernatural Aid, his magic wand, also fulfills the function of informing the boy of his heritage and destiny. As Mr. Ollivander, the owner-operator of the only wand shop in Diagon Alley, revealed to Harry as he gave him his wand: "It so happens that the phoenix whose tail feather is in your wand, gave another feather — just one other. It is very curious indeed that you should be destined for this wand when its brother — why, its brother gave you that scar ... the wand chooses the wizard."[21] Here, Mr. Ollivander is referring to the wand belonging to Voldemort, the dark lord who killed Harry's parents and nearly killed him, the villain that Harry is destined to destroy.

The Crossing of the First Threshold in the myth is when the boy leaves behind the world he grew up in (the world of mortals), and enters the realm of adventure, where reside the gods and monsters that he must encounter in order to become a hero. This stage is a symbol for the stage of transition in life from boy to man, and more so than the other stages, recalls the initiatory rites of passage at puberty. The chapter in the first Harry Potter book when Harry finally disembarks for the Hogwarts School is an initiatory crossing. He knows that the train he needs to get on must be boarded from "Platform Nine and Three-Quarters" at the King's Cross station; but of course, there is no such platform visible to the naked eye, because it is a magical platform, leading to a magical train, which will take Harry to a magical world. Harry must figure out a way to make this critical transition from the "muggle" world of his childhood (the mortal world), into the magical world of his adolescent and adult life (the "wizarding" world). Notably, Harry is cruelly abandoned at the station by his muggle family, his aunt and uncle, Petunia and Vernon Dursley, and his cousin Dudley; but he is taken in by a wizarding family, the Weasleys, who guide him onto the magical invisible platform and onto the equally magical train, the Hogwarts Express. This transfer of family attachments at the King's Cross station from the Dursleys to the Weasleys is the first step in Harry's complete transition from the muggle world to the magical world. By the end of the first book in the series, Harry will have replaced the bullying Dudley Dursey with the loyal and affable Ron Weasley as his surrogate brother. By the end of the second book, he will also have replaced the neglectful and abusive Aunt and Uncle Dursley with the lovable and nurturing Mr. and Mrs. Weasley as his surrogate parents. And finally, by the end of the series, Harry will actually become a real member of the Weasley family by marrying Ron's little sister, Ginny. The Crossing of the First Threshold for Harry Potter is a first crossing from muggle to magical world, from muggle family to magical family, and ultimately, from a muggle identity to a magical identity.

The passage in and out of the Belly of a Whale (or Beast) is an archetypal theme in myth and literature. In the Judeo-Christian tradition, the Biblical tale of Jonah is the most well-known example of this motif. Campbell explains that "the passage of the magic threshold is a transit into a sphere of rebirth ... symbolized by the worldwide womb image of the belly of the whale."[22] The boy, having passed through the magic threshold, dies in spirit, only to be reborn as a man. Jonah, as the Bible tells, enters the belly of a giant fish as he is fleeing the command of God to deliver the sacred message of repentance to Nineveh. After suffering in the fish "womb" for three days and three nights, Jonah communes with his tormentor and finally accepts his sacred mission, whereupon he is vomited out by the great fish onto dry land— "reborn"—no longer an anonymously reluctant Israelite, but a prophet of God. Bettelheim, in his psychoanalytic reading of the fairytale, provides a psychosexual take on the Belly of the Beast theme:

> Little Red Riding Hood lost her childish innocence as she encountered the dangers residing in herself and the world, and exchanged it for wisdom that only the "twice born" can possess: those who not only master an existential crisis, but also become conscious that it was their own nature which projected them into it. Little Red Riding Hood's childish innocence dies as the wolf reveals itself as such and swallows her. When she is cut out of the wolf's belly, she is reborn on a higher plane of existence; relating positively to both her parents, no longer a child, she returns to life a young maiden.[23]

In using the term "twice born," Bettelheim is referring to the Hindu concept of Dvija, which states that while the first birth of the individual is physical, the second birth is existential, occurring when one is initiated into a fulfilling and functional role in society. In this sense, both Jonah and Little Red Riding Hood are twice born or reborn via the passage through the womb-like belly of the beast/whale. Coming in, they knew not what they feared, they ran in ignorance of the inevitabilities and the responsibilities of life. Coming out, they have encountered their fears and integrated into themselves a better sense of who they are and what their roles are to be in society.

The Road of Trials is the stage in which the boy becomes a hero by proving his worth through a series of trials, tasks, and tribulations. There are many examples of trials and tests that heroes must overcome in myth and legend. Moses had to deliver the Ten Plagues to Egypt. Hercules had to complete his Twelve Labors for Eurystheus. Odysseus' long voyage home in *The Odyssey* is a seemingly endless Road of Trials, fraught with danger and peril at every turn. In *The Lord of the Rings*, Frodo's journey to Mordor is a Road of Trials, in which a monster or enemy emerges at nearly every step of the way. This stage of the hero's adventure recapitulates the ordeal aspect of the initiation ritual, in which the pubescent boy must demonstrate his masculinity and strength by withstanding some type of painful or injurious physical trial without fleeing or crying or otherwise betraying fear or weakness. Anthropological records abound with examples of the excruciating ordeals that both boys and girls must withstand in many cultures in order to pass through the invisible, mystical barrier between childhood and adulthood. They are referred to by anthropologists as "mortification rituals," because the initiate is placed in a situation in which they may actually die or get critically wounded, or in some cases the rituals are so gruesome and terrifying that the initiate might be "scared to death," or in other cases, the ritual itself symbolizes the death of the child and his spiritual rebirth as an adult. One lucid example is the initiation ritual of "a Thousand Cuts," that boys in the Sepik tribes of New Guinea undergo after puberty. The boys are cut hundreds of times along their back, chest, and buttocks, until their scarified skin resembles the scales of a crocodile. The tribesmen believe that the "Crocodile Spirit" consumes the boy, leaving behind a man. To add insult to injury, the boys are referred to as women and are treated as women throughout the entire painful, bloody ordeal — in order to make it clear that they will not be considered men until they have undergone the entire ceremony without showing pain or weakness. After the excruciating ritual, which takes weeks to complete, the boy — in dire need of some tender loving care — is returned to his mother for convalescence, which leads us into the next stage.

The Meeting with the Goddess is typically experienced by the hero at the point of the journey where he needs either spiritual or physical healing — which is usually just after the most grueling ordeal on his Road of Trials. If the Initiation portion of the hero's journey can be seen, in a Jungian interpretation, as a succession of stages in which the hero encounters and integrates different archetypal figures, in order to become a complete and balanced Self, then the Road of Trials represents the integration of the Hero archetype itself, which is the cultural ideal of the masculine ego. In the subsequent Meeting with the Goddess, the Earth Goddess figure is encountered and integrated.

She is the representation of the ideal mother — the healing, forgiving, nurturing, and embracing mother.

In one legend of Arthur, the king breaks his sword, Excalibur, while fighting a knight who was more powerful than he (in some accounts that knight is Sir Lancelot). As the sword is the symbol of Arthur's identity, representing both his heritage and his destiny, Arthur is crestfallen. Merlin tells Arthur to cast the broken shards into a lake, whereupon the Lady of the Lake arises from the misty waters, wielding Excalibur, now made whole again, which she returns to Arthur. In doing so, she repairs Arthur's broken spirit, and makes him whole again. In *The Lord of the Rings*, Frodo is heartbroken and crestfallen after his dear friend and most trusted mentor, Gandalf, is killed by a balrog in the abyss of Khazad-dûm. Galadriel, the Elven Queen of Lórien, plays the role of goddess to Frodo. She allows him to gaze into her magical reflecting fountain, which is a gift often given by the goddess ... the gift of intuition and self-reflection. In the fountain, Frodo sees his beloved Gandalf reborn as a figure in white, and is somewhat relieved. Overwhelmed by Galadriel's wisdom and empathy, Frodo offers her the one Ring of power. And here, briefly, we see the goddess in both dimensions, the motherly goddess of light who gives life and nurtures it; as well as the motherly goddess of shadow, who smothers and devours her children, dominating them completely in body and soul:

> And now at last it comes. You will give me the Ring freely! In place of the Dark Lord you will set up a Queen. And I shall not be dark, but beautiful and terrible as the Morning and the Night! Fair as the Sea and the Sun and the Snow upon the Mountain. Dreadful as the Storm and the Lightning! Stronger than the foundations of the earth. All shall love me and despair![24]

Galadriel, of course, overcomes her temptation to take the ring.

Temptation, as a stage in the journey, must be overcome by the hero before he can proceed to the climactic battle with the dark father figure. Campbell refers to this test as the stage in which the hero encounters the Woman as the Temptress, as Temptation is so often embodied in myth by the female seductress. The Sirens in the myth of Odysseus are perhaps the most vivid depiction of the temptresses power to sway the hero away from the straight path and lure him into perilous folly. But temptation must not always take the form of a seductress. At the heart of the stage is the concept that the hero's quest is a symbol for the spiritual quest of enlightenment, which is a universal quest for all men and women. Temptation as an archetypal theme is dangerous because it draws the hero back down towards the physical world of sensual desires, while the hero must direct his focus upwards towards the spiritual world of divine illumination.

While in the wilderness, Jesus is tempted three times by the Devil.

> After fasting forty days and forty nights, he was hungry. The tempter came to him and said, "If you are the Son of God, tell these stones to become bread.
>
> Jesus answered, "It is written: 'Man shall not live on bread alone, but on every word that comes from the mouth of God. [Matthew 4: 2–4].

Clearly, Jesus is stating that his concern is for spiritual rather than physical nourishment.

> Then the Devil took him to the holy city and had him stand on the highest point of the temple. "If you are the Son of God," he said, "throw yourself down. For it is written: "He will command his angels concerning you, and they will lift you up in their hands, so that you will not strike your foot against a stone.'"
>
> Jesus answered him, "It is also written: 'Do not put the Lord your God to the test.'" [Matthew 4: 5–7].

Here, Jesus resists the urge to put his spiritual connection with God to a physical test. The power of spirituality resides in pure faith. When a physical proof of this spirituality is demanded, it displays a lack of faith and therefore a feeble spirit.

> Again, the Devil took him to a very high mountain and showed him all the kingdoms of the world and their splendor. "All this I will give you," he said, "if you will bow down and worship me."
>
> Jesus said to him, "Away from me, Satan! For it is written: 'Worship the Lord your God, and serve him only'" [Matthew 4: 8–10].

The most common temptation for the hero, even more common than the seductress, is the temptation of power. Satan's last temptation of Jesus is the lure of pure, unadulterated power. The hero, once he has completed his Road of Trials and has been healed by the Goddess, is an extremely powerful figure. However, he has yet to face his biggest challenge, the inevitable encounter with the dark father. If only the hero allied himself with the dark forces rather than opposing them, he would become all-powerful, and one day he would rule the world himself as a dark lord. This temptation to join the dark father rather than depose him must be overcome. Jesus clearly tells Satan that he is not interested in ruling the kingdoms of the world, but only in serving his God, so that he may earn his position in the Kingdom of Heaven (which, as Jesus explains, is within ourselves).

Moses was tempted to stay in Egypt as a royal prince, but he chose to abandon his heritage as the Pharoah's daughter's adoptive son, and instead identify himself as an Israelite, a slave people oppressed by Egyptian tyranny. In *The Empire Strikes Back* (1983), Darth Vader delivers the archetypal temptation to his son Luke: "Luke, you can destroy the Emperor. He has foreseen this. It is your destiny! Join me, and together, we can rule the galaxy as father and son!" Luke, by allowing himself to fall into the abyss, chooses death over dark power. In the first Harry Potter book, Voldemort tells the hero: "Don't be a fool.... Better save your own life and join me ... or you'll meet the same end as your parents...."[25] In the film version, Voldemort ups the ante. He not only tempts Harry with power, but with his heart's deepest desire: "Harry, would you like to see your mother and father again? Together, we can bring them back.... There is no good and evil, there is only power.... Together, we'll do extraordinary things!"[26] And finally, in *The Lord of the Rings*, Frodo is tempted by the power of the Ring at every step of his journey. The Ring, in and of itself, is nothing more than a symbol of power — how power corrupts Man's soul — and how Man seems to be irresistibly drawn to power. In the end, even our hero, Frodo, cannot resist the temptation of power: "I have come ... but I do not choose now to do what I have come to do. I will not do the deed. The Ring is mine!" Ironically, it is the poor creature who loves the Ring more than anything — the creature whose entire body and spirit was devoured by the power of the Ring — it is Gollum who destroys, albeit accidentally, the one true Ring of Power.

Atonement with the Father is the psychological climax of the hero story, the moment of epiphany, when the hero gazes at the true nature of his own Self, and slays the dragon of his most primordial fears. "Atonement (at-one-ment) consists in no more than the abandonment of that self-generated double monster — the dragon thought to be God (superego) and the dragon thought to be Sin (repressed id). But this requires an abandonment of the attachment to ego itself, and that is what is difficult."[27] In Freudian terms, the oedipal drama climaxes at the moment when the son conquers the father, not by actually killing him, but by identifying with him. When the son can finally understand his own urges and overcome them, this triumph of the ego's will allows the son to see father not as a rival, but as a mentor and identification figure. The son, in this way, integrates and internalizes the father. The id is subdued, the superego reformed, and the ego of the boy dies and is reborn as the ego of a man. The hostile relationship with the father is atoned, as the son and father are now at-one.

In the myth, the father is represented as an ogre-tyrant or a dark lord, he is the embodiment of the undeveloped, immature psyche, in which the id is unrepressed and the superego is yet unformed. The ogre-tyrant/dark lord is pure desire, pure lust, a pure will to power. It craves total and complete control over everything. (In other words, it is the psyche of a two-year-old child.) The job of the developing ego is to outgrow this stage in which the unrepressed id's penchant for greed and lust and the unformed superego's penchant for power and control are intertwined in the form of a ravenous ogre. The hero, in the role of the ego, represents the new order that must defeat the old. The hero-ego must slay the ogre-id/superego, while at the same time recognizing the subtle truth, that all of these figures are one in the same — they are all different parts of the same psyche, that need to become integrated and unified.

> Stated in direct terms: the work of the hero is to slay the tenacious aspect of the father (dragon, tester, ogre king) and release from its ban the vital energies that will feed the universe. "This can be done either in accordance with the Father's will or against his will; he [the Father] may "choose death for his children's sake," or it may be that the Gods impose the passion upon him, making him their sacrificial victim. These are not contradictory doctrines, but different ways of telling one and the same story; in reality, Slayer and Dragon, sacrifice and victim, are of one mind behind the scenes, where there is no polarity of contraries, but mortal enemies on the stage, where the everlasting war of the Gods and the Titans is displayed. In any case, the Dragon-Father remains a Pleroma, no more diminished by what he exhales than he is increased by what he repossesses. He is the Death, on whom our life depends; and to the question "Is Death one, or many?" the answer is made that "He is one as he is there, but many as he is in his children here." The hero of yesterday becomes the tyrant of tomorrow, unless he crucifies himself today.[28]

As the psychological complexity of this stage is great, its manifestation in myth and fantasy is manifold. Sometimes the father is actually killed by the hero, as in the case of Oedipus. Sometimes a creature representing the father is killed, as in the case of the dragon-slaying, giant-slaying, and ogre-slaying heroes. In some stories, the son is a willing sacrifice, as in the Old Testament story of the Akedah, (Abraham's sacrifice of his son, Isaac); or as in the New Testament story of the Crucifixion. In other stories the father and son atone, as in the Greek myth of Phaëthon and Phoebus, or in the last episode of the Star Wars films, *The Return of the Jedi* (1987). In some stories, atonement is achieved via an act of retribution or restitution that avenges the death of a father, such as in Shakespeare's *Hamlet* or Disney's *The Lion King* (1994). In the last Harry Potter novel, atonement is achieved on all of these levels.

1. Voldemort, the Dark Lord, is killed by Harry in their final showdown. Though Voldemort is not Harry's actual father, it is established that they are spiritually linked, like father-and-son, in a somewhat complicated plot involving horcruxes and spells.

2. Prior to the final showdown, Harry allows himself to be killed by Voldemort — a willing sacrifice he makes in order to save his friends. However, unbeknownst to both Harry and Voldemort, the Dark Lord cannot actually

kill Harry, because of the aforementioned spiritual link between the hero and villain.

3. Though there is no reconciliation between Harry and Voldemort, a reconciliatory atonement occurs between Harry and his deceased mentor, Dumbledore, when Harry meets with Dumbledore on a spiritual/psychological plane, in between the scene where Voldemort nearly kills Harry, and the scene in which Harry finally kills Voldemort.

4. By killing Voldemort, the killer of Harry's mother and father, atonement with Harry's real father, James, is achieved, not just through the act of avenging his death — but by becoming the great wizard his father was — and by realizing the destiny he was born to fulfill.

The character arc of the mythological hero is a full circle, from the prophecy before his birth through the legends that arise after his death, which usually foretell of either a second coming, or the birth of another hero-king who will take his place. Within this arc there is an infant who grows to be a boy, a boy who is initiated into manhood, a man who becomes a leader of other men, a leader who teaches a younger hero how to lead, and finally, an old man who passes on into the stuff of myth, legends, and dreams. The end of the mythological hero's saga is typically tragic. All of this stands in contrast to the fantasy story hero, who's character arc is not a full circle, but a bow. The fantasy hero's story climaxes following his Atonement with the Father. His story ends with a great victory, and we leave him at his peak — a triumphant hero, a beloved husband, and a benevolent king. The stage following this climax — Apotheosis — is more typically experienced in the stories of the mythological hero.

Jesus, for example, has a moment of atonement with his disciples during the Last Supper, where his disciples become one with him by eating his body (the Passover matzoh) and drinking his blood (the Seder wine). (As this is a living myth, this Atonement is re-experienced by Christians in the ritual of Communion.) Following the Atonement with his disciples, Jesus has an Atonement with his Father, as he dies on the cross. Campbell points out that the cross itself, a shape in which the four directions intersect, is an ancient symbol of Atonement or Unification. It represents the "Axis Mundi," the World Axis, where the higher and lower realms unite, the connecting point between Heaven and Earth. The iconic image of Jesus on the Cross symbolizes this connection between Heaven and Earth, the Atonement between God the Father and his Son, Jesus, who serves as a mediator between God and his other children, the descendants of Adam and Eve. On the cross, Jesus atones with God, a willing sacrifice, accepting his destiny in return for the forgiveness of all men's sins.

There is a reconciliation with God, as Jesus finally understands the purpose of his life on Earth. And then ... then there is Apotheosis, the symbolic death and spiritual rebirth of the hero. This is the final initiation, the passage from mortal existence to immortality. Jesus, following his death on the cross, arises in spirit. The hero is now a god.

In fantasy stories, the stage of true apotheosis is usually never reached, though it is often alluded to, in that the hero often has a near-death experience at the apex of his climactic battle, which changes him from a purely physical to a more spiritual being. Harry nearly dies in all seven of the Harry Potter novels (often times more than once), and each near-death experience only strengthens his resolve. Frodo nearly dies after the Ring is destroyed at Mount Doom, but he is saved at the brink of death. The character that usually does experience the true Apotheosis is the hero's mentor, the character that plays the archetypal role of the Wise Old Man, which is the embodiment of the positive father figure. As the Wise Old Man is himself a hero at the end of his own character arc, it is fitting that he should experience this latter stage of ego development. In terms of the main hero's story, the death and apotheosis of his mentor at the climax of his journey is perfectly timed, as the hero is now ready to stand alone. He no longer needs the physical presence of a mentor, as he is a fully functioning individual who has integrated all of the disparate elements of his psyche into a complete whole.

In *The Lord of the Rings*, Gandalf the Grey, Frodo's mentor, experiences apotheosis after he sacrifices himself in battle with the balrog in Khazad-dûm, in order to save the Ringbearer and the rest of the Fellowship. His death is not only functional in terms of the development of Gandalf's character, it also furthers the development of Frodo's character as well. Frodo, following Gandalf's death, must now carry on alone, without the old wizard's arm to lean on. Frodo also learned, by witnessing Gandalf's death, what his own destiny must be. He learned that the ultimate act of the hero is self-sacrifice, which is a lesson that Frodo carries with him and reminds himself on every step of his journey, all the way to the cracks of Mount Doom. When Gandalf returns to the story, he has changed. No longer Gandalf the Grey, he is now Gandalf the White, a wizard with the spiritual power to overcome obstacles that the earlier Gandalf could not withstand. The exact same theme is played out in the *Star Wars* films. Luke's mentor, Obi Won Kenobe, sacrifices himself in battle with Darth Vader. But his physical death is transitory. His spiritual rebirth allows him to communicate with Luke more fluidly. As an internalized part of Luke's psyche, Obi Won is an even more powerful mentor than he was before. And in the Harry Potter books, Harry's mentor, Dumbledore, dies; but he reappears as a mystical/spiritual presence in the final book, once again giving Harry the final bit of wisdom and instruction that he needs in order to destroy the Dark Lord.

Though the symbolism of the Hero's Journey lies in the concept that this is truly an inner quest for psychological unity, the outer journey is focused on the physical quest, which usually involves the destruction of a shadow figure (dragon, ogre, tyrant) and/or the retrieval or destruction of a significant object (golden treasure, hostage princess, sacred/magical relic). This is the Ultimate Boon. It is a boon because it represents, in some way, the thing that will bring prosperity, peace, or unity to the hero's community. The Boon is usually a link between mortals and the gods, such as Prometheus' fire, Percival's Holy Grail, or Moses' Ten Commandments. In this sense, the Boon is also a symbol of the hero himself, as the hero — a semi-divine being — is also a link between mortals and the gods. Jesus, for example, is the actual Ultimate Boon in his myth. His story and his spirit and his message are the things that will redeem mankind. His symbol, the Cross, is merely a reminder of this concept. In every Harry Potter book, there is an Ultimate Boon that must be retrieved and/or destroyed in order to keep the powerful object out of Voldemort's hands. In the final book, there are seven Ultimate Boons, called "horcruxes," but the most important horcrux is Harry himself. The fact that Harry himself (like Jesus) is the ultimate Ultimate Boon, not only serves the plot of the series, in that it makes Harry the only one who can destroy Voldemort — it also serves the symbolism of the story, in that Harry himself, not any magical object, retains the spiritual power to rid the word of evil.

> The full round, the norm of the monomyth, requires that the hero shall now begin the labor of bringing the runes of wisdom, the Golden Fleece, or his sleeping princess back into the kingdom of humanity, where the boon may redound to the renewing of the community, the nation, the planet, or the ten thousand worlds. But the responsibility has been frequently refused....[29]

The Refusal of the Return recapitulates the reluctance of the hero demonstrated in the early part of his journey, but the reasoning has changed. In the Refusal of the Call, the hero is plagued by self-doubt, he does not think he is good enough to meet the challenge of the adventure before him. In the Refusal of the Return, the hero's problem is the exact opposite ... he thinks he is too good to return to the lowly world of mortals from which he has ascended. His challenge now is not to find the courage to proceed, but to summon the *humility* to return to the humble beginnings from whence he came, in order to save a community that may very well be undeserving of a savior.

Moses, atop Mount Sinai, communing with God for forty days and forty nights, descends the mountain to find the Israelites prostrating themselves before a pagan idol of Egyptian divinity, the Golden Calf. Moses smashes the stone tablets on which were written the Ten Commandments by the finger of God himself, forever destroying the physical testament of God's word, given to the Children of Israel. This is a Refusal of the Return. Though the Israelites are undeserving of God's love, undeserving of a messiah, Moses must now find the humility within himself to serve the Israelites, even though they are ungrateful and unworthy, and he must find forgiveness within his heart, even though the Israelites had forsaken their savior and their god. He must return to the mountaintop to retrieve a second copy of the Ultimate Boon.

Though Jesus' ultimate Return, the "Second Coming," is in the form of a promise for the future, one could imagine the reluctance of a savior to return to the world where he was tortured, humiliated, and crucified for the sins of men, who since his death have committed war and genocide and atrocities against each other that would sicken even the most forgiving of heroes, and all too often these acts were committed in Jesus' name. If ever there was a messiah too good for his people, this would seem to be the case, yet nevertheless, the "norm of the monomyth" would require the hero to return.

In the new genre of superhero movies — the modern mythical heroes — the superhero usually exhibits a Refusal of the Return, in his reluctance to remain a superhero, as the job requires complete self-sacrifice and the inability to lead a normal human life. In *Superman II* (1980), Superman gives up his superpowers so he can lead a normal life with his love interest, Lois Lane. Similarly, in *Spider-Man II* (2004), Spiderman gives up his spidey-powers so he can devote all of himself to his love interest, Mary Jane Watson. In both cases, the heroes quickly regain both their superpowers and their sense of responsibility to their communities, but only after the emergence of a new super-villain that is more powerful than any villain that had come before. In the end, the central character trait required of all heroes — self-sacrifice — is the attribute that empowers the hero to complete his journey.

"If the hero in his triumph wins the blessing of the goddess or the god ... the final stage of his adventure is supported by all the powers of his supernatural patron."[30] The Magic Flight is the passage of return to the mortal world by the now divine hero. Whereas the hero's departure away from home was fraught with trials and tests that stressed and fatigued the hero to the point of defeat, the Magic Flight is a demonstration of the prowess and supernatural powers of the hero, who returns to his home not a boy nor a man nor even a hero, but as a god. Moses descends the mountaintop with horns of light, the spiritual presence of the Lord, shining from his forehead. He then leads his people towards the Chosen Land, where the fearsome giants Sihon and Og are dispatched without the slightest bit of trouble or delay. The once meek and reluctant hero is now a formidable warrior-king. In *The Hobbit*, Bilbo and his dwarf companions are rescued in the nick of time by the Great Eagles of Middle Earth, who fly them on their backs to safety. In *The Lord of the Rings*, a similar flight occurs when Frodo and his companion, Sam, after destroying the Ring, return from Mordor on the wings of the Great Eagles, sent by Gandalf to save them. After defeating the wicked witch in Frank Baum's *The Wonderful Wizard of Oz* (1900), Dorothy employs a magical Golden Cap to summon the Winged Monkeys to fly her and her companions back to Emerald City. Later, Dorothy uses the power of her Silver Shoes to whisk herself home to Kansas.

The return to the mortal world for the now divine hero may occur in a fashion other than the Magic Flight, especially if the hero finds himself stuck in the realm of the gods. In these cases, a Rescue from Without is called for. "The hero may have to be brought back from his supernatural adventure by assistance from without. That is to say, the world may have to come and get him."[31] The passage from death's door on the backs of eagles, experienced by Bilbo and the dwarves in *The Hobbit* and by Frodo and Sam in *The Return of the King*, are examples of a Magic Flight and Rescue from Without combined. At the Crossing of the Return Threshold, the hero brings the wisdom of transcendental unity back to his society and his psyche, which is his home and his Self:

> The hero adventures out of the land we know into darkness; and his return is described as a coming back out of that yonder zone. Nevertheless — and here is a great key to the understanding of myth and symbol — the two kingdoms are actually one. The realm of the gods is a forgotten dimension of the world we know. And the exploration of that dimension, either willingly or unwillingly, is the whole sense of the deed of the hero.[32]

Upon crossing the threshold and returning to the world of mortals, the hero, having grasped the wisdom of the gods, is now a Master of the Two Worlds, he is both mortal and divine. For the brief time that he stays in the mortal world, the hero has much to teach to his disciples, and his powers to reform the evils of the common-day world are at their peak. In *The Return of the King*, when Frodo and his hobbit companions finally return to the Shire after their long journey, they do not return as the meek little hobbits that departed. They are now heroes, masters of warfare, fearless warriors who bow and make obeisance to no one. In the chapter entitled "The Scourging of the Shire," the returning hobbit heroes discover that their peaceful home has been overrun by invading foreigners, men once allied with the evil wizard, Saruman, who fled following the defeat of their dark lord and took possession of the Shire from the feeble hobbit inhabitants. Frodo, Sam, Merry, and Pippin waste no time in rising a force of insurgent hobbits against the invaders and routing them out with all due haste. Notably, Saruman, the evil wizard, is not killed in Mordor or Isengard — the great bastions of dark power and the primary battlefields of the Great War. He is killed in the Shire, amongst the little folk that he thought too insignificant to reckon in the tide of great events that swept over Middle Earth. As Jesus declared: "The meek shall inherit the Earth" (Matthew 5: 5).

In the story of the young man who comes of age via the confrontation with and displacement of an evil and invariably older figure of menacing tyranny, we see a symbol for the common, everyday boy who's challenge is to initiate himself into the company of men, and eventually live up to all of the social expectations heaved upon him by his elders, his peers, and himself. The final stage of Campbell's model of the Hero's Adventure is Freedom to Live:

> For the mythological hero is the champion not of things become but of things becoming; the dragon to be slain by him is precisely the monster of the status quo: Holdfast, the keeper of the past. From obscurity the hero emerges, but the enemy is great and conspicuous in the seat of power; he is enemy, dragon, tyrant, because he turns to his own advantage the authority of his position. He is Holdfast not because he keeps the past but because he keeps.[33]

The hero represents the future generation, and the hope that this generation can develop in freedom of the cultural chains and obstructive conventions that bound the parent generation in its day. He is the quintessential rebel, forever shaking up the status quo, never allowing the seat of tyranny to rest easy on its throne, forever making uneasy the head that wears the crown. And it is this perpetual uneasiness, this chronic state of conflict between the father and the son — the generation holding and the generation becoming — that makes freedom to live possible.

FOUR

The Princess

"Being a princess isn't all it's cracked up to be."
— Diana, Princess of Wales

While the pubescent male's rite of passage from boyhood to manhood is traditionally completed through a trial or ordeal that represents a triumph or achievement over some obstacle in the external world, the female rite of passage is traditionally accomplished via the completion of an internal metamorphosis — her body itself changes from that of a girl to a sexually matured, nubile, fertile woman. Hence, while the symbolism of the male hero's journey depicts the accomplishment of an external goal, which in turn precipitates the transformation of the boy into a man; in the case of the princess, the heroine figure in myth and fairytale being most commonly portrayed as a princess, the trials of her journey symbolize the psychological conflict and turmoil that she must undergo while her body itself transforms of its own accord. Like it or not, she will change from a girl into a woman. But is she psychologically ready for the social and physical transitions from maiden to wife, from daughter to mother, from virgin child to sexually mature and active woman?

The focus in this psychoanalysis of the princess archetype is on themes that symbolically represent the girl's apprehension towards her upcoming pubertal changes (menarche), as well as the physical acts and ordeals that these changes portend (sex, pregnancy, childbirth). In traditional cultures, these fears are fueled by menstrual taboos directed towards menstruating women. Menstruating women in primitive cultures and orthodox religions are often considered "unclean" and may even be temporarily exiled from society while menstruating. According to Orthodox Jews, a woman who is menstruating is referred to as a "Niddah"—she is ritually impure. Not only is her husband or any man forbidden to have sex with a Niddah, he may not sleep in the same bed with her, and he cannot even touch her. Any physical contact with a Niddah will render the man ritually impure.[1] James Frazer, in *The Golden Bough*, lists numerous menstrual taboos in primitive cultures from around the world, many of them even more severe than the Niddah laws of Orthodox Jews. Some anthropologists and psychoanalysts believe that the menstrual taboos among primitive peoples represent a primal male fear of the female reproductive area.[2] Nevertheless, even modern, liberated women in the 21st century often feel inhibited when it comes to talking about menstruation, especially in the presence of men, and these feelings of anxiety and inhibition are felt the strongest among adolescent girls.[3]

'Menses Anxiety' is the term I will use to indicate the general feeling of fear and apprehension that is typically portrayed symbolically in coming-of-age stories, especially fairytales, in which a girl, usually a princess, must overcome obstacles in order to achieve her goal, usually a marriage with a prince. The fear of the passing time, getting older, is more acute for the female, as the ticking of the biological clock towards menarche, as well as the ticking of the clock towards menopause, is more strongly felt by the female than the male, whose sexual maturity and sexual decline are not as decisively distinguished. "Menstruation, indeed, is named time, *menses* being the Latin word for 'months.' In our vernacular we refer to menstruation also in terms of time ... one's period."[4] The Wicked Witch's hourglass in the film *The Wizard of Oz* (1939) is a particularly vivid symbol of menses anxiety. The hourglass is filled with red sand. When the final grain of sand falls, Dorothy will die. In this case, the hourglass and the sand within it represent time and the clicking of the biological clock. The hourglass points to the sexually mature female figure, which will replace Dorothy's childlike physique, and the red color of the sand reminds her of the imminent emergence of menstrual blood, which will precipitate the physical change. The death of Dorothy is a symbolic death. It is the death of childhood and innocence, which is feared by the child as much as a literal death, for whom the hope of rebirth into a new and mature form is not completely understood. It is the job of fantasy and fairytale to help the girl prepare herself psychologically for these changes, by showing her in story (through symbolic themes), that although the inevitable changes of life are scary and even painful, they must not be avoided, but embraced, as the maiden's sorrow over the imminent death of her childhood will ultimately be prevailed by the joys of womanhood.

The Goose Girl

The Grimms' version of the ancient fairytale *The Goose Girl* begins as follows:

> There once lived an old queen whose husband had died many years ago, and she had a beautiful daughter ... the time came for her to be married and the child had to travel into the alien country.... When the hour of parting had arrived, the old mother went into her bedchamber, took a small knife and cut her fingers until she bled; then she let three drops of blood fall onto a white handkerchief, gave it to her daughter and said, "Preserve this carefully, dear child, it will be of great service to you on your trip."[5]

First, it should be noted that the princess fairytale very often begins with the death of the girl's mother. As the first stages of life (infancy and childhood), are marked by a strong attachment with the mother figure, the death of the mother at the very beginning tells us that the story will be dealing with the transition from the first stages of life to the next stage, in which a primary attachment is created with a male husband. "The three drops of blood [serve] as a symbol of achieving sexual maturity..."[6] The dying mother, in her last act, imparts a symbol to her daughter of the changes to come — the changes that, unfortunately, the mother will not be able to help her go through. The girl in the story loses the handkerchief with the three drops of blood. Consequently, she is forced to undergo a series of grueling trials and ordeals before she ultimately marries her prince and lives happily ever after. Nevertheless, the three drops of blood represent the mother's guiding hand to her daughter. "With the three drops of blood on the clean white rag, she minimizes and beautifies the three things connected with blood in a woman's life: menstruation, loss of virginity, and childbirth."[7]

Little Red Cap

Known more commonly as *Little Red Riding Hood* in America, *Little Red Cap* is perhaps the most clear and vivid depiction of the fairytale's use of symbolism to represent menses anxiety in the girl's psyche, especially as it relates to the fear of sex. The story begins with the girl's separation from mother:

> Come, Little Red Cap, take this piece of cake and bottle of wine and bring them to your grandmother ... when you're out in the woods, be nice and good and don't stray from the path, otherwise you'll fall and break the glass...[8]

Erich Fromm provides a simple psychoanalytic interpretation:

The "little red cap of velvet" is a symbol of menstruation ... and the warning "not to run off the path" so as not "to fall and break the glass" is clearly a warning against the danger of sex and of losing her virginity.[9]

Bettelheim draws out the psychoanalytic interpretation a bit more:

The name "Little Red Cap" indicates the key importance of this feature of the heroine in the story. It suggests that not only is the red cap little, but also the girl. She is too little, not for wearing the cap, but for managing what this red cap symbolizes, and what her wearing it invites. Little Red Cap's danger is her budding sexuality, for which she is not yet emotionally mature enough. The person who is psychologically ready to have a sexual experience can master them, and grow because of it. But a premature sexuality is a regressive experience, arousing all that is still primitive within us and all that threatens to swallow us up.[10]

The fairytale's portrayal of the Big Bad Wolf as a figure who is at once ravenous and charming, dangerous and inviting, cunning and seductive, offers a conflicted view of the male sex. If read as a warning, the parent is telling the girl: "Beware of the Big Bad Wolf, he will trick you into his bed and consume you with his lust!" If read as a symbol of the girl's own anxiety, the story is telling the girl: "Be aware of the wolf *inside* of you. Follow the straight path, control your impetuous desire to disobey the warnings, and you will master it. Stray off the path, and you allow yourself to be devoured by your own desires!" Bettelheim noted the psychological ambivalence of Little Red Cap in his description of Gustave Doré's famous illustration of the story:

The wolf is depicted as rather placid. But the girl appears to be beset by powerful ambivalent feelings as she looks at the wolf resting beside her. She makes no move to leave. She seems most intrigued by the situation, attracted and repelled at the same time. The combination of feelings her face and body suggest can best be described as fascination. It is the same fascination which sex, and everything surrounding it, exercises over the child's mind.[11]

Little Red Cap, of course, is lured from the straight path by the wolf, who entices her to pick some pretty wild flowers, the flower a symbol of the virginity of a pubescent girl, who has not yet been "deflowered". However, she is rescued from the belly of the wolf in the end by the good huntsman, suggesting that even girls who make a mistake early in life — if they are good and pure at heart — can sometimes be offered a second chance. Little Red Cap demonstrates that she learned her lesson well, as in the Grimms' version of the tale, there is a short secondary tale tacked on to the main story, in which Little Red Cap is not lured off the path by the wolf, and the wolf is killed by Little Red Cap herself.

Cinderella

It has been noted that the Cinderella type folktale is the most famous and widespread story type in the world.[12] It is particularly well-loved because the girl in the story is not born a princess, she becomes one after overcoming her trials and ordeals. In olden times, the highest social level a young woman could reach, given her lack of access to education or professional work, was that of a princess who would one day become a queen. The status of princess could only be achieved via station of birth or by marriage. Therefore, the Cinderella story, in which a girl rises above her ignoble social status to marry a prince, represents the highest achievement a girl could strive for. Obviously, there are other elements within the story that fascinate girls as well.

The figure of the evil stepmother (who will be discussed at length in the subsequent chapter) is a complex and multifaceted archetype. Suffice it to say at this point that for the princess, the evil stepmother represents a negative image of the good biological mother, who dies in the beginning of the story. While the function of the good biological mother is to help her daughter through the passage from maidenhood to womanhood; the function of the evil stepmother is to hinder and block her stepdaughter's development. In olden times, it was quite common for women to die in childbirth, and the rate of maternal mortality is still shockingly high in third world countries. As girls growing up in olden times were more likely to have stepmothers, and because stepmothers may have been more likely to favor their own biological children over their stepchildren, it is quite likely that the evil stepmother figure in the Cinderella story found an attentive audience among girls in those days. Similarly, the figure of the wicked stepsister was equally relevant to young girls in olden times, whose typical sibling rivalries and jealousies would have been amplified by their strained relationship status. It should also be noted that, since the only means of social mobility available to young women was the prospect of marrying well, the competition among girls, even sisters, to win the affection of an eligible, handsome, young prince, would have been fierce.

Moving on to the more oblique motifs within in the story, the glass slipper lends itself most directly to psychoanalytic interpretation.

> Two of the unique properties of glass are its transparency (purity) and its fragility, thus making it an appropriate symbol of virginity, as exemplified, for instance, in the bridegroom's breaking of a glass at a traditional Jewish wedding.[13]

Bettelheim noted in even more depth:

A tiny receptacle into which some part of the body can slip and fit tightly can be seen as a symbol of the vagina. Something that is brittle and must not be stretched because it would break reminds us of the hymen; and something that is easily lost at the end of a ball when one's lover tries to keep his hold on his beloved seems an appropriate image for virginity, particularly when the male sets a trap — the pitch on the stairs — to catch her. Cinderella's running away from this situation could be seen as her effort to protect her virginity.[14]

The girl's name, Cinderella, is derived from the fact that her wicked stepsisters tortured her by tossing peas and lentils into the hearth, forcing her to pick them out from the ashes. Hence, she was always covered in cinders and ashes. (The original German name of the girl was Aschenputtel, which does not hit the ear as nicely as Cinderella, but is certainly closer to the spirit of the tale, in which the girl's nickname was used in a mocking, derogatory fashion by her stepsisters.) The task of picking out peas and lentils from the ashes is reminiscent of the trial forced on Psyche by Venus (separating the different grains in a huge pile of mixed grains). In the myth, the trial is completed by Psyche in order to win back her lover, Cupid, the goddess' son. In the fairytale, Cinderella is unaware that she will eventually be rewarded for her trials with the love of a prince, but the theme of trial and reward remains similar. In the myth, Psyche is aided in her task by a colony of sympathetic ants. Similarly, in the fairytale of Cinderella, the girl is aided in her task by pigeons and turtledoves.

Cinderella's most significant helper is the spirit of her departed mother, who is resurrected in the Grimms' version of the fairytale as a white bird who lives in the tree planted above her mother's grave, and in the Perrault version, she is the Fairy Godmother. In both versions, the true mother's spirit dresses Cinderella in a beautiful gown, so she can attend the ball and enthrall the prince. In the Grimms' version, the stepsisters try to fool the prince in the end. The first stepsister cuts off her toe to fit into the slipper, but the prince sees the blood on the shoe and discovers the trick. The second stepsister cuts off her heel to fit into the slipper, but once again, the prince sees the blood and the jig is up. In this case, the appearance of blood points to an inappropriate connubial match, possibly alluding to the medieval superstitions regarding the evil spirits that exist within the "virgin blood," i.e. the blood released when the hymen is broken. At the end of the Grimms' version of the tale, the stepsisters are punished for their wickedness by having their eyes pecked out by pigeons, while Cinderella marries the prince. The retribution of blindness seems just, as the stepsisters were blind to their own malevolence, and could not see that mistreating Cinderella was unfair and cruel.

Rapunzel

Maternal cravings during pregnancy were often deemed dangerous in primitive cultures, creating the association in folklore between cravings and the socially forbidden or taboo.[15] In *Rapunzel*, the pregnant mother's craving for the witch's forbidden rapunzel lettuce is tragically succumbed to by the weak father, but it is the daughter that is punished for her mother and father's sin. In this sense, the forbidden craving could be seen as a symbol for forbidden (premarital) sex, which, when resulting in an unwanted conception and illegitimate child, results in a child who indeed must pay for her parents' sin. Perhaps this is why Rapunzel's parents are so oddly willing to give up their child in return for nothing more than a head of lettuce. The witch, however, does not lay claim upon Rapunzel until her twelfth birthday, (just before menarche is likely to occur). Playing the role of the negative mother, the witch locks Rapunzel up in a tower, forbidding her to see any man, thus inhibiting her ability to become sexually mature.

But nature cannot be impeded. Just as the Goose Girl's beautiful golden hair drew her prince to her, Rapunzel's long golden hair, a symbol of feminine beauty and sexuality, draws a handsome prince to her tower. Falling instantly in love, they commit the sin of premarital sex (later we learn that Rapunzel, in exile, gives birth to twin babies). Once again, the sin of fornication must be punished. Before the prince can return to rescue Rapunzel, the witch discovers their plot. She cuts off Rapunzel's hair in an attempt to cut off her sexuality, and banishes her to a faraway land. The prince falls off the tower and is blinded by thorns. Again, the retribution of blindness is just, because the impetuous prince was blind to the repercussions of his libidinous act. He did not see that having sex before marriage would cause Rapunzel to be shunned socially and exiled until after her pregnancy, a fate typical of young unwed girls who find themselves "in trouble." In the end, the prince, Rapunzel, and their children are reunited, but not before a long period of misery and separation.

The Maiden Without Hands

There are many variants throughout the world of the type of folktale in which a girl is mutilated, either by her father or by herself, after she refuses his sexual advances. In many instances, the heroine "responds by mutilating herself, then giving the amputated parts (usually hands or breasts) to her tormentor."[16] A person's hands relate directly to her social power, so cutting off the hands represents her total loss of empowerment. Another association with the girl's hands is the rite of marriage, in which the father gives his daughter's hand in marriage to her bridegroom. In the Grimms' tale *The Maiden Without Hands*, a father mistakenly promises his daughter's hand to the Devil. Whenever the Devil comes for the girl, he cannot take her because she protects herself by washing her body with clear water and drawing a circle around herself with white chalk. (Water represents purity, while white represents virginity, and the circle represents the girl's Self or Ego.) The Devil commands the father to chop off the girl's hands, so she cannot protect herself. When the father tells his daughter what he intends to do, she meekly replies: "Do what you want with me. I'm your child."[17] This telling bit of dialogue lends itself to a psychoanalytic interpretation, in which the tale represents a girl who has been despoiled by her own father, resulting in a maiden who is unfit for marriage, and therefore must remain at home with her father, stuck in the unfavorable position of being a sexual slave to her father's perverse desires (which are embodied in the figure of the Devil). Neither a proper daughter nor a proper wife, she is imprisoned by the ogre-like king, never to be rescued by the virtuous prince. Having no hands means she has no proper hand to be given in marriage, and no power or future in her society. Nevertheless, she decides to leave home, in the lowly state of a deformed and penniless beggar. After many ordeals, she is at last redeemed by the grace of God.

The amputation of the breasts in similar folktales represents a parallel theme. The development of breasts in the pubescent girl signifies both her sexual maturation, and the resultant awakening of her father's incestuous desire (or if one prefers the Electra interpretation, the reawakening of the daughter's incestuous desire, projected onto the father). The amputation of the breasts represents a desire for the daughter to return to the prepubescent state of childhood, a time in which the girl was free from her father's sexual advances. Amputation of the breasts may also represent the girl's desperate attempt to make herself sexually undesirable to her father, and by default, to make herself appear sexually immature to all men. And finally, the maternal association with the breasts may be interpreted as another expression of despoilment by the father. Here, the father, by treating his daughter as if she were his wife, the daughter's mother, makes his own daughter unfit for marriage to another man, thus disallowing her the freedom to become a proper mother to her own children. In all of these psychoanalytic interpretations, the chopping off of the hands or breasts represents menses anxiety as a manifestation of fear, reluctance, or inability to mature into the adult female roles of wife and mother, via a psychic regression to the Electra complex of early childhood.

Incest, as a theme in myth, fantasy, and fairytale, is ubiquitous.

While it is often portrayed in terms of shame and horror, incest can be viewed positively when it constitutes the foundational myth of a particular culture, and it is extremely common in creation myths around the world. Usually, incest between gods is a divine marriage, but incest between mortals is profane.[18]

If, symbolically, gods are parents and mortals are their children, then the incest of the gods represents the young child's naïve misunderstanding of the social rules pertaining to sexuality. "Why is father forbidden to me," asks the little girl, "when he is not forbidden to mother?" According to Freud, the task of the developing ego (and by extension, the tales that inform the ego) is to project carnal desires away from the same-sex parent and onto a socially appropriate love object. Hence, in the Electral interpretation of the incest theme, the father's sexual advances in the fairytale are actually the girl's own inappropriate incestuous desires projected onto the father.

An alternate interpretation, (which is a conclusion that a young Dr. Freud deduced but ultimately rejected), was that these tales and fantasies express the true fears and anxieties faced by girls who find themselves in the psychologically traumatic position of being the sexual object of a perverted father, brother, or any other elder male relative. Sexual abuse of children, especially girls, is rampant in the modern world. We may only imagine how much more common this problem was in the distant past, when daughters were treated as the literal property of their fathers, and fathers themselves were legally free to do whatever they wanted with their female children, without fear of repercussion from the law or even from the censure of their own cohort. Many researchers assume that the practice of a widower father to take one of his own daughters as a sexual partner was widespread and common in cultures throughout the world, including Europe in the Middle Ages.

Returning to the psychoanalytic interpretation, the unconscious expression of a forbidden desire (i.e. the "rape fantasy"), which expresses itself as unwilling intercourse, may be understood in light of the fact that the superego or moral structure of the female in ancient societies was required to forbid the wanton act of sex by a woman of high social stature. A woman of the higher class is considered to be either above or bereft of sexual desire; hence, for these women, the erotic desire is transformed into an aggressive fantasy, in which the female is allowed sexual contact, but through no voluntary act on her part, thus relieving her of the shame and guilt of wanton sexuality. A good woman cannot want sex, but if she is pursued and overpowered, then it is not her fault, and her repute remains untainted. Freud, when first using dream analysis and hypnosis as primary methods of psychoanalytic practice, discovered an unexpected tendency for his female patients to recall dreams or memories of sexual trauma or abuse at the hands of their fathers or other male relatives. At first he believed that he was uncovering actual memories of rape, incest, and sexual abuse. He later revised this theory, however, as he was apparently reluctant to assume that sexual abuse in the home could be so widespread as to be the basis of all neurosis. Also, since he himself was neurotic, the theory of sexual trauma as the root cause of all neurosis would mean that he himself was molested by his mother or father, an assumption that he was not willing to make. Once again, the tendency for Freud to over-generalize his theories — his determination to reveal the universal cause to all neuroses — led to an incorrect conclusion. Nevertheless, his rejection of the repressed memory theory for the "rape fantasy" led to some of his most important insights, culminating in the oedipal theory itself. In the oedipal (or in this case "electral") interpretation, the rape, when it occurs in dreams, is an unconscious expression of taboo incestuous desires. Since the actual desire is considered too taboo for direct expression, even in fantasy, the act of rape is conjured, which frees the victim of any guilt or shame for her part in the sexual act. Thus, *The Maiden Without Hands* is a fairytale expressive of an unconscious fantasy, which is cathartic for the girl as it releases the neurotic energy of the unconscious desire in a way that is not traumatic to the ego.

Myths from around the world, especially the Greek myths, are full of tales which involve the sexual pursuit of an unwilling female by a determined and undaunted male. The unconscious expression of what may be considered perverse or deviant desires, in which the act of sex is joined with the act of violence, is often referred to as the "submission fantasy," which is still claimed by psychoanalysts to be a widespread phenomenon among women. The fantasy of being pursued, overtaken, overpowered, and ravished, combines the primal urges of sex and aggression with the equally primal emotions of passion and fear. Contemporary psychoanalysts typically encourage their patients to accept submission fantasies in their dreams, emphasizing the difference between fantasy and reality.

Alice's Adventures in Wonderland

In Tim Burton's very broadly adapted 2010 film version of Lewis Carroll's *Alice's Adventures in Wonderland*, the title character is given psychological issues that are reminiscent of the themes from fairytales. Alice is an adolescent on the verge of womanhood. She is expected by everyone in her repressed Victorian social circle to give up her childish dreams of wonder and fantasy and adopt the adult role of a corset-wearing, etiquette-obsessed, uptight English lady. But young Alice is still mourning her recently deceased father, who represents both her lost childhood and her attachment to the world of fantasy. Nevertheless, she is being forced into an unwanted engagement with a foppish, lordly, twit, when — quite unexpectedly — she spots a watch-bearing white rabbit. Alice impulsively chases after it and falls down a tree hole, entering the enchanted realm. Here we are introduced to a number of ripe symbols.

The rabbit, a symbol of fertility, carries a clock, a reminder of the problem of menses, and even exclaims repeatedly: "I'm late! I'm late!" The theme of rapid growth and equally rapid shrinkage, evident in Carroll's book, is even more apparent in the film, as a symbol of the nubile girl's anxieties over maturation. On the one hand, she looks forward to growing up and experiencing all that adult life has to offer; but at the same time, she fears all of the pain and ordeals associated with the roles of mother and wife, while she also grieves the loss of her childish innocence and whimsy. Once she enters Wonderland, Alice is informed by its inhabitants that she is the "wrong Alice"— not the little Alice who had visited the fantasy world as a child — but the grown up Alice. She's lost her "muchness," they tell Alice — her childish tendency towards grandiosity and imaginary flights of fancy. In the film, Alice finds a happy medium, regaining her "muchness" by expanding her ego, and finding the inner strength to reject her unwanted suitor and live her life on her own terms.

Briar Rose

The Grimms' version of the fairytale *Briar Rose* is more commonly known as *Sleeping Beauty,* due to the immensely popular Disney movie from 1950. In the Grimms' version, a baby daughter, Aurora, is born to a king and queen. Twelve wise women are invited to bless the child, but when an uninvited thirteenth wise woman appears (insulted at being snubbed), she curses the baby: "In her fifteenth year the princess shall prick herself with a spindle and fall down dead!"[19] The spindle and spinning wheel is a worldwide symbol of femininity and especially of motherhood, as mothers in olden times spent much of their day spinning flax and wool to make clothes for their children. Similarly, the round shape of the wheel reminds us of the womb. Frazer reported in *The Golden Bough* that many cultures have superstitions regarding knots and pregnancy. In essence, knots are bad luck because they represent the tying up of the fallopian tubes and/or umbilical cord, which will result in infertility, miscarriage, stillbirth, or complications during pregnancy. To avoid such bad luck, a pregnant woman must make sure that there are no knots to be found in her household, and any string, thread, or rope found to be knotted must be untangled and spread out at once. The pricking of the finger on the spindle, more simply, represents menarche, the appearance of the first blood.

> In times past, fifteen was often the age at which menstruation began. The thirteen fairies in the Brothers Grimm's story are reminiscent of the thirteen lunar months into which the year was once, in ancient times, divided. While this symbolism may be lost on those not familiar with the lunar year, it is well known that menstruation typically occurs with the twenty-eight day frequency of lunar months, and not with the twelve months which our year is divided into. Thus, the number of twelve good fairies plus a thirteenth evil one indicates symbolically that the fatal "curse" refers to menstruation.[20]

Fortunately, after the curse is made, the twelfth wise woman offers a blessing: "The princess shall not die.... Instead, she shall fall into a deep sleep for one hundred years."[21] Although the king had burned all the spinning wheels and spindles in his kingdom to protect his daughter, on the day of her fifteenth birthday, the princess is inexplicably left all alone in the palace, and equally inexplicably, she comes across a door that she'd never seen before, with a phallic symbol sticking out of it. "A rusty key was in the lock, and when she turned it, the door sprang open, and she saw an old woman in a little room sitting with a spindle and busily spinning flax."[22] After pricking her finger, the princess falls into a deep slumber that spreads throughout the entire palace. A briar hedge grows around the palace, surrounding it, thus giving the princess her name, "Beautiful Sleeping Briar Rose." Sleep, in this case, represents the psychosexual stage of Latency, in which the libido is temporarily dormant before it matures during the subsequent Genital stage of adolescence.[23] Rollo May made an association between the briar of twisted thorns and the pubic hair that grows around the vagina at puberty. Yolen also sees a sexual symbol in the briar: "The briar in Sleeping Beauty encapsulated the Druidic language of trees, which sees the briar as signifying eroticism."[24] The princes who come too soon to fetch Aurora get stuck on the briar and "died miserable deaths." However, when the hundred year curse was over (or, in other words, when the princess' body and mind were ready), the "beautiful flowers" blossoming on the briar surrounding the palace "opened of their own accord." The consummate moment of maturation comes with the kiss of the lucky prince. Here the flower, especially the red rose, is associated with feminine passion and sexuality in general, and the female genitalia (which buds and opens at the time of sexual maturation) in particular. Hence, the loss of virginity is a "deflowering." If the flower is plucked too soon, it is traumatic.

But if it is plucked at just the right time, when it opens of its own accord, it is beautiful.

The theme of *Briar Rose* is that of the reawakening of the dormant libido following its long exile in Latency, which is represented by the extended slumber of the princess. Her libido is finally released by the power of "Love's First Kiss." The sleeping curse is a fixation in the Latency stage, symbolic of the girl's reluctance to proceed from the innocence of childhood to the Genital Stage ... the stage of sexual maturity, loss of innocence, as well as the acceptance of adult responsibilities and obligations. The handsome prince's first kiss represents the inevitability of sexual maturation, just as the prince himself is irresistible. Once the sleeping princess gives in to her repressed, latent desire, her soul is reanimated — or in Jungian terms — her repressed anima is released.

Snow White

The Grimms' version of *Snow White* begins:

> Once upon a time, in the middle of winter when the snow flakes fell like feathers from the sky, a queen sat at a window which had a frame of black ebony. And as she was sewing while looking at the snow, she pricked her finger with the needle and three drops of blood fell on the snow. The red looked so beautiful on the white snow that she thought to herself, "I wish I had a child as white as snow, as red as the blood, and with hair as black as the wood of the window frame." Soon after she got a little daughter who was as white as snow, as red as blood, and had hair as black as ebony, and she was therefore called Snow White...

Bettelheim explains:

> Fairy tales prepare the child to accept what is otherwise a most upsetting event: sexual bleeding, as in menstruation and later in intercourse when the hymen is broken. Listening to the first few sentences of "Snow White," the child learns that a small amount of bleeding — three drops of blood (three being the number most closely associated in the unconscious with sex)[25] — is a precondition for conception, because only after this bleeding is the child born.[26]

The good mother dies and the father is remarried to a vain and wicked woman. The archetypal stepmother in this tale is evil because she's trying to stop nature, attempting to hold off forever the natural development of her daughter from girl to woman. She's trying to keep the princess' budding sexual desires forever repressed within the straightjacket of a "sleeping death." The stepmother is also revolting against a harsh but inevitable truth of life: as the daughter comes of age and reaches the peak of her beauty and sexual attractiveness, her mother is simultaneously declining in beauty and attractiveness.

Thus, the biological clock that ticks towards menarche for the daughter, resulting in menses anxiety, is concurrently ticking towards menopause for the mother, resulting in aging anxiety — (female anxiety over declining attractiveness, health, and fertility). *Snow White* is a story in which both of these anxieties come to a head within a single relationship.

When the magic mirror tells the stepmother, "You, my queen, may have a beauty quite rare, but Snow White is a thousand times more fair,"[27] the queen commands her huntsman to kill the girl and bring back her lungs and liver as proof of her death. When the stepmother eats the lungs and liver (secretly replaced by the huntsman with the organs of a boar), she believes that by devouring Snow White's flesh (as if in a primitive ritual),[28] she will acquire the youth and beauty of her stepdaughter. But the huntsman had secretly taken pity on the child and allowed her to go free. In the deep of the woods, Snow White is taken in by a group of dwarfs. Here, the little people symbolize the desirable state of being a little child. Though Snow White lives, her stepmother is victorious, because she has successfully stunted Snow White's development, and has forced her to regress to a state of early childhood.

However, the stepmother is still driven by her envy and anxiety, so when the mirror tells her that Snow White still lives, she disguises herself as a peddler and comes to the dwarfs' cottage selling staylaces (corsets). A corset, of course, is a garment worn by women to accentuate the hourglass figure. When the stepmother ties the staylaces around Snow White's torso, she is playacting at the role of the good mother, who encourages her daughter's development into a woman; but the stepmother actually tightens the laces so hard that she suffocates the child, and she leaves, thinking once again that she has killed her. If the psychoanalytic interpretation of the "sleeping death" is made here, we see Snow White moving forward towards the Genital Stage of sexual maturation, but her wicked stepmother hinders her by forcing her back down into the dormant stage of Latency, in which the libido is suffocated, i.e. repressed. Fortunately, the dwarfs return home in time to resuscitate the girl. The next day, the stepmother returns with a poisoned comb. As in *The Goose Girl* and *Rapunzel*, the girl's long, luscious hair is a potent symbol of her sexual attractiveness. So the stepmother once again pretends to be the good mother in combing Snow White's hair, but the poison knocks the girl unconscious. Fortunately, once again, the dwarfs return in time to remove the comb and save Snow White. The stepmother returns for a third time with a poisoned apple. The sexual connotation of the apple is firmly established in the biblical story of Adam and Eve, in which the forbidden fruit (typically depicted as an apple) represents sexual temptation. When Snow White bites into the red part of the apple, she falls into a sleeping death so powerful that not even the dwarfs can revive her. In the Grimms' version of the tale, the piece of apple lodged in Snow White's throat is released when the prince carries her off to his castle, causing her to be revived; but the Disney film version (1939) depicts the theme of reawakening a bit more vividly, when the princess is brought back to life by "Love's First Kiss." Sexual maturation, just like a handsome young prince, cannot be stopped. In a fitting denouement, the ever-jealous stepmother cannot resist attending Snow White's wedding, where she is forced to put on red-hot iron slippers, and dances until she falls down dead.

Fitcher's Bird *and* Bluebeard

The Grimms' fairytales *Fitcher's Bird* and *Bluebeard* are quite similar in theme, yet with distinguishing features that are worthy of noting. In *Fitcher's Bird*, a maiden is kidnapped from her father by a sorcerer, who keeps her prisoner in his "house in the middle of a dark forest." He tells her one day:

> I must go on a journey and leave you alone for a short time. Here are the keys to the house. You may go wherever you want and look at everything except one room, which this small key here opens. If you disobey me, you shall be punished by death.[29]

The sorcerer then hands her an egg.

> "I'm giving you this egg for safekeeping. You're to carry it wherever you go. If you lose it, then something awful will happen."[30]

The sorcerer is a negative father figure, representing illicit or incestuous sexual desires. The egg, "with its obvious symbolism of femininity, fertility, and fragility," represents both virginity and potential maternity, while the key is an obvious phallic symbol.[31] The forbidden door clearly represents sexual temptation, and the threat of death represents the death of childhood innocence.

> Finally she came to the forbidden door ... curiosity got the better of her.... She stuck the key into the lock, turned it a little, and the door sprang open. But, what did she see when she entered? There was a large bloody basin in the middle of the room, and it was filled with dead people who had been chopped to pieces. Next to the basin was a block of wood with a glistening ax on top of it. She was so horrified by this that she dropped the egg she had been holding in her hand, and it plopped into the basin. She took it out and wiped the blood off, but to no avail: the blood reappeared instantly. She wiped and scraped, but she could not get rid of the spot.[32]

When the sorcerer returned home, he was none-too-pleased to find blood on the egg.

He threw her down, dragged her along by the hair, cut her head off on the block, and chopped her into pieces, so that her blood flowed on the floor. Then he tossed her into the basin with the others.[33]

The same exact fate befell the girl's younger sister, but the third sister fared better. She stored the egg in a safe place before passing through the forbidden door, and when she found her vivisected sisters in the bloody basin

she gathered the pieces together and arranged them in their proper order: head, body, arms, and legs. When nothing more was missing, the pieces began to move and join together. Both the maidens opened their eyes again.[34]

The dead, bloody, butchered women in the basin were girls who had passed through that mystic barrier from girlhood to womanhood. In the end, the girl sees that the maidens who passed through the forbidden door were not dead after all, they just seemed dead to the perception of a child who doesn't know any better. They're still alive, really — just in a different form. Though the trials of womanhood (menstruation, the first sexual act, and childbirth) seem to the girl to be just a painful gory bloody mess, the lesson to be learned is that these ordeals can be survived.

The sorcerer returns, but when he found no blood on the egg, "he no longer had any power over her and had to do what she requested."[35] She told him to carry a basket of gold to her father's house as a dowry for their wedding, and she hid her sisters in the basket. (As the first two sisters did not pass the initiatory test, they must return to the childhood state, under their father's roof, until they are ready to mature.) While the sorcerer was away, the third sister "dipped herself into a barrel of honey, cut open a bed, and rolled around in the feathers so she looked like a strange bird, and it was impossible to recognize her."[36] This blatantly erotic symbol of transformation shows that when the girl is ready for the connubial bed, the sexual act can be sweet as well as transformative. The maiden has now changed beyond recognition, she has become "Fitcher's Bird," i.e. a woman, not a girl. (In German, the word for bird, "vogel," is also an antiquated slang term for the sexual act. In England, a similar association is made, as the word "bird" refers to a sexually mature girl; while in America, the corresponding slang word is "chick.") At the end of the tale, the evil sorcerer is burned alive by the sisters' brothers, the traditional guardians of a maiden's sexual sanctity.

In *Bluebeard*, there is no egg, but the golden key (phallus) that Bluebeard gives the maiden is stained with blood (virgin blood from the hymen). The maiden cannot resist opening the forbidden door, which in and of itself represents an "eternal Temptation."[37]

Despite all warnings about the dire consequences if she tries to find out, woman is not satisfied with remaining ignorant about sex and life.... Notwithstanding all the hardships woman has to suffer to be reborn into full consciousness and humanity, the stories leave no doubt that this is what she must do.[38]

Giving in to sexual temptation, as an archetypal theme, is almost always punished with some form of death.[39] The beata culpa or "fortunate guilt" for the sin of disobedience is an archetypal theme found throughout mythology, from Eve eating the forbidden fruit, to Pandora opening the forbidden box, to Prometheus stealing the forbidden fire. The adolescent sin of disobedience, represented in myth as Man's disobedience towards God, leads to pain, but through this pain comes wisdom or spiritual enlightenment. The insight gained from the Tree of Knowledge is the child's key to the forbidden door of adult relations. As Ludwig Tieck wrote in his version of the *Bluebeard* fairytale:

Cursed curiosity! Because of it sin entered the innocent world, and even now it leads to crime. Ever since Eve was curious, every single one of her worthless daughters has been curious.... The woman who is curious cannot be faithful to her husband. The husband who has a curious wife is never for one moment in his life secure.... Curiosity has provoked the most horrifying murderous deeds.[40]

Just as Bluebeard's maiden was punished for opening the forbidden door, so was Psyche punished for opening the jar of beauty, and Eve for eating the apple, and Little Red Cap for straying off the path. The moral of the theme is not necessarily that girls should be warned against flowering into the beauty and sexuality of their adolescence; but rather, like all things in life, every blessing is accompanied by a curse as well. The lesson we learn from the fairytales is, don't be impetuous about growing up, it will happen eventually and all too soon, and when it's all over we often realize that we lost more than we gained. Every great pleasure is paid for by a corresponding pain, and every deep desire has its equal and corresponding fear.

FIVE

The Goddess and the Witch

"These are three essential aspects of the mother: her cherishing and nourishing goodness, her orgiastic emotionality, and her Stygian depths."

— Carl Jung

The mother archetype is perhaps the most fundamental of all the archetypes, as it relates to the primary human relationship, the earliest love object and emotional attachment, which existed, perhaps in its strongest manifestation, even before the birth of the individual. As the mother is the primary attachment in the formative stages of life, it is essential to the health of the ego that the unconscious image of mother remains pure and positive. Hence, there exists the necessity of "splitting" any negative associations with the mother figure into a separate archetype, thus creating two separate archetypal figures from the original one.[1] The positive archetype retains the primary association with the original nurturing birth mother — the Earth Goddess, goddess of fertility, life, and nature. And the negative archetype takes on all of the destructive attributes of the mother figure that begin to appear once the initial separation, the birth trauma, is experienced. The negative archetype continues to grow in power and ferocity with each subsequent experience of separation anxiety or conflict (weaning, termination of co-sleeping, toilet training, etc.).[2] She is the Wicked Stepmother and/or Witch, goddess of death, pain, and destruction.[3] As Jung explains:

These attributes of the mother archetype ... I formulated ... as "the loving and the terrible mother." Perhaps the historical example of the dual nature of the mother most familiar to us is the Virgin Mary, who is not only the Lord's mother, but also, according to the medieval allegories, his cross. In India, "the loving and the terrible mother" is the paradoxical Kali. Sankhya philosophy has elaborated the mother archetype into the concept of *prakṛti* (matter) and assigned to it the three *gunas* or fundamental attributes: *saltva, rajas, tamas:* goodness, passion, and darkness. These are three essential aspects of the mother: her cherishing and nourishing goodness, her orgiastic emotionality, and her Stygian depths.[4]

Bettelheim explains how a maternal archetype in fairytale is split into two separate figures, using Little Red Cap as an example:

Unable to see any congruence between the different manifestations, the child truly experiences Grandma as two separate entities — the loving and the threatening. She is indeed Grandma *and* the wolf. By dividing her up, so to speak, the child can preserve his image of the good grandmother. If she changes into a wolf—well, that's certainly scary, but he need not compromise his vision of Grandma's benevolence. And in any case, as the story tells him, the wolf is a passing manifestation — Grandma will return triumphant. Similarly, although Mother is most often the all-giving protector, she can change into the cruel stepmother if she is so evil as to deny the youngster something he wants.[5]

And Campbell, as was his wont, delineates the split maternal archetype categorically:

For she is the incarnation of the promise of perfection; the soul's assurance that, at the conclusion of its exile in a world of organized inadequacies, the bliss that once was known will be known again; the comforting, the nourishing, the "good" mother — young and beautiful — who was known to us, and even tasted, in the remotest past. Time sealed her away, yet she is dwelling still, like one who sleeps in timelessness, at the bottom of the timeless sea. The remembered image is not only benign, however; for the "bad" mother too —(1) the absent, unattainable mother, against whom aggressive fantasies are directed, and from whom a counter-aggression is feared; (2) the hampering, forbidding, punishing mother; (3) the mother who would hold to herself the growing child trying to push away; and finally (4) the desired but forbidden mother (Oedipus complex) whose presence is a lure to dangerous desire (castration complex)—persists in the hidden land of the adult's infant recollection and is sometimes even the greater force.[6]

The Goddesses of Light and Dark

Encapsulating all of the loving and life-giving attributes of the maternal archetype, the Goddess figure is ubiquitous throughout mythology. She is the Goddess of Life, Birth, and Rebirth, such as the Egyptian Isis and the Christian Mother Mary. She is also the Chthonic Mother or Earth Mother — Mother Nature — Gaia in Greek mythology, whose body itself both gives birth to all life and still nurtures it. She is the Goddess of Love, Sex, Passion, Beauty, and Fertility, such as the Greek Aphrodite and Demeter, the Indian Parvati, and the Egyptian Nut; but she can also be the Goddess of Purity, Fidelity, and Chastity, as in the Christian Virgin Mary and the Greek Hera. She is the Protective Goddess, the Goddess of Nurturing, Kindness, and Forgiveness (the Greek Artemis and Hera, the Egyptian Bast, and the Christian Mary). She is also the Goddess of Light, Wisdom, Compassion, and Understanding (the Greek Sophia, the Jewish Shechina, the Greek Athena, and the Chinese Kwan Yin). She also is the Goddess of Music and the Arts (the Greek Muses).

The negative or contrary aspects of the mother are depicted in myth as witches, destructive goddesses, or sorceresses. She is the harbinger of death or the medium between mortals and the spirits of death. The Witch of Endor in the Bible converses with the spirit of the deceased prophet Samuel. Hecate, the Greek goddess of sorcery and witchcraft, mistress of darkness and of the underworld, was a fearful deity, whose spiritual presence in the night elicited the barking of dogs. Medea, arguably the most villainous mother in Greek mythology, slaughtered her own children. The Graeae, in Greek mythology, were a trio of sisters who shared one eye and one tooth. They were portrayed as old hags and powerful sorceresses. A similar trio of goddesses in Greek myth, the Fates, sewed the thread of life for each mortal on earth, and thus were goddesses of death and destruction.

Shakespeare evoked the image of the Fates in his casting of the three witches in *Macbeth*. The three witches appear in Lloyd Alexander's fantasy novel *The Black Cauldron*, but their character is more in line with the Greek myth than with the medieval version of the witch. The Three Sisters in *The Black Cauldron*, Orddu, Orwen, and Orgoch, are immensely powerful enchantresses. Though they initially appear as hags, they later transfigure for a brief time into beautiful maidens; and they are neither good nor evil, being more-or-less disinterested in human affairs. They admit to enjoying the taste of human flesh (the cannibalistic trait of witches will be discussed in depth later), but they do no harm to Taran, the hero. Rather, they help him find and destroy the unholy cauldron. In Rick Riordan's series of *Percy Jackson and the Olympians* fantasy novels, the Fates make an appearance in the initial novel, *The Lightning Thief*, as three old ladies who knit the socks of death. In the second novel, *The Sea of Monsters*, a different trio of Fates operate as taxi drivers in New York City. Another death goddess from Greek mythology appears in *The Lightning Thief*. Medusa, the villainous witch who can turn heroes into stone with just a look of her face, masquerades in the novel as Aunt Em, the owner of a shop that sells stone garden gnomes ... (Aunt *M* ... get it?).

The traditionally feminine task of sewing is often used to impart a mater-nal quality to a fictional character. In *Taran Wanderer*, Lloyd Alexander's fourth fantasy novel in the *Chronicles of Prydain* series, Dwyvach, an Old Weaver Woman, takes poor Taran into her home and becomes a much needed mother figure to the orphan hero. In Greek myth, Arachne was a mortal woman who was more gifted in weaving than any woman who ever lived. But her pride and hubris was punished by the goddess Minerva, who turned her into a spider, thus creating the creature that can weave so well. In Native American mythology, the Grandmother Spider is a Goddess of Life who is nurturing and inspires creativity. The Grandmother Spider archetype is recapitulated in the character of Charlotte from E.B. White's classic fantasy novel, *Charlotte's Web*. In the story, Charlotte the barn spider is a motherly and nurturing figure to the hero, Wilbur the pig, whose dying acts include weaving a miraculous web that saves Wilbur's life, and the laying of an egg sack that hatches into a future generation of arachnids.

In the Judeo-Christian tradition, Lilith, Adam's first wife, was envisioned as the witch-mother of all demons. According to Jewish mystical texts like the Kabbalah, Lilith was created by God from the same earth with which Adam was created, rather than being created from Adam's rib, as was Eve. Hence, Lilith was Adam's equal, and therefore demanded equal rights, including, according to some texts, the right to the top position during sexual intercourse. Because Adam would not yield to Lilith, the first woman was either banned from Eden or left on her own accord (texts disagree on this point), and went on to develop into a fearsome legendary figure, who seduced men while they slept (i.e. a succubus), which enabled her to give birth to demons. Lilith also stole the souls of babies as they slept, resulting in crib death (SIDS). Lilith reemerged in the Victorian era as a more sympathetic character, and was the subject of many significant poems and works of art. George Mac-Donald, a key author in the early years of the genre of fantasy literature, published a fantasy novel entitled *Lilith* in 1895, which was extremely influential for future fantasy writers such as C.S. Lewis and Tolkien. More recently, Lilith has been adopted by the feminist movement, resulting in the popular "Lilith Fair" concert tour, and a host of empowered fantasy figures, from comic book super-heroines to erotic novel vampiresses. It is worthwhile to note that Harry Potter's saintly mother was also named Lilith.

The character of Jadis, the White Witch, in C.S. Lewis' Narnia novels, is based primarily on the mythological figure of Lilith. In the first book of the series, *The Lion, the Witch, and the Wardrobe,* the White Witch appears in the fantasy world at the same time that the children, in the real world, feel abandoned by their real mother, who sent them off to live in the country during the Battle of Britain. In this way, she symbolizes the fear of abandonment attached to the mother figure. Later in the book, it is explained that she was descended from Adam's first wife, and is not a "Daughter of Eve."[7] In *The Magician's Nephew*, the hero's central conflict in the real world is his mother's terminal illness. His feelings of anger and fear, i.e. separation anxiety, are projected onto Jadis, the shadow mother in the fantasy world. Later in the same story, Jadis eats the Fruit of Everlasting Life, a fruit much like the forbidden fruit in the Garden of Eden. There are, however, some elements of the Jadis character that seem to be derived from Greek myth. For example, Jadis has the magical ability to turn people into stone, like Medusa the Gorgon in Greek mythology. Jadis, as a goddess of Winter, appears to be the antithesis of the Greek goddesses of Spring, Demeter and Persephone.

The Phallic Mother

A rather obscure term in psychoanalytic literature, the "phallic mother" refers to a dominating female who, though lacking a proper penis, retains a figurative phallus in that she wields the societal manifestation of the phallic symbol ... aggressive power. The uncanny expression of masculine aggression in the form of a female figure recalls infantile fears of an omnipotent mother. Campbell noted that the image of the phallic mother was "perfectly illustrated in the long fingers and nose of the witch,"[8] though the motif can just as easily be seen in the traditional witch's wand, a potent phallic symbol. Melanie Klein believed that the weapons of the phallic mother are an absent breast that threatens the child's survival, an orally intrusive breast, a devouring mouth/vagina, and an anally penetrating phallus, terrifying images that elicit separation anxiety in the infant and castration anxiety in the male child. Thus, the phallic mother is a "bad mother," combining both the abandoning aspects of the negative mother and the aggressive qualities of the negative father, creating a figure who serves as "the bearer of the infant's sadistic projections."[9] In fairytale, the phallic mother is cast as the ubiquitous evil stepmother/wicked witch.

The Grimms' fairytale *The Raven* begins as follows:

> Once upon a time there was a queen who had a daughter.... One day the child was very naughty.... The mother became impatient, and as she looked at the ravens flying around outside the castle, she opened the window and said, "I wish you were a raven and would fly away! Then I'd have my peace and quiet." No sooner had she said those words than the child was changed into a raven and flew from her arms out through the window.[10]

In this tale, the mother's Freudian slip is revealed through poetic metaphor. The raven is a widely recognized symbol of death. The mother, in her anger and haste, wished the bothersome child to be dead. The child, taking the mother at her word, takes on the guise of death by transfiguring into a raven and flying to a "dark forest"—the dark place in the mind where the deepest and most distressing childhood issues are addressed.

In *Snow White*, though the evil stepmother, as opposed to the real mother, is clearly designated as the villain, later on in the story, at the climax of her villainy, after she delivers a poisoned apple to Snow White, the story reads:

> No sooner had the child taken a morsel of the apple into her mouth than she fell to the ground dead. And the queen, casting on her a terrible glance, laughed aloud and cried, "As white as snow, as red as blood, as black as ebony! This time the dwarfs will not be able to bring you to life again."[11]

So we see that the evil queen, guised in the form of a stepmother, is actually none other than Snow White's own mother, who long ago used the same words—"As white as snow, as red as blood, as black as ebony"—to wish her daughter into life; but now, in her conversely evil form, she uses the same words to curse her maturing daughter, and wish her dead. This slip in continuity reveals a truth—that earlier versions of the story do not split the character of mother into two characters—good mother and bad stepmother. The tale of a mother who contrives to kill and eat her daughter in order to suppress and devour her youthful appeal is psychologically resonant, but perhaps too close to the feelings it is trying to represent. Splitting the mother in two provides a more palatable story for the young reader, who nevertheless construes the true meaning on a subconscious, intuitive level. The darkest, most perverse desire a woman can have—to kill her own child—is given voice in the figure of the wicked witch, if only as the projected fear of the child's anxious unconscious mind.

The public has a morbid fascination with news stories about parents, especially mothers, who kill their own children.[12] This horrific act intrigues the public's interest because it seems to be in direct contrast to the most basic instinct a person can have ... to protect one's own child. However, at the same time, the public fascination with filicide may allude to a primordial anxiety, the fear that a small child has that his parent may want to kill him, a form of Freudian castration anxiety. And, even more terrifying, the fear that a parent has that she may be capable, if driven to the breaking point, of harming or even killing her own child. In both cases, whether it is a remembered projection of the child or a repressed anxiety of the adult, the mere thought of filicide must be disguised and condensed, like an image in a dream, and projected onto a safe archetype—the wicked witch—the universal object of all childhood fears and parental anxieties. There is no reason to believe that the contemporary fascination with cases of filicide is new in any way. Certainly, filicide has always been one of the most reviled social taboos. It is also reasonable to assume that in the past, when birth control was not nearly as available or culturally acceptable as it is now, and when abusive and brutal treatment of children was accepted as the norm, that the act of filicide was even more common. Hence, the widespread folktale/fairytale theme of child murder at the hand of a witch or stepmother may have been, to some degree, fictionalizations of actual murder stories, told as scary horror tales to adults and children alike, in the days before the common folk read storybooks or newspapers.

The filicidal actions of fairytale stepmothers could also be interpreted as outlets of childhood aggression felt towards their parents, as Tatar explains:

> A child's murderous hostility towards his parents (which manifests itself in the form of disavowal and repudiation of parents in childhood fantasies) shows up in folklore as parental hostility toward a child. To obviate the profound sense of guilt aroused by unacceptable thoughts, an aggressor can take advantage of a willfully clever stratagem. He turns himself into an innocent martyr and casts the victim of his guilt-tainted thoughts into the role of a nefarious villain. The psychological mechanism at work here, known as projection, was neatly illustrated by Freud in the syntactical conversion of the sentence "I hate him" into "He hates me...." There is no doubt much truth in Otto Rank's view that adults invest the lives of folkloric heroes with the details of their own infantile history and that they thereby create the stuff of fairy tales by means of retrograde childhood fantasies.[13]

Tatar's interpretation of the fairytale as the child's projection of hostility onto the parental figure is based on Rank's theory of the "paranoid structure" of the fairytale, in which the fairytale serves as the repository for all of the repressed fears and unexpressed feelings of hostility, guilt, and anxiety felt by children towards their parents. This unilateral interpretation, however, belies the fact that children throughout history and throughout the world have always been the victims of the most brutal and aggressive forms of violence, suffered at the hands of their parents. Like the "rape fantasies" of Freud's first patients, when we dismiss the material as "pure projection," we risk losing the truth of abusive behavior and real trauma, in favor of a bowdlerized vision of the average parent.

Cannibalism

The common fairytale theme of abandonment, epitomized in the story of *Hansel and Gretel,* in which the parents abandon the children because they are starving, often hints to an even darker theme — the fear that if they allow the children to stay, the parents might resort to eating the children. Abandoning the children is a way of avoiding this fate. However, when Hansel and Gretel enter the witch's house, their deepest fears are projected onto the witch, who would eat the children without thinking twice. Stories in which children face a devouring father or mother figure allow the readers to project their deepest fears and most paranoid suspicions regarding their own parents. Food is the most basic and fundamental symbol of love. The parent who withholds food from his child withholds love. And the parent who actually transforms his child into food for herself ... well, this goes beyond the range of normal human experience.[14] The theme of parental cruelty and malice is driven to its most depraved extreme when the parent moves beyond simple withholding (neglect), rejection (abandonment), and beating (abuse), to the most heinous and inconceivable of social taboos.

The myths abound with stories of gods and mortals who eat their own children. Cronos, the father of the gods in Greek mythology, swallowed his children, who survived by escaping from his belly. Tantalus, an arrogant mortal, slays his son Pelops and serves him to the gods for dinner. Atreus, another arrogant mortal, slaughtered his two nephews and served them to their father in a feast. Campbell notes:

> We all know the fairy tale of a witch who lives in a candy house.... She is a cannibal. (And for some six hundred thousand years of human experience cannibals, it should be born in mind — and even cannibal mothers — were grim and gruesome, ever-present realities). Cannibal ogresses appear in the folklore of peoples, high and low, throughout the world; and on the mythological level the archetype is even magnified into a universal symbol in such cannibal-mother goddesses as the Hindu Kālī, the "Black One," who is a personification of "all-consuming Time"; or in the medieval European figure of the consumer of the wicked dead, the female mouth and the belly of Hel.[15]

When Hansel and Gretel's mother refuses to feed her own children and casts them out of the house to starve, the children recreate the all-giving goddess-like mother of their infancy, from whose body they fed freely, in the image of a candy house, upon which they graze greedily. But no sooner do they taste of the forbidden house than the shadow of the mother figure appears. The witch is so evil and savagely inhuman that she represents the polar opposite of the nurturing mother figure. Rather than feeding her children, she feeds *on* them. However, while we may interpret the cannibalistic ogress/witch as a product of early childhood fantasies, the archetype herself, as Campbell pointed out, may be an archaic vestige from an earlier stage of human existence.

Cannibalism in fairytales and fantasy is often used as a symbol of perversion. In the Grimms' fairytale *The Juniper Tree*, we are told in the beginning, "All this took place a long time ago, most likely some two thousand years ago,"[16] so we are prepared for a story with some primordial themes. The stepmother favors her own daughter but is cruel to her stepson: "She could not forget that he would always stand in her way and prevent her daughter from inheriting everything ... she pushed him from one place to the next, slapped him here and cuffed him there, so that the poor child lived in constant fear."[17] In due time, the stepmother decapitates the boy and makes a stew out of his body, which she feeds to the father. The boy's stepsister, who loved him, buries his bones under the Juniper Tree that retains the spirit of his dead biological mother, and he is soon reborn as a bird who avenges himself against the stepmother. In this story, the motif of cannibalism is simply used as a device to show the extent of greed and malice that a parent can exhibit toward her child.

In the Grimms' tale *The Robber Bridegroom*, an unwilling girl is engaged to an evil man. When she visits his cabin, she's greeted by an old woman sitting by a fire:

> Oh, you poor child.... This is a murderer's den! You think you're a bride soon to be celebrating your wedding, but the only marriage you'll celebrate will be with death. Just look! They ordered me to put this big kettle of water on the fire to boil. When they have you in their power, they'll chop you to pieces without mercy. Then they'll cook you and eat you, because they're cannibals.... The old woman then led her behind a large barrel, where nobody could see her.... No sooner was the maiden hidden than the godless crew came home, dragging another maiden with them. They were drunk and paid no attention to her screams and pleas. They gave her wine to drink, three full glasses, one white, one red, and one yellow, and soon her heart burst in two. Then they tore off her fine clothes, put her on a table, chopped her beautiful body to pieces, and sprinkled the pieces with salt....[18]

In *The Robber Bridegroom*, the act of cannibalism is clearly used to represent the visceral aspects of the sexual act, particularly when it is forced upon an unwilling young girl. To an innocent child furtively witnessing an experience of passion, the sexual act may seem horrifyingly cannibalistic, as certain organs are taken into the mouth or tasted by the sexual partner, and other acts of feeding, such as licking, sucking, and biting, are engaged in.

Cannibalism is also often used to refer to an excessive form of love, especially between a mother and her child. How often does a mother say to her baby, "You're so cute ... I can just eat you up!" The use of the cannibal motif was expressed most eloquently by Maurice Sendak in his classic children's book, *Where the Wild Things Are*. When the young boy, Max, in the midst of his play as a "wild thing," roars at his mother, "I'll eat you up!"—he is expressing love, only in a wild, inappropriate, uncontrolled way. He's punished for his wildness by his mother, who sends him to his room "without eating anything," thus depriving her child of the maternal love, symbolized by food, and attention that he desires. As Max sits alone, trying to figure out what went wrong, he enters a fantasy world where his wild feelings are embodied in the "Wild Things." When he misses his mother and leaves the fantasy world, the Wild Things beg him, "Please don't go! We'll eat you up, we love you so!"—and finally Max understands that the desire to eat someone up comes from a good, loving place; but when it is uncontrolled and unrestrained, it appears to the other as wild and aggressive. Perhaps the strong desire for the child to eat the mother, both figuratively and literally (as in the Oral Stage of breastfeeding), is reflected in the myths and fairytales of cannibalistic mothers as the projected desires of young boys like Max, who want nothing more than to express love to their parents, but are rejected when their expressions of affection are too wild and aggressive.

And finally, there is the form of cannibalism that refers to the emotional devouring of one person by the other (again, most typically, between mother and child). The "devouring mother," as an archetype, is a mother that devours her children emotionally, keeping them dependent upon her for everything, and making them feel guilty for wanting to separate and develop independent lives. As the psychoanalyst Carl-Heinz Mallet explains:

> Many children suffer what Hansel is threatened with. They are devoured by their mothers—devoured out of love, to be sure. First the son is tied to his mother's apron strings for too long a time; then the mother refuses to let him go. She refuses to do without his love, devotion, and attachment; she "keeps him in"—body and soul, if possible, and systematically. She spoils him, shining his shoes, doing his laundry, ironing his shirts. And she cooks him "the best food," because she knows that the way to a man's heart is through his stomach.[19]

Here, separation anxiety is experienced by the mother rather than the child; and the child, who is everyday devoured by his mother, experiences the anxiety of Hansel, who is being fattened up as he is kept in the witch's cage:

> Anyone who sits in a stable, unfree and dependent, and regards his condition as heaven on earth is doomed. He becomes part of his mother—as though he has really been eaten up—and his filial love usually delights her until she is well on in years, walking on crutches like the witch and waggling her head. Skillfully tamed sons are more faithful than many husbands.[20]

In this interpretation, the wicked witch who lives in the gingerbread house is not the abandoning mother who would eat her own children out of selfishness, envy, aggression, or greed. She is a loving, doting, devoted mother. If anything, she is too loving, she gives too much, nothing is ever withheld. But the child unconsciously knows that this mother is just as dangerous, because the house of candy becomes a prison that cannot be escaped. The mother who would let her child devour her own body until it appears that there is nothing left, the martyr-mother who is all-giving and forever self-sacrificing, becomes the mother who would devour her own child, smothering him in love, until the child is nothing more than a lifeless stew, a fattened Hansel in a warm, womblike oven.

SIX

The Wizard and the Dark Lord

"One for the Dark Lord on his dark throne In the Land of Mordor where the Shadows lie."
                                        –Tolkien, *The Lord of the Rings*

Just as the maternal archetype is split into two figures, the positive (Goddess) and the negative (Witch), the paternal archetype is likewise split. For Jung, the positive father is encapsulated in the archetype of the Wise Old Man, who may take the form of a sage, scholar, teacher, hermit, wizard, sorcerer, or god.[1] In fantasy literature, the Wizard archetype is standard. The negative father, who will typically play the role of antagonist in the hero's journey, and who will also embody many of the psychological components of the Shadow archetype, is typically represented as a devil, demon, necromancer, ogre, tyrant, or evil warlord. The ubiquitous figure of the Dark Lord is general enough to encapsulate all of these variants and more.

An interesting inversion exists in the relationship between the hero and his biological father, as opposed to the relationship between the princess and her mother. The princess' biological mother is usually the good mother, who often dies in the beginning of the story, only to be resurrected as a helpful bird, spirit, or fairy godmother. The princess' stepmother, on the other hand, is almost invariably wicked and cruel. In the case of the hero, whose journey is so often staged as an oedipal battle between father and son, the biological father is frequently evil or at least fatally flawed, while the positive father figure is a mentor who guides and inspires the hero, but who is not the real father. The Arthur myth is a perfect illustration of this kind of scenario. Arthur's true father, Uther Pendragon, though a powerful king, was a rash and impetuous man, whose sins would come back after his death to haunt his son. Arthur's mentor, Merlin the Wizard, was a wise and nurturing guide who taught Arthur about his true identity and instructed him on his path to glory.

The wizard mentor is usually met early on the road of the hero's journey, and is often the herald who draws the hero out of his commonday world.[2] Gandalf the wizard acts as herald for both Bilbo Baggins in *The Hobbit* and Frodo Baggins in *The Fellowship of the Ring*. In the Harry Potter novels, Albus Dumbledore, a wise teacher and powerful wizard, is the mentor of the title character. It is worthwhile to note that powerful wizards in the Harry Potter books are known as members of the "Order of Merlin"—a clear link to Arthurian myth. In Lloyd Alexander's Prydain novels, the aged Dalben is a wise and powerful enchanter who plays the role of mentor to the hero, Taran. And in C.S. Lewis' Narnia novels, though the heroes change in each book, Aslan the lion plays the role of wizard and mentor in all of the stories. Nicholas Flamel (1330–1418), the legendary medieval alchemist who purportedly discovered the Philosopher's Stone, is a key prototype of the wizard figure in fantasy literature. The Philosopher's Stone enables its owner to transform lead into gold and, more importantly, to create the magical potion known as the "Elixir of Life," which bestows immortality. As a character in fantasy books, Flamel is featured prominently in the first Harry Potter novel, *Harry Potter and the Philosopher's Stone*, as well as in the *The Alchemyst* series of fantasy novels by Michael Scott.

Dark Lords exist in nearly every fantasy story. In the *Percy Jackson & the Olympians* series of novels, the Greek gods Hades, Lord of the Underworld, and Kronos, King of the Titans, reprise their mythological roles as evil tyrants. In the Prydain novels, the dark lord Arawn was drawn from Welsh mythology, where Arawn was the god of Annwn, the Welsh underworld, which literally means—"not-world"—the kingdom of the dead. In Tolkien's Middle Earth novels, Sauron the Great plays the role of the Dark Lord, and Saruman the Wizard is his powerful accomplice. In *The Silmarillion*, the book which lays the mythological groundwork for the world of Middle Earth, the original Dark Lord was Morgoth, (originally Melkor), who was one of the godlike beings called Valar, the initial residents and creators of Middle Earth. Morgoth was a Lucifer-esque figure, who rebelled against Eru, the Creator God of the universe. All evil and corruption in Middle Earth can be said to exist because of Morgoth's presence. After many epic battles, Morgoth is eventually banished by the other Valar and exiled out of Middle Earth into the Void, where he remains. However, his evil will remained in Middle Earth via the presence of his cunning lieutenant, Sauron, who sought to control all of Middle Earth. In the Harry Potter novels, the Dark Lord in every book is Lord Voldemort, the evil wizard who, while being no direct relation to Harry Potter, shares a bit of Harry's soul, and vice versa, thus making Harry and Voldemort spiritually related, almost like father and son.

Sacrifice

The history of the practice of animal and human sacrifice in primitive cultures provides an outline of theological thought in myth and legend that sheds light on the origin of the paternal archetypes. Animal sacrifice is possibly the oldest form of ritualized religious practice. It originated in the earliest period of human history, the age when all humans were hunter/gatherers, whose lives depended upon the hunting, killing, and eating of wild animals.[3] In terms of religious thought, this was a period of universal spiritualism or animism, when primitive peoples believed that there was a spirit force or "mana" in everything. Hunters, therefore, had to deal with feelings of guilt and remorse for having killed another living being, which has a spirit just the same as they did.[4] The ritual sacrifice, therefore, was an atonement for the horrific yet necessary crime of slaying the animal. The ritual sacrifice atoned for the sin by making sure that, although the animal's body died, its spirit was released and would be reborn to live again. Far from being a selfish or wanton act, the eating of the roasted body was also part of the ritual, as it completed the process of atonement, making the animal's body and spirit "at-one" with the hunter.

In the age of animism, it was believed that, since spirit existed in everyone and everything, rituals and magic were available to everyone. Therefore, any hunter could perform a ritual sacrifice. However, in keeping with the human tendency towards creating a power structure within social circles, it became standard practice in early primitive peoples to designate the role of priest or shaman to the member of the tribe or clan, typically the elder male, who was chosen to be the medium between mortals and the spirit world. This individual, thought to be more in touch with the spirits and their magic, was the original prototype for the Wise Old Man or Wizard archetype. The emergence of the "divine king" came about via the combination of the priestly and kingly roles within the tribe. The priest-king was both a spiritual and political overlord, a person set apart from the other people as he retained both physical and magical powers, and who was generally considered to be part human and part god. The origin of both the Hero and the Dark Lord archetypes are found in the divine king figure. When the divine king was good and in touch with both the spirits and his people, he was a Hero. When he was perceived as being evil or maleficent, the divine king provided the prototype for the Dark Lord archetype.

The emergence of the divine king figure in the Fertile Crescent of the Near East coincided with the Agricultural Revolution, approximately 10,000 B.C., when Neolithic peoples made the transition from a livelihood primarily based on hunting and gathering, to livelihoods based primarily on farming and ranching. As ancient peoples changed from nomadic to agricultural and pastoral lifestyles, early city-states were formed, and the divine king became an even more powerful and significant figure. As the medium between the people and their gods, he was "at-one" with the land and spirits. Therefore, the fertility of the land itself was directly related to the vitality and fertility of the king. The divine king was considered a hero only when he was perceived as fulfilling this connective role between the people, the land, and the gods. The divine king was considered a Dark Lord when he was perceived in the following ways:

1. If he was the divine king of an enemy nation.
2. If he abused his power for evil or selfish purposes.
3. If he refused to step down from his position, even though he had lost his powers over the spirit world, and the land, flocks, or people were suffering as a result.

Since the vitality of the divine king was directly linked to the vitality of the people, when the divine king's body or spirit was no longer vital, he was required to sacrifice himself or be sacrificed, much like the original animal sacrifices of the hunters, in order for a successor to replace him and revitalize the land. For the divine king, his willing self-sacrifice (apotheosis) elevated him from semi-divine to completely divine status in the eyes of his people. As Campbell notes:

> "The hero of yesterday becomes the tyrant of tomorrow, unless he crucifies *himself* today."[5]
>
> "The work of the hero is to slay the tenacious aspect of the father (dragon, tester, ogre king) and release from its ban the vital energies that will feed the universe."[6]

In this way, Hero (demigod), Wizard (God), and Dark Lord (Devil), can all be seen as different aspects of the same archetype. The Hero becomes a demigod by killing a tyrant; but later in his lifecycle, he can either become a fully divine god by sacrificing himself, or he can become a Dark Lord, if he chooses to sacrifice others in his stead.

> "The hero is ... the champion not of things become but of things becoming."[7]
>
> "A god outgrown becomes immediately a life-destroying demon."[8]

In slaying the demon, the hero becomes divine, and the cycle goes on and on.

In *The Golden Bough*, Frazer relates numerous examples from around the world of the ritual of the sacrifice of the divine king.[9] He also relates how, in many instances, the king, rather than willingly sacrifice himself, co-opted another suitable person to be sacrificed:

When kings were bound to suffer death, whether at their own hands or at the hands of others, on the expiration of a fixed term of years, it was natural that they should seek to delegate the painful duty, along with some of the privileges of sovereignty, to a substitute who should suffer vicariously in their stead.[10]

Since the divine king was thought to hold within him a spark of the celestial spirits, and since this spark in many cases was hereditary, as the line of kingship was handed down from father to son or from father to son-in-law, it seemed only logical that the most appropriate sacrifice, in lieu of the divine king himself, would be a daughter or a son. A classical example of daughter sacrifice can be seen in the Greek myth of Andromeda, who was chained to a rock by her father, King Cepheus, as a sacrifice to the sea monster, Cetus, in order to atone for his wife's insult to Poseidon. She is fortunately rescued at the last minute by the hero, Perseus. This mythological theme would become the origin of the common motif in folktales, in which a princess is taken captive by a dragon. A biblical example of daughter sacrifice can be found in the Book of Judges:

> And Jephthah made a vow to the Lord: "If you give the Ammonites into my hands, whatever comes out of the door of my house to meet me when I return in triumph from the Ammonites will be the Lord's, and I will sacrifice it as a burnt offering." Then Jephthah went over to fight the Ammonites, and the Lord gave them into his hands. He devastated twenty towns from Aroer to the vicinity of Minnith, as far as Abel Keramim. Thus Israel subdued Ammon. When Jephthah returned to his home in Mizpah, who should come out to meet him but his daughter, dancing to the sound of timbrels! She was an only child. Except for her he had neither son nor daughter. When he saw her, he tore his clothes and cried, "Oh no, my daughter! You have brought me down and I am devastated. I have made a vow to the Lord that I cannot break...." After the two months, she returned to her father, and he did to her as he had vowed. And she was a virgin."[11]

There are even more Biblical examples of son sacrifice, the first being the "Akedah," when Abraham, upon God's command, bound his son Isaac and prepared him as a sacrifice. In the Book of Kings II, the king of Moab sacrifices his firstborn son in order to achieve a military victory over the Israelites. In Leviticus and Deuteronomy, the Bible explicitly forbids child sacrifice, prohibitions which presuppose the ritual practice of child sacrifice in the ancient Near East. Historical and archaeological evidence point to the widely practiced existence of child sacrifice in ancient Carthage and Phoenicia, as well as among the Aztecs and Incas of Mesoamerica and South America, while the Koran contains passages that describe the practice of pagan Arabians sacrificing their children. There is even some archaeological evidence that child sacrifice was practiced in prehistoric Britain, Germany, and France. Shockingly, the practice of child sacrifice is not completely extinct, as cases of the ritual are occasionally uncovered in the more remote regions of the Third World. However, the most significant example of son sacrifice is found in the myth of Jesus, whose crucifixion is most commonly interpreted as the sacrifice of God the Father of his only son, as a means of atonement for the human race. Hence, the theme of child sacrifice, which is found in religion, myth, legend, and folktale throughout much of the world, can be seen as a prime motif in the fantasy literature derived from both the Judeo-Christian and Greco-Roman traditions.

In Tolkien's *The Return of the King*, Denethor, the Steward King of Gondor, is a tyrant guilty of treason. He allowed himself to be manipulated by the Dark Lord, Saruman, because of his desire to stay on the throne, rather than handing it over to the proper heir and king. At the depths of his paranoia and madness, Denethor prepares to sacrifice his unconscious son, Faramir, as a burnt offering. Pippin the hobbit warns Gandalf the wizard about the unholy act that is about to transpire:

> Pippin: "The Lord [Denethor] is out of his mind, I think. I am afraid he will kill himself, and kill Faramir too.... But Faramir.... He is not dead, and they will burn him alive..."
> Gandalf: "...only the heathen kings, under the domination of the Dark Power, did thus, slaying themselves in pride and despair, murdering their kin to ease their own death."

And when Gandalf and Pippin confront Denethor to stop him:

> Denethor: "I would have things as they were in all the days of my life ... and in the days of my longfathers before me: to be the Lord of this City in peace, and leave my chair to a son after me, who would be his own master and no wizard's pupil. But if doom denies this to me, then I will have naught: neither life diminished, nor love halved, nor honor abated."[12]

Here, Denethor plays the role of the Dark Lord/Tyrant King, the man who, driven by his own lust for power and glory, will destroy the innocent life of his own son, for his own selfish purposes.

In C.S. Lewis' *The Lion, the Witch, and the Wardrobe*, Aslan offers himself up as a willing sacrifice to Jadis, the White Witch, in exchange for the life of the child, Edmund. Aslan, the son of the "Emperor-Over-the-Sea," is clearly a Christ figure. This parallel is most clear at the moment of his self-sacrifice. As a witch, Jadis is represented as a pagan figure, so we see in this confrontation between Aslan and Jadis, the conflict between Christianity and Paganism. Aslan is sacrificed on the "Stone Table"—another reference to the fact that human sacrifice was a ritual of the Neolithic (Stone Age), pre–Christian pagans. Similarly, Jadis uses a stone knife in a twisted shape, rather than a straight metal knife, as a sign that this is an unholy pagan rite. But because he was a "willing victim,"[13] the magic of Aslan's self-sacrifice broke the stone table, and he was resurrected; just as Jesus' self-sacrifice and resurrection, according to his followers, broke the Stone Age rituals of pagan sacrifice.

In the Harry Potter series as well as in *The Lord of the Rings*, we see sacrifice used as a theme to distinguish between the actions of the Hero, the Wizard, and the Dark Lord. The Wizard displays the correct behavior of the divine king by allowing himself to be sacrificed. In *The Fellowship of the Ring*, Gandalf sacrifices himself in the mines of Moria by taking on the ferocious balrog all by himself, so that the rest of the Fellowship could escape. He subsequently descends into the Abyss as he fights the balrog to death, only to be resurrected as Gandalf the White. Similarly, in *Harry Potter and the Half-Blood Prince*, Dumbledore allows himself to be killed by Professor Snape, so that (as the convoluted plot turns) the dangerous Elder Wand could be kept out of the hands of Voldemort. Though these acts of the wizards do not destroy the Dark Lord, they fulfill the function of the wizard archetype's role, which is to serve as a mentor to the hero, and to demonstrate to him exactly what he must do. In contrast, the Dark Lord displays the incorrect behavior of the divine king by selfishly sacrificing others in order to grasp power for himself. The Dark Lord Voldemort in the Harry Potter series and the Dark Lords — Sauron, Saruman, and Denethor — in *The Lord of the Rings*, demonstrate numerous times their eagerness to sacrifice others, especially the hero, for their own personal gain. And finally, the hero, at the climax of his journey, invariably must sacrifice himself in order to destroy evil and banish the destructive forces from his world. Though Harry Potter survives the death curse placed on him by Voldemort, and though Frodo the Hobbit is rescued from the Cracks of Doom after destroying the Ring of Power, the point is that they willingly sacrificed themselves, knowing full well that they would die, in order to defeat the Dark Lord. In doing so, they proved that they learned their lessons well from their wizard mentors. The seeds sown by positive father figures blossom later in the good deeds of their sons.

SEVEN

Man and Beast

"Homo homini lupus" [Man is a wolf to man]."

What is the difference between Man and Beast? For some, there is no difference. Man *is* a beast, he is Homo Sapien, a hominine in the family of Great Apes. For others, it is important to distinguish between Man and Beast, but what is the distinguishing characteristic? The defining quality of Homo Sapien is "sapience" or wisdom, which includes such features as language, reasoning, problem solving, and self awareness. However, we cannot be completely certain that other animals, such as chimpanzees and dolphins, do not possess the same sapient abilities, only to lesser degrees or in different forms. Nevertheless, based on the ubiquitous existence since primordial times of the man-beast archetypal figures in myth, legend, and art, it seems that the need to understand the relationship between humankind and other beasts is a basic and universal preoccupation.

Kurt Lewin (1890–1947), the renowned psychological theorist, once said that Freud's theory was the "third great blow" to human self concept. The first blow, delivered by Copernicus, was the realization that the Earth, and therefore humanity, was not located at the center of the universe. The gods and the cosmos were not focused entirely on us. The second blow, delivered by Darwin, was the realization that humans in our current form were not, as previously believed, divinely created. Rather than being the children of God, humankind evolved from apes. We are beasts. And the third blow, delivered by Freud, was the realization that the quality of humanity that we believed to be the differentiating characteristic between humans and beasts — sapience — was not necessarily true. Man, according to Freud, is controlled primarily by his beastly drives and desires. He is not the "master of his own house." Rather, he is a rudderless boat adrift in an ocean of unconscious desire, memory, and emotion. His behaviors are determined primarily by the primal desires that drive him. However, he desperately wants to understand how these drives propel him, and how he can better control his body and mind. Perhaps this desire, the human need to understand how we can be different from other animals, is in-and-of-itself the primary distinction between Man and Beast.

Totemism

In attempting to understand the most basic drives in the human psyche, the Id, and in trying to discern the origin of the Oedipal Complex, Freud looked back to the earliest conflicts in human history. He looked back to the primordial period in the development of our species, when archaic homo sapiens were still essentially just apes living in the wild, in order to understand the primordial period of human development, when the psyche of the infant and child were being formed. Freud came to the conclusion in his book, *Totem and Taboo: Resemblances Between the Mental Lives of Savages and Neurotics* (1913), that totem reverence is at the psychological root of the incest taboo, which in turn is the psychosexual catalyst of the Oedipal Complex. Since the concept of totemism lies at the heart of the psychological relationship between Man and Beast, we must understand the psychological principles of totemism in order to see how this system of thought gave rise to the man-beast archetypes in myth, folktale, and fantasy.

Freud defined the totem as follows:

> As a rule, it is an animal, either edible or harmless, or dangerous and feared; more rarely the totem is a plant or a force of nature (rain, water), which stands in a peculiar relation to the whole clan. The totem is first of all the tribal ancestor of the clan, as well as its tutelary spirit and protector; it sends oracles and, though otherwise dangerous, the totem knows and spares its children.[1]

The totem animal is frequently directly related to the physical survival of the clan, i.e. the buffalo for the Native Americans of the Western plains. But even when this is not so, the totem animal is *believed* to be spiritually connected with the natural and supernatural forces upon which the clan depend upon for survival. Freud posited that the totem animal is worshipped as an ancestral spirit because, on an unconscious level, the totem is connected with the father figure:

> Psychoanalysis has revealed to us that the totem animal is really a substitute for the father, and this really explains the contradiction that it is usually forbidden to kill the totem animal, that the killing of it results in a holiday and that the animal is killed and yet mourned.[2]

Freud goes on to describe an oedipal scenario within a horde of apelike primitive hominids that, in essence, establishes both totem reverence and the incest taboo at the core of the human psyche.

> The Darwinian conception of the primal horde does not, of course, allow for the beginning of totemism. There is only a violent, jealous father who keeps all the females for himself and drives away the growing sons.... One day the expelled brothers joined forces, slew and ate the father, and thus put an end to the father horde.... This violent primal father had surely been the envied and feared model for each of the brothers. Now they accomplished their identification with him by devouring him and each acquired a part of his strength. The totem feast, which is perhaps mankind's first celebration, would be the repetition and commemoration of this memorable, criminal act with which so many things began, social organization, moral restrictions and religion...[3]

So, driven to rage by sexual desire, primordial man kills his own father and copulates with the female harem, which includes his own mother. This "alpha male" behavior can be seen in other animal groups, and in Great Apes in particular, so there is no reason to believe that Freud is being too imaginative in his description of this scenario, though his assumption of cannibalism is not necessarily supported. Nevertheless, Freud goes on to explain how this primordial drama would establish the psychological roots of totem reverence, incest taboos, and the Oedipal Complex:

> They hated the father who stood so powerfully in the way of their sexual demands and their desire for power, but they also loved and admired him. After they had satisfied their hate by his removal and had carried out their wish for identification with him, the suppressed tender impulses had to assert themselves.... They undid their deed by declaring that the killing of the father substitute, the totem, was not allowed, and renounced the fruits of their deed by denying themselves the liberated women [their mothers]. Thus they created two fundamental taboos of totemism out of the sense of guilt of the son, and for this very reason these had to correspond with the two repressed wishes of the Oedipal complex. Whoever disobeyed became guilty of the two only crimes which troubled primitive society.... The surrogate for the father was perhaps used in the attempt to assuage the burning sense of guilt, and to bring about a kind of reconciliation with the father.[4]

Freud then goes one step further, explaining how totemism as a basic thought process became the basis for both primitive and modern religious belief:

> In the Christian myth man's original sin is undoubtedly an offence against God the Father, and if Christ redeems mankind from the weight of original sin by sacrificing his own life, he forces us to the conclusion that this sin was murder. According to the law of retaliation which is deeply rooted in human feeling, a murder can be atoned only by the sacrifice of another life; the self sacrifice points

to a blood-guilt. And if this sacrifice of one's own life brings about a reconciliation with god, the father, then the crime which must be expiated can only have
been the murder of the father. Thus, in the Christian doctrine mankind most
unreservedly acknowledges the guilty deed of primordial times because it now
has found the most complete expiation for this deed in the sacrificial death of the
son.[5]

Hence the ritual of sacrifice, which Frazer and other anthropologists believe
originated as a hunter's rite of atonement with the spirit of the slaughtered
animal, is seen differently in a Freudian view. For Freud, the sacrifice is indeed
an atonement, even when the being that is sacrificed is an animal rather than
a person; but the atonement itself is with the "primordial father," the Adam-
like father of the "primal horde," who was murdered by his sons. This type
of symbolic thinking (referred to in the previous chapter as animism) was
referred to by Freud as the "animistic mode of perception"— the belief that
everything around us has a spirit or a life force, and that animals, plants, and
even inanimate objects have a sense of consciousness.[6] According to Freud,
the animal that was sacrificed in the primitive ritual was a totem, a symbol
or substitute for the father, who was revered and worshipped via the sacrificial
rite. Thus the totem sacrifice becomes the origin of all subsequent religious
ritual and thought:

> In the same deed which offers the greatest possible expiation to the father, the
> son also attains the goal of his wishes against the father. He becomes a god him-
> self beside or rather in place of his father. The religion of the son succeeds the
> religion of the father. As a sign of this substitution the old totem feast is revived
> again in the form of communion in which the band of brothers now eats the
> flesh and blood of the son and no longer that of the father, the sons thereby
> identifying themselves with him by becoming holy themselves. Thus through the
> ages we see the identity of the totem feast with the sacrificial animal, the thean-
> thropic human sacrifice, and the Christian eucharist, and in all these solemn
> occasions we recognize the aftereffects of that crime which so oppressed men but
> of which they must have been so proud. At bottom, however, the Christian
> communion is a new setting aside of the father, a repetition of the crime that
> must be expiated. We see how well justified is Frazer's dictum that "the Christian
> communion has absorbed within itself a sacrament which is doubtless far older
> than Christianity.[7]

The question of whether the totem is perceived as a substitute father, a
protective spirit, or as the metaphysical connection between a tribe and the
animal-spirit world, is not necessarily important. Indeed, in relating the following Native American legend of the buffalo totem, Campbell explains how
the totem ritual and myth encapsulates all of these perceptions as part of the
mythology and religion of the tribe:

"This story is of a Blackfoot tribe, long, long ago, who couldn't get the buffalo to go over the cliff. The buffalo would approach the cliff and then turn aside. So it looked as though the tribe wasn't going to have any meat for that winter. One day, the daughter of one of the houses got up early in the morning to draw the water for the family and happened to look up to the cliff. There on the cliff were the buffalo. And she said, "Oh, if you would only come over, I would marry one of you." To her surprise, they all began coming over. Now, that was surprise number one. Surprise number two was when one of the old buffalo, the shaman of the herd, comes and says, "All right, girlie, off we go."

"Oh, no," she says.

"Oh, yes," he says, "you made your promise. We've kept our side of the bargain. Look at all my relatives here — dead. Now off we go."

Well, the family gets up in the morning and they look around, and where is Minnehaha? The father looks ... and he says, "She's gone off with a buffalo. And I'm going to get her back." So he puts on his walking moccasins, his bow and arrow, and so forth, and goes out over the plains.... He grabs her by the arm and says, "Come!"

But she says, "No, no, no! This is real danger. The whole herd will be right after us. I have to work this thing out. Now, let me just go back."

So she gets the water and goes back. And the buffalo says, "Fe, fi, fo, fum, I smell the blood of an Indian"— you know, that sort of thing.... And he gives a buffalo bellow, and all the buffalo get up, and they all do a slow buffalo dance with tails raised, and they go over, and they trample that poor man to death, so that he disappears entirely. He is just all broken up to pieces. All gone. The girl is crying, and her buffalo husband says, "So you are crying."

"Yes," she says, "he is my daddy."

"Well," he says, "but what about us? There are our children, at the bottom of the cliff, our wives, our parents — and you cry about your daddy." Well, apparently he was a kind of compassionate buffalo, and he said, "Okay, if you can bring your daddy back to life again, I will let you go."

So she ... puts the bone down on the ground and covers it with her blanket and sings a revivifying song, a magical song with great power. And presently — yes, there is a man under the blanket. She looks. "That's Daddy all right!" But he is not breathing yet. She sings a few more stanzas of whatever the song was, and he stands up.

The buffalo are amazed. And they say, "Well, why don't you do this for us? We'll teach you our buffalo dance, and when you will have killed our families, you do this dance and sing this song, and we will all come back to live again."[8]

Besides demonstrating how the totem can represent both animal-spirit and ancestral-spirit, this story shows quite clearly how totem reverence in both ritual and myth can be seen as the originator of the man-beast archetype. When the man-beast figure appeared incarnate in primitive ritual, the figure was typically embodied by the shaman, priest, or chief, who was garbed in costume to resemble the totem figure:

A primitive chief is not only disguised as the animal; when he appears at initiation rites in full animal disguise, he *is* the animal. Still more, he is an animal spirit, a terrifying demon who performs circumcision. At such moments he incorporates or represents the ancestor of the tribe and the clan, and therefore the primal god himself. He represents, and is, the "totem" animal.[9]

Hence, the appearance of the half-man/half-beast figure (i.e. centaurs, minotaurs) in art, such as prehistoric cave paintings and in ancient legends and myth, could be a remembrance or representation of primitive rites, in which the shaman portrayed and embodied, in costume, the tribe's totem. However, it was not only the shaman who became the man-beast during the rituals. Sometimes, a segment of the tribe or the entire tribe itself would don the sacred costumes and become the man-beast figure incarnate:

> Dr. Jung has pointed out the close relation, or even identification, between the native and his totem animal (or "bush soul"). There are special ceremonies for the establishment of this relationship, especially the initiation rites for boys. The boy enters into possession of his "animal soul," and at the same time sacrifices his own "animal being" by circumcision. This dual process admits him to the totem clan and establishes his relationship to his totem animal. Above all, he becomes a man, and (in a still wider sense) a human being.[10]

For Jung, the man-beast archetype represents a psychological relic or unconsciously remembered link with humankind's primitive past. It not only signifies our most basic connection with the animal kingdom, but also our striving to use this connection, the collective totem, as a means of establishing one's identity within the community:

> "The Australian concept of the *alcheringamijina,* ancestral souls, half man and half animal, whose reactivation through religious rites is of the greatest functional significance for the life of the tribe. Ideas of this sort, dating back to the Stone Age, were widely diffused..."[11]

For Campbell, the "totem-ancestors" were spiritual protectors of the wilderness who were identified with by the tribe out of their necessity for survival within the wild:

> For the primitive hunting peoples of those remotest human millennia when the sabertooth tiger, the mammoth, and the lesser presences of the animal kingdom were the primary manifestations of what was alien — the source at once of danger, and of sustenance — the great human problem was to be linked psychologically to the task of sharing the wilderness with these beings. An unconscious identification took place, and this was finally rendered conscious in the half-human, half-animal figures of the mythological totem-ancestors.[12]

Totemism is very much alive today. We see it in the form of team mascots such as the St. Louis Cardinals' Freebird and the Seattle Mariners' Moose, in national animals such as the American Bald Eagle and the Russian Bear, and in astrological/zodiac animals such as Scorpio and Leo. Though these totems do not, for the most part, have religious significance, they are potent symbols of identity and community. In fantasy literature, where magic is as powerful and real a force as it was in the minds of our primitive ancestors, totem animals are extremely important. In *The Golden Compass* and the other two novels in Philip Pullman's *His Dark Materials* trilogy of fantasy novels, every individual has a "daemon," an animal companion which is an outward projection of certain elements of her identity or psyche. Because the protagonist, Lyra, is a child, her daemon, Pantalaimon, like the daemon of all children, changes form frequently, morphing from a moth to a mouse to an eagle, based on the present condition of Lyra's emotional state. But when Lyra comes of age and her identity is stabilized, her daemon stabilizes as well and enters into its final immutable form, a pine marten.

Pullman's use of daemons borrows heavily from an ancient but very widespread form of totemism among primitive peoples, in which every person has their own totem animal. As Jung explains:

> Many primitives assume that a man has a "bush soul" as well as his own, and that this bush soul is incarnate in a wild animal or a tree, with which the human individual has some kind of psychic identity.[13]

This belief was also common among Native American tribes, who believed that when a boy comes of age, he discovers his spirit animal, usually as a function of some sort of initiation rite, such as a "vision quest." Once his spirit animal is identified, the boy's identity is forever linked with that animal, and he is given a new name based on that animal, i.e. "Runs with Elk," and he is then initiated into the community of adult men. The term "daemon" refers to the notion that a spirit is not internal, but external. "Spirit was originally a spirit in human or animal form, a *daimonion* that came upon man from without."[14] For the ancient Greeks, daemons were spirits, independent of specific human beings, but capable at anytime of possessing the body of a human and controlling his behaviors and thoughts. While daemons in Greek mythology could be either good or bad, demons in the Judeo-Christian tradition were always evil, as they were sent by the Devil.

In the Harry Potter novels, every witch or wizard has a "patronus," which is more of a psychological image than a physical or spiritual being. For Harry Potter, the significance of the patronus is that it can be used to ward off dementors, the ghoulish guards of Azkaban prison. "The Patronus is a kind of positive force, a projection of the very things that the dementor feeds upon — hope, happiness, the desire to survive...."[15] Naturally, an individual's patronus is significant to him on a psychological level. Harry's patronus, for example, is a stag, the same patronus as his father's. So for Harry, his patronus, as indicated by the etymological root of the word, was quite literally a paternal protector.

Also in the Harry Potter novels, there is a good deal of totem symbolism found in the "mascots" of the Hogwarts Houses. The evil house is named Slytherin. Its totem is a snake. The snake is a totem symbol linked with paganism, and is often associated with the deceptive serpent in the Garden of Eden, who is generally interpreted as a devil figure. In the Judeo-Christian tradition, anything remotely pagan or pre-monotheistic is automatically associated with evil. However, because Harry Potter is a "parselmouth" — he can converse with and command snakes — we see that there is a bit of the dark side within Harry as well. If Harry were living in a primitive culture, his ability to talk to snakes would have escalated him to the position of a shaman, a medium between the physical and spiritual worlds. However, in the very Judeo-Christian world of England (despite the fact that the stories take place in a pagan-esque parallel world of witches and wizards), Harry's ability to talk with snakes is observed with suspicion and misgiving among his peers. In addition, the most infamous alumnus of Slytherin house, the dark lord Voldemort, is a parselmouth as well. Voldemort has a "pet" named Nagini, a huge snake, who also retains part of Voldemort's soul. (In Sanskrit, "nagini" refers to a spirit that takes the form of a great snake.) Furthermore, there are menacing basilisks in the Slytherin house, evil creatures from European mythology, that are massive snakes (kind of like wingless dragons).

Opposed to Slytherin in every way is Gryffindor, Harry Potter's house, whose totem is a lion. The lion is a very potent symbol in England, as it is linked with King Richard the Lionhearted, and is therefore a symbol of England and of English nobility. The lion is also associated with the Juedo-Christian God and with Jesus (C.S. Lewis chose to represent Christ in his Narnia novels as the great lion, Aslan). On a broader level, the lion is generally associated with courage, pride, strength, and majesty, as the lion is the "king of the jungle," and his cohort is named a "pride." The third Hogwarts house, Ravenclaw, has as its totem the raven, which is generally associated with death (as in Edgar Allan Poe's famous poem), though it is revered in some Native American and Asian cultures as a god. There is an English legend that England would not fall to foreign invaders as long as ravens roost in the Tower of London. The fourth house, Hufflepuff, has a badger for its totem. As badgers are small and chubby with soft fur, and because they burrow for themselves cozy little homes in the ground, they are often thought of as cute and cuddly creatures, causing people to see in badgers the need for comfort and security that is such a basic facet of human existence, and so we can see in the badger a symbol of the modern suburban middle class. C.S. Lewis noted of the badger:

Consider Mr. Badger in *The Wind in the Willows*—that extraordinary amalgam of high rank, coarse manners, gruffness, shyness, and goodness. The child who has once met Mr. Badger has ever afterwards, in its bones, a knowledge of humanity and of English social history which it could not get in any other way.[16]

Perhaps it is this association that made Rowling assign the badger as the totem of the house that represents the honest, hardworking middle class within the wizarding world.

Centaurs

The archetypal figure of the half-man/half-beast is extremely old. Paintings of man-beasts can be seen in prehistoric cave paintings in Southern France that are over 50,000 years old, though scholars debate as to whether these pictures depict actual man-beasts, or shamans in man-beast costumes engaging in ritual. Centaurs, half-man/half-horse, are common mythological figures. It is possible that when ancient peoples first saw a stranger from a foreign tribe astride a horse, that they mistook the figure for a magic creature that was part man and part horse. Also, there was a prehistoric creature called Chalicotheres, that somewhat resembled a centaur. Though they became extinct millions of years ago, it's possible that the discovery of fossils of this creature by ancient peoples gave birth to the centaur myth. In Greek mythology, centaurs are descended from Centaurus, a deformed and depraved man, who mated with mares. Centaurs are wild, fierce creatures, who, when intoxicated for the first time at the wedding party of Pirithous, attacked and raped all of the women and boys. As such, they represent (as do all man-beasts) the co-existence of the untamed and the civilized within mankind.

However, there is the contrary figure of Chiron, an intelligent, peaceful, and insightful centaur, who was a talented oracle and a great teacher and mentor to many of Greek Mythology's greatest heroes. As a reward for giving up his immortality for the release of Prometheus, the god who gave to mankind the gift of Fire, the constellation Centaurus was named in memory of Chiron. Chiron was clearly the inspiration for the character of Ronan in the Harry Potter novels, a wise centaur who has the ability to read the stars and tell the future. Similarly, centaurs in C.S. Lewis' Narnia novels can read the stars, and they are also wise and kind, though ferocious in battle. In *The Lightning Thief*, Chiron the centaur is Percy Jackson's teacher and mentor, and in Dante's *Inferno*, Chiron is the captain of a band of centaurs that guard the river of fire.

Satyrs

A satyr is a creature that is half-man, half-goat. The satyrs were the consort of Dionysus and were thus associated with drunkenness, sex, and debauchery. The Greek god Pan is the most famous mythological satyr. As ancient Greece was in large part a shepherding nation, it is possible that the figure of a half-man, half-goat arose from the shaman costumes of totemistic sacrificial rituals. Because Pan was the god of nature and fertility, and therefore associated with pantheistic beliefs and rites, his image was syncretically infused into Christian dogma as the embodiment of everything that is unchristian and unholy — the antichrist — Satan. Pan's association with the Devil may also stem from the lingering practice of paganism in the first few centuries after the ascendancy of the Roman Catholic Church, and the practice of Neopaganism in the past few centuries of the modern era, both of which would cause pious Christians to consider the pagan god as an embodiment of the Devil. It may also be possible that, since Pan was also linked in mythology with the drives for sex and uncontrollable passion, he may have been marginally associated with the act of bestiality between men and sheep, which is particularly reviled in the Judeo-Christian tradition. The passage in Genesis 6: 12 — "And God saw the earth, and behold, it was corrupt, for all flesh had corrupted their way on the earth" — is often interpreted to mean that the species of man and beast that God had created were "corrupted," because they intermingled and, through bestiality, gave rise to mutant species such as centaurs and satyrs ... hence the need to wipe out all of the "corrupt" species on Earth with a cleansing flood, sparing only a breeding pair of each of the pure and uncorrupted species.

Pan's Roman counterpart was Faunus, thus giving rise to the word "faun" as an alternate term for satyr. Tumnus, the faun in C.S. Lewis' *The Lion, the Witch, and the Wardrobe,* plays an important role in the beginning of the story, as does Grover the satyr in *The Lightning Thief.* In both stories, they are friends of the young hero and serve as herald figures, but they are also somewhat cowardly, weak, and powerless. The faun in the fantasy film *Pan's Labyrinth* (2006) is a herald figure, who at different points in the film appears as either kind or maleficent, though he is ultimately good. It is possible that the somewhat dubious nature of fauns and satyrs in modern fantasy arises as a result of the ambivalent associations with Pan/Satan in the Greco-Roman and Judeo-Christian traditions.

The Minotaur and the Sphinx

There is only one minotaur in Greek Mythology, Asterion, the monstrous son of Pasiphaë, the wife of King Minos and the Cretan Bull. As he is half-man and half-bull, the Minotaur is ferocious and wild, so he is caged in the famous labyrinth in Knossos, where it hunted and fed on sacrificial men and virgin maidens, until he is slain at the hand of Theseus. Minotaurs appear in fantasy stories from Dante's *Inferno* to C.S. Lewis' Narnia books to *The Minotaur Trilogy* by Thomas Burnett Swann. A sphinx is a creature that is half-human, half-lion. The Greek sphinx that appears in the Oedipus myth is female, while the Egyptian sphinx, upon whom the great monument at Giza is based, is male. The sphinx is often depicted as a threshold guardian, as in the Oedipus myth. She asks a riddle, and if it is answered correctly, the traveler may pass; but if answered incorrectly, the sphinx kills and/or consumes the traveler.

Therianthropes

A therianthrope is a creature that transforms from man to beast and vice versa. As such, like the previously discussed man-beast archetype, the therianthrope represents the duality of man, who is part civilized and part wild. Classical Mythology is filled with therianthropic transformations. Ovid's *Metamorpheses* is an epic in which each tale recounts the metamorphosis of a character from one form to another, usually as a result of unrequited love or uncontrolled erotic passion. Likewise, folktales and fairytales feature therianthropic transformations as a standard and frequent motif. Most frequently, it is the male character who is transformed by a witch into a beast such as a frog, and who is later re-transfigured into a handsome prince (i.e. the "animal groom" motif).

> It may be that these sorceresses translate the metaphorical wisdom of old wives on sexuality ("men are beasts") into literal terms.... The animal groom motif in fairytales may have been told by women to women in the context of covert reflections on maturity, marriage, and sexuality.[17]

In a similar vein, Bettelheim noted that the "animal husband" is a symbol of the girl's sexual anxieties."[18] The fact that the initial transformation from man to beast usually occurs before the beginning of the story, so that the princess' initial meeting with the prince is when he is still in his beastly form, points to the notion that the pubescent girl's anxiety over sex arises in childhood, before her own transformation into a young woman:

The change from the "natural" or beautiful appearance took place in the unfathomable past when we did not know why something happened to us, even when it had the most far-reaching consequences. Shall we say that repression of sex occurred so early that it cannot be recalled? None of us can remember at what moment of our life sex first took on the form of something animal-like, something to be afraid of, to hide, to shun; it usually is tabooed much too early.[19]

The symbolism at the climax of the tale, when the beast is transformed into a handsome young prince, represents the transformation that takes place in the mind of the pubescent girl, when she no longer perceives the sexual act and the one who perpetrates it as a bestial act committed by a beastly being, but as a desirable act that is shared with a loving and desirable partner.

Werewolves (or lycanthropes) are an extremely common figure in folktales from around the world, and play a particularly significant role in the folktale and fantasy literature of Europe and America. Some scholars believe that the werewolf myth arose as an explanation for the exploits of serial killers, who, like werewolves, tend to prey at night on young girls, attack cyclically, and often mutilate and cannibalize their victims.[20] An alternate theory of origin is that the evolution of early hominids from a primarily fruit gathering primate to a predatory hunting beast is remembered at a symbolic level deep within the human unconscious, giving rise to the archetype as an elemental idea.[21] As a symbol of the dual nature of man, the man who appears civilized and evolved during the day, only to regress into a wild, libidinous wolf at night, reflects the conflicted nature in all of us. Vampires, who appear human on the outside, but who are actually wild and libidinous creatures on the inside, fulfill the same archetypal role as the werewolf. Also, like the werewolf, the wild side of the creature is only revealed at night, and the vampire can also transfigure into menacing beasts, such as a wolf or a vampire bat. The equally famous Jekyll/Hyde character from Robert Louis Stevenson's *The Strange Case of Dr Jekyll and Mr. Hyde* (1886), presents a science-fiction version of the werewolf archetype, in which the means of transfiguration is achieved through science, via a chemical concoction, rather than through a magical curse.

In Michael Scott's *Nicholas Flamel* series of fantasy books, therianthropes are shape-shifters such as werewolves and were-boars, referred to as the "Torc clans." They are descended from the antediluvian races, the generations of mythical creatures who lived before the mythical Flood. This is a reference to the race of "Nephilim," mentioned briefly in Genesis 6: 4. Literally translated as the Fallen Ones, they are the half-breed descendants of the "Sons of God," angels who came down to the earth and mated with the "Daughters of Men." The Torc clans were also the demigod heroes of Classical Mythology, envisioned as superhuman beings that preceded the existence of the human race on Earth. They are credited with everything from the erection of the Egyptian pyramids and the pillars of Stonehenge to the invention of fire and tools and even the initial idea of divinity.

> When the earliest humani first appeared, the Torc clans taught them how to work wood and stone and how to create fire. The humani worshipped the Torc clans as gods — why do you think so many of the earliest gods have animal shapes? Think of the cave paintings of creatures that are neither man nor beast but something in between. You must have seen statues of the Egyptian gods Sobek, Bastet and Ahubis: humani bodies, but with animal heads. Think of the dances where humani pretend to be animals: they are just memories of the time when the Torc clans lived side by side with the humani.[22]

In the Harry Potter books, "Animagi" are "wizards who can transform at will into animals."[23] The word, clearly, is a combination of the words "animal" and "magi." In the very beginning of the first novel, Professor Minerva McGonagall appears in her cat form. Wormtail, one of Voldemort's allies, appears mostly as a rat named "Scabbers," while Sirius Black, Harry's godfather, spends a good deal of his time as a wolf. Harry's own father was known to take the shape of a stag. There are other therianthropes in the books as well. Professor Lupin, a major character in the series, is a werewolf. Boggarts, one of the many kinds of spooks that appear in the series, are shapeshifters: "It's a shapeshifter.... It can take the shape of whatever it thinks will frighten us the most."[24]

Wild Men

A wild man or "woodwose" is a hairy bipedal primate that is not quite human and not quite beast, but something in between. Many people claim to have encountered these so called "missing links," known variably as Apeman, Bigfoot, Sasquatch, the Abominable Snowman, Yeti, etc. Though the actual existence of these creatures is arguable, the public's fascination with them and their appearance in fantasy literature are unequivocal. The origin of the archetype could be based on encounters with formerly unknown primates that were misconstrued by early European explorers as man-beasts — i.e. gorillas, orangutans, and chimpanzees. This would also explain why this particular archetype is not widely found in ancient myths, folktales, and fairytales, appearing initially in medieval European literature and artwork of the late 15th Century. A similar explanation of origin may lie in the encounters of early European explorers with primitive peoples, so called "savages," that were similarly misconstrued — i.e. Australian aborigines, African pygmies, etc.

And, of course, there is always the possibility, though remote, that actual relics of our archaic hominid ancestors, such as the Neanderthals, actually exist, or existed in the not-so-distant past, and that the archetypal figures are actually real "missing links," encountered by modern homo sapiens, who caught a fleeting glimpse through the rearview window of time at the human race's primordial past.

A psychoanalytic explanation of the man-beast archetype is that the figure is representative of atavistic traits still existent in the human mind. In other words, primitive man still exists in the primal areas of the psyche, and is given form in the outward projection of the Wild Man figure. For Freud, the primal areas of the psyche, expressed by the primary drives of sex and aggression, are found in the libidinal structure of the psyche, the "Id." For Jung, the symbolism of the Persona/Shadow archetypes presupposes a civilized, repressed side of the psyche — the Persona — as well as a manifestation of everything that is uncivilized, all of the repressed or hidden urges — the Shadow.

Wild Men are found in the fantasy realm of Tolkien's Middle Earth. The wild men, a.k.a. Drúedain, were a primitive forest-dwelling folk who were naked (though covered in hair) and wild in nature. Though they were previously reviled by modern men, when they came to the aid of the Riders of Rohan during the War of the Ring, they gained the respect and allegiance of the kingdoms of men in Middle Earth. In Lloyd Alexander's *Prydain* series, Gurgi is a hairy apelike creature who is the best friend and sidekick of Taran, the hero. Though not necessarily the brightest tool in the shed, Gurgi is loyal, generous, affectionate, loving, and faithful till the end. In form and temperament, Gurgi is almost exactly like the character of Cha-Ka from the popular television fantasy series *Land of the Lost* (1974–1976), later reprised in a television series remake (1991) and a film adaptation (2009). Cha-Ka was a member of the Pakuni race, hair-covered human-like creatures that were gentle and peaceful in nature. Another primitive but friendly and loyal manlike beast is Chewbacca the Wookie in the *Star Wars* films. Though, since Chewbacca is from the planet Kashyyyk, one cannot assume that he is any way a relation of the human species.

The Man of Nature

In direct contrast to the Wild Man archetype, there is the Man of Nature, a civilized man who has chosen to leave society and live alone in the wilderness. This hermit, usually wise and ascetic, represents a unity between Man and Nature. In this way, he also represents unity within the Self. He lives in a state of atonement with the natural order which man (Adam) enjoyed briefly in his primary state (Eden) before the Fall. The male counterpart to the female Chtonic Mother archetype, i.e. the Earth Goddess or Mother Nature, the Man of Nature embodies the post-modern yearning to reconnect with Nature and reclaim the purity and innocence of pre-modern society. If Modern Man is Fallen Man, the man who has lost his essential connection with Nature, symbolized by his exile from Eden, then the Man of Nature represents a drive towards reconnection with what was lost. He is Nature's Child, yearning to return to the womb of Mother Earth. In the realm of Faërie, the reader vicariously experiences the earth in its pristine, primeval form, (i.e. Narnia, Prydain, and Middle Earth), worlds that are not yet despoiled by modern technology, pollution, and industry. Furthermore, in Faërie, Man interacts with Nature in a fashion more representative of Primitive Man's "animistic mode of perception," in which the spirits of Nature, Beast, and Man are still unified. Not only does the Man of Nature commune with Nature, he actually communicates verbally with the birds and beasts of the forest.

The biblical Noah, based on his apparent ability to communicate with the animals in the Ark, serves as a template for the Man of Nature archetype in fantasy. (Noah finds his parallel in Greek Mythology with Deucalion, and he is also very similar to the character of Utnapishtim in the Sumerian myth, *The Epic of Gilgamesh*.) In *The Book of Three,* the first installment of the *Prydain Chronicles,* Taran and his companions encounter Medwyn in a secret and remote hideaway in the woods. In keeping with his function as the male counterpart to the Goddess archetype, Medwyn heals the injured heroes and offers them both kindness and sage advice. The hermit is described as a "strange-looking figure, broad and muscular, with the vigor of an ancient but sturdy tree. His white hair reached below his shoulders and his beard hung to his waist." Medwyn speaks to animals and lives in the hull of an ancient ship that had settled upon a mountain top long ago, in a bygone age. It is implied that Medwyn is actually "Nevvid Nav Nevion," who, "when the black waters flooded Prydain, ages ago ... built a ship and carried with him two of every living creature ... the animals who came safe again into the world remembered, and their young have never forgotten." Medwyn's "hidden valley" is a refuge and hospice for injured and lost animals, for as Medwyn knows but Man has forgotten: "Every living thing deserves our respect."[25]

A similar character appears in *The Horse and His Boy,* C.S. Lewis' second Narnia novel. The Hermit of the Southern March is described as "a tall man dressed, down to his bare feet, in a robe colored like autumn leaves, leaning on a straight staff. His beard fell almost to his knees." The hermit lives in a garden hidden in the woods, in the shade of "the hugest and most beautiful tree," and he refers to the animals in his care as his "cousins." [26] He heals Aravis, who was injured by a lion, assists Shasta on his quest to save Narnia, and he offers Bree some much needed empathy and advice. In *The Hobbit*, Bilbo Baggins encounters "Beorn. He is very strong, and he is a skin-changer … sometimes he is a huge black bear, sometimes he is a great strong black-haired man with huge arms and a great beard … as a man he keeps cattle and horses which are nearly as marvelous as himself. They work for him and talk to him. He does not eat them; neither does he hunt or eat wild animals."[27] As an archetypal figure, Beorn the bear-man is a combination of both the man-beast and the Man of Nature archetypes, while the Hermit of the Southern March and Medwyn combine the wizard and Man of Nature archetypes; but in any case, all of these figures are derivative of the good father archetype, which Jung referred to as the Wise Old Man.

Anthropomorphic Beasts

Animals that can talk and otherwise behave just like humans are commonplace in myth, fairytale, and fantasy. Even in the Bible, we find a talking serpent in the Garden of Eden and a talking donkey in Moab.[28] As the setting of Faërie recaptures the "animistic mode of perception" (which Freud attributed to the minds of primitive peoples), it is natural to assume within this scenario that since an animal has a spirit just like a human, then that animal should be able to think and feel and even speak like a human. In the same vein, the cognitive mode of "animistic thinking," which Jean Piaget observed in the "Preoperational" stage of cognitive development in young children, is not based on reason but on imagination, as well as the irrational tendency to project one's own thoughts onto other beings. Hence, a small child who thinks and feels and speaks will naturally project these facilities onto animals, and so the appearance within a children's story of animals that can act and speak like humans is easily accepted, requiring little suspension of disbelief, as it only reaffirms an assumption that they had already made. This may be why the types of fantasy stories and fairytales in which speaking animals appear are generally more appealing to children rather than adults, whose thoughts tend to be circumscribed within the confines of operational (logical) thinking.

C.S. Lewis noted of talking beasts:

> The presence of beings other than human which yet behave, in varying degrees, humanly: the giants and dwarfs and talking beasts. I believe these to be at least (for they may have many other sources of power and beauty) an admirable hieroglyphic

which conveys psychology, types of character, more briefly than novelistic presentation and to readers whom novelistic presentation could not yet reach. Consider Mr. Badger in *The Wind and the Willows*— that extraordinary amalgam of high rank, coarse manners, gruffness, shyness, and goodness. The child who has once met Mr. Badger has ever afterwards, in its bones, a knowledge of humanity and of English social history which it could not get in any other way.

A talking beast immediately endows his own character with the humanlike qualities we tend to project onto particular animals, such as stubbornness in mules, courage in lions, loyalty in dogs, etc. In this way, the talking beast provides a virtual shorthand for personality description and character development within the fantasy scenario.

Tolkien observed, "Beasts and birds and other creatures often talk like men in real fairy-stories. In some part (often small) this marvel derives from one of the primal "desires" that lie near the heart of Faërie: the desire of men to hold communion with other living things."[29] According to Josephus, in Eden, humans and beasts spoke together directly in a shared tongue.[30] The loss of our ability to speak to animals came as a consequence of the Fall of Man. Hence, the fantasy of communing with talking animals is a fantasy of Return, return to the primordial or primitive mindset, return to the magical age of early childhood, and a return to the innocent age of Man in Eden, before the Fall brought disunity between Man, God, Beast, and Nature.

Apes

Apes, when they appear in fantasy, are often portrayed negatively. Because apes are the closest existent relatives to Man, when they are anthropomorphically depicted, they often take on Man's corrupt instincts, including his power, greed, deceit, and craftiness, as well as his tendency to move against Nature, and his desire for unnatural things that inevitably destroy the beauty and balance of the natural order. Jung noted that the devil in medieval descriptions is often labeled as "*simian dei* (the ape of God)."[31] In *The Last Battle*, the final chronicle in the Narnia series, the devious old ape with the apt name of Shift is the central villain: "he was the cleverest, ugliest, most wrinkled ape you can imagine."[32] His greatest evil was his diabolical plot to transform Narnia into a modern industrial, commercial, secularized, market driven nation: "There'll be oranges and bananas pouring in — and roads and big cities and schools and offices and whips muzzles and saddles and cages and kennels and prisons — oh everything."[33] Here, the Ape epitomizes Man's state of disharmony with Nature, displayed in his perverse desire to enslave his fellow beasts and to build artificial structures that despoil the natural landscape, all in the name of "progress."

Bears

Bears in fantasy (due to the fact that they are simultaneously big, cuddly, and powerful) often take on a paternal role. Like a huge stuffed animal with retracted but nonetheless lethal razor-sharp claws, the Bear's blend of potential fierceness and gentle cuddliness is associated with the child's relationship to a playful, lovable father, who engages in rough-and-tumble play and tick-ling-cuddling games; but who at times can surprisingly turn round with such anger and impatience and punitive rage that he is at once transformed from a fuzzy cuddly teddy-bear into a fearsome, massive beast. Tolkien's shapeshift-ing man/bear, Beorn, in *The Hobbit,* is such a figure. He is gentle, supportive, and kind — but we are warned many times by Gandalf to be careful — as Beorn has a sharp temper, and can turn ferocious at the drop of a hat. Iorek Byrnison, one of the "Armored Bears of Svalbard" in Philip Pullman's *His Dark Materials* fantasy series, plays a protective paternal role to Lyra, the heroine. And, of course, who can forget Baloo from Kipling's *The Jungle Book*, the gentle father figure to young Mowgli.

Dogs

Dogs in myths, fairytales, and fantasy stories tend to recapture their real life roles as loyal and obedient friends to Man. Because dogs often bark in the middle of the night in response to sounds and smells that are unperceived by their human masters, it is assumed that dogs can sense spirits and demons, making them valuable allies when unholy ghosts are lurking about. Hecate, the Greek witch-goddess, was invisible, but her presence was betrayed by the barking of dogs. Cerberus, the three-headed giant dog in Greek mythology, is a faithful and obedient guard-dog, standing sentry at the gates of Hades. Likewise, Fluffy, the three-headed giant dog in the Harry Potter books, is used by Dumbledore to guard the "Sorcerer's Stone." (Hagrid, the giant groundskeeper at Hogwarts, mentions to Harry that Dumbledore "bought him off a Greek chappie" in a pub.)[34]

Frogs and Toads

Since frogs metamorphosis from fish to amphibian, they are seen as sym-bols of metamorphosis in humans — the ability to transform from one state to another — such as the transformation at puberty from boy to man or girl to woman. Rollo May wrote:

Appearing in many of Grimms' fairy tales and in mythology of all sorts since, the frog is that creature with one foot in our previous evolutionary development, the water, and another foot on land. It represents the archaic element in its cold and slimy qualities, and also in its big eyes, primitive as they are, which can at least peer powerfully. The frog here stands for the point in evolution when our human forebears crawled out of the swamps and slime but kept the possibility of living in water as well.* Some persons regard the frog as symbolic for intercourse and thus conclude that the queen met a man at her bathing spot and cuckolded the king. This is entirely possible since frogs in Grimms' tales often have this sexual role." *(footnote) "The relation of this level of water and slime to levels of the unconscious, by way of both Freud's and Jung's theories, is obvious.[35]

In a similar vein, Bettelheim wrote of the frog in fairytale:

It might seem a remote connection to think that frogs stand for the evolutionary process in which land animals, including man, in ancient times moved from the watery element onto dry land. But even today we all begin our life surrounded by a watery element, which we leave only as we are born. Frogs live first in water in tadpole form, which they shed and change as they move to living in both elements.... Thus while on the deepest level frogs may symbolize our earliest existence, on a more accessible level they represent our ability to move from a lower to a higher stage of living.[36]

The Grimms' fairytale *The Frog King* (oftentimes referred to as *The Frog Prince*) is the best known example of the frog archetype. In the tale, transfiguration or metamorphosis is represented by the frog, who becomes a king or prince upon the bestowal of a kiss from the princess. Just as the frog begins as a different creature and changes completely via its maturational development, so too does the human — especially the young human — change greatly and completely as a function of development. The moral of the story is that change is inevitable, it is part of growing up. Change is perceived as evil (black magic) when it is feared, and it is perceived as good magic when it is accepted, and especially when it is earned through hard work and pro-social deeds.

Bettelheim discussed the sexual connotation of the frog archetype in more depth:

The story of the frog — how it behaves, what occurs to the princess in relation to it, and what finally happens to both frog and girl — confirms the appropriateness of disgust when one is not ready for sex, and prepares for its desirability when the time is ripe.... By using the frog as a symbol for sex, an animal that exists in one form when young — as a tadpole — and in an entirely different form when mature, the story speaks to the unconscious of the child and helps him accept the form of sexuality which is correct for his age, while also making him receptive to the idea that as he grows up, his sexuality too must, in his own best interest, undergo a metamorphosis.[37]

Ernest Jones noted that the disgust humans often feel towards the slimy frog is similar to a young girl's initial feelings towards sex:

> The frog is in the unconscious a constant symbol of the male organ when viewed with disgust. So we have to complete the interpretation by saying that the story represents the maiden's gradual overcoming of her aversion to intimacy with this part of the body.[38]

Like humans in the womb, frogs start life as a water creature until they eventually emerge onto land, hence they are also seen as symbols of birth, rebirth, and fertility. Campbell noted, in reference to *The Frog King*:

> The frog, the little dragon, is the nursery counterpart of the underworld serpent whose head supports the earth and who represents the life-progenitive, demiurgic powers of the abyss. He comes up with the golden ball, his dark deep waters having just taken it down...[39]

Von Franz observed that toads are often associated with the chtonic mother, and are seen as symbolic representations of the uterus. In many cultures, frogs and toads are used in rituals and potions as magical aid in the process of childbirth.[40] In the Grimms' tale *Briar Rose*, a frog plays a magical role in the birth of the princess:

> In times of old there lived a king and queen, and every day she said, "Oh, if only we had a child!" Yet they never had one. Then one day, as the queen went out bathing, a frog happened to crawl ashore and say to her, "Your wish shall be fulfilled. Before the year is out, you shall give birth to a daughter."[41]

In the fantasy film *Pan's Labyrinth* (2006), a giant toad is used to represent the heroine's feelings about her mother, who is pregnant and will soon give birth. The frog archetype is a potent symbol of both our primordial beginnings and our ability to transform into ever-higher stages of physical and psychological development.

Giant Birds and Flying Beasts

Ever since ancient humans gazed up at the skies in envy of the winged bird in flight, he longed to fly, to glide gracefully above the ground and all its toils and troubles, to soar regally and at ease to distant realms, perchance to rise above the clouds and meet the gods. The dream of flight has been captured in myth and fairytales in many ways: the Magic Carpet of Tangu in the Arabian *One Thousand and One Nights*, Icarus' wings of feathers and wax in the Greek myth, the witch's broom in medieval folktales (and, of course, Harry Potter's state-of-the-art "Nimbus 2000" flying broom), are but a few examples. When the fantasy hero cannot fly through a magical means of his own possession, he must rely on the help of giant birds, who often fly in to save the day at the end of a story, recapturing the "Magic Flight" stage of Joseph Campbell's model of the Hero's Adventure.

In *The High King,* the last of the Prydain Chronicles, the hero Taran is rescued by Caw, the Gwythiant, a giant bird that Taran saved as a fledgling. Later in the same book, Edyrnion, the king of the eagles, rallies the eagle hosts to battle the evil hordes, helping to achieve victory for the heroes. Giant eagles in particular are the most common last minute saviors in fantasy. Eagles rescue the heroes at the climax of both *The Hobbit* and *The Lord of the Rings.* It is also a bird — the "old thrush" — who achieves victory for the heroes in *The Hobbit,* by telling Bard about the secret weak-spot in the dragon Smaug's armor of scales.

Flying magical creatures such as Pegasus the flying horse, Griffons (which have the head of a lion and the body of an eagle), and dragons, exist in many mythologies from around the world, and are also found in folktales and fantasy. In *The Last Battle,* the final Chronicle of Narnia, Tash appears as a portent of doom. Tash is part man and part bird, and is worshipped as a god by the Calormenes, a nation of people who are very similar to the Arabs of the Middle Ages, at least from a Victorian English perspective. Hippogriffs appear in Western European legends as creatures that are half horse and half griffon. Buckbeak the hippogriff is a significant character in the third Harry Potter book. It should also be mentioned that the legendary wisdom of owls in Western culture can be traced back to the fact that the Greek Goddess Athena, goddess of wisdom, kept an owl as her talisman. In many other cultures, however, in places such as Africa, the Middle East, and among the native peoples of both North and South America, owls are perceived as evil omens and portents of death, possibly because of their nocturnal habits. Hedgwig the owl, in the Harry Potter books, is a friend and servant to the hero, as owls are the postmen in the wizarding world.

Horses

As heroes in myth, fairytale, and fantasy are often very close to their horses, (since riding horseback is the most frequent form of transportation in these stories), it is not uncommon for horses in Faërie to talk or to display uncanny wisdom. In *The Lord of the Rings,* Gandalf's horse, Shadowfax, can understand the language of men, though he cannot speak it. Shasta, on the other hand, the title character in *The Horse and His Boy,* speaks incessantly throughout the fifth Chronicle of Narnia. Falada, the horse in the Grimms' fairytale "The Goose Girl," can also speak. Of this horse, Bettelheim noted:

> Even more ancient is the motif of the talking horse. Tacitus reported that among the Germans horses were presumed to be able to predict the future and were used as oracles. Among the Scandinavian nations, the horse is viewed in similar ways.[42]

Referring to the same fairytale figure, Mallet commented:

> In mythology and popular superstition, horses are male animals, so we may surmise a paternal element in Falada.[43]

The paternal role that Falada plays in the fairytale is quite clear, not only because he is the only connection that the Goose Girl has with her old home, which is lost to her, but because he reminds her of her parents repeatedly with the recurring rhyme: "Oh if your mother knew, her heart would break in two."

It is frequently observed that girls often form special and deep-seated bonds with horses and ponies, and the notion that girls feel in horses a paternal or male aspect, even if the horse is a mare, is a common interpretation. Other interpreters disagree, arguing that girls love horses because they are empowering.[44] Horses are not chauvinistic towards their riders, they respect women just as much as they respect men, and the mastery of a horse, no matter how robust the animal, is more easily achieved with nurturing and kindness than with power and aggression.

Wolves

Wolves, as the embodiment of wildness, are commonly used as a metaphor for the savage and feral nature of man, as the ancient Latin phrase dictates, "Homo homini lupus...." (Man is a wolf to man). The wolf, thanks in large part to *Little Red Riding Hood*, is one of the most common villains in children's stories. Fairy tales (or "nursery tales"), were scary stories told by nursemaids to get children to stop being naughty. In *The Boy Who Cried Wolf*, for instance, the little boy is eaten by a wolf as a direct result of his pathological lying. Thus, the moral of the story is "Stop lying." But the story could also be told to correct a child's incessant crying or whining about nothing. "Stop crying." The moral could be anything, because the motif that makes the story so powerful is that of the wild animal attacking and eating an innocent child. The child identifies with both the child and the wolf. The child knows what it's like to be small and vulnerable and naïve. The child also knows how it feels to be angry, out of control, and wild. At the end of *The Boy Who Cried Wolf,* the child is consumed by the wildness of his own nature. Similarly, in Maurice Sendak's *Where the Wild Things Are,* the little boy Max dons his wolf suit in order to allow himself to go wild. When he tells his mother — "I'll eat you up!" — he is expressing his love for her in its most primal and raw form. The expression is too wild for his mother to accept, so Max must go to his room without eating anything (i.e. without the love of his mother) till he learns to subdue the wild side of himself, which is only released when he is in the guise of a wolf.

Dwarves and Giants

The very small and the very large mythical creatures known as dwarves and giants exist in almost every mythology and are common figures in fairytale and fantasy. Of course, it should be noted that dwarves and giants do exist in real life (the medical conditions of dwarfism and gigantism), and that the discussion of dwarves and giants here is directed exclusively at the symbolic representation of dwarves and giants in fantasy literature. Dwarves in their many forms — elves, hobbits, munchkins, etc. — can often be seen as metaphors of childhood. They are not children, per se, but their small size recalls memories of the "happy, vanished time."[45] Childhood ... when the body and the world itself were young and filled with fanciful little people, when magic and wonder were everywhere and in everything, and when giants — both benevolent and fierce — shook the earth with the awesome force of their massive footfalls.

Bettelheim saw in dwarves a representation of nascent yet puerile masculinity:

> There are no female dwarfs. While all fairies are female, wizards are their male counterparts, and there are both sorcerers and sorceresses, or witches. So dwarfs are eminently male, but males who are stunted in their development. These "little men" with their stunted bodies and their mining occupation — they skillfully penetrate into dark holes — all suggest phallic connotations. They are certainly not men in any sexual sense — their way of life, their interest in material goods to the exclusions of love, suggest a pre-oedipal existence.[46]

Giants, on the other hand, in Bettelheim's view, represent parents, but more specifically, the parent from the point of view of the small child. He recounts a vignette about a mother who told her son the tale of "Jack and the Beanstalk." The young boy asked: "There aren't any such things as giants, are there?" Before the mother could respond, the boy continued: "But there are such things as grownups, and they're like giants." Bettelheim noted: "This theme [giants] is common to all cultures in some form, since children everywhere fear and chafe under the power adults hold over them."[47] Similarly, Jones explains,

> the conception of giants, with their clumsy stupidity and their alteration of kindliness and ogerish devouring of children, is a projection of various infantile thoughts about grownups, particularly the parents.[48]

In myth, giants are often represented as an elder race of beings that preceded humans.

> Mythologically, giants often appear as the "older people" in creation, a race that has died out: "There were giants in the earth in those days [Gen. 6:4].[49]

Here, von Franz is referring to the race of Nephillim in the Bible, the offspring of the "sons of God" who intermingled with the daughters of men prior to the Great Flood, and who later reappear as the inhabitants of Canaan in Numbers 13:32–33. The most famous giant in Jewish mythology is Og. According to legend, Og was one of the original Nephillim. He survived the flood by sitting atop of Noah's ark. The Titans, in Greek mythology, were a similar race of giants that were descended from the gods:

> Giants, therefore, are a supernatural race, older and only half human. They represent emotional factors of crude force, factors which have not emerged into the realm of human consciousness. Giants possess enormous strength and are renowned for their stupidity. They are easy to deceive and are a prey to their own affects, and therefore helpless for all their might.... A similar state of affairs prevails now in the world at large, where giants — uncontrolled collective, emotional forces — lord it over the earth. Society is unconsciously led by primitive archaic principles.[50]

In Tolkien's children's story "Farmer Giles of Ham," the childish nature of giants is articulated:

> And among other things still at large there were giants: rude and uncultured folk, and troublesome at times ... he [the giant] was the ruin of roads and the desolation of gardens, for his great feet made holes in them as deep as wells; if he stumbled into a house, that was the end of it ... he lived far off in the Wild.[51]

Here, we get a sense of the giant as a projection of the toddler-child's own clumsiness. Self-consciousness of this childish trait results in a simultaneous projection of his wish to grow up into a big boy, who is no longer clumsy. Hence, the giant is clumsy because he is a small child, but he is also very big, because the child wishes to be big. Quite similar characterizations of giants are found in the depiction of Glew, the bumbling giant in the Prydain Chronicle, *The Castle of Llyr,* and in the obtuse giant-king of Harfang, in the Narnian

Chronicle, *The Silver Chair*. Hagrid, in the Harry Potter books, is only a half-giant, which accounts for him being only half an oaf. (Pureblood giants in the wizarding world are fierce, brutal, and oftentimes malevolent beings.) Nevertheless, the figures in these fantasy books all portray the giants in the image that was interpreted by the psychoanalytic readers as the "bumbling father" trope. If we could imagine how adults appear to little children, we might see ourselves as lovable giants, beneficent and kind, carrying the little ones on our shoulders, tossing them about like tiny dolls, and bestowing great treasures and delicacies for their pleasure. When we're cross, we become laughable, stupid, clumsy, oafish lummoxes, spouting our insensible nonsense and, when outwitted by the faster and more nimble little ones, resorting to our last recourse, the use of brute force, at which time we can become fearsome and even terrifying in our rage.

Monsters

Monstrous creatures not already mentioned, such as trolls, orcs, goblins, etc., were identified by Tolkien as "Fell" creatures; that is, creatures that relate to the corrupt nature of man subsequent to his Fall. There is an interesting duality in the quality of magical creatures in Middle Earth. Each of Tolkien's magical creatures has its dark or "fell" counterpart. The breed of orcs are descended from elves of the time of the ancient wars, who were held captive by Melkor for endless years in the pits of Utumno, tortured and corrupted in his dungeons until they became fell creatures, a "mockery of the Elves, of whom they were afterwards the bitterest of foes."[52] (Orcs, in *Beowulf*, are the descendants of the fallen biblical figure, Cain.) The dwarves of Middle Earth, whose downfall is their greed and lust for the gold and gems found at the heart of mountains, have as a fell counterpart the goblins, who share the greed of the dwarves as well as their penchant for delving underground. Unlike dwarves, goblins have no respect for the mountains they defile in their mining, and though they share with dwarves a talent for engineering, they invariably use this ability for evil purposes.

> It is not unlikely that they have invented some of the machines that have since troubled the world, especially the ingenious devices for killing large numbers of people at once, for wheels and engines and explosions always delighted them, and also not working with their own hands more than they could help; but in those days and those wild parts they had not advanced (as it is called) so far.[53]

Trolls were also created by Melkor, as the fell counterpart to the Ents, the walking, talking trees. The primary features of the trolls, besides their massive bodies and brute strength, is their penchant for eating dwarves and hobbits, and the fact that they turn to stone when exposed to sunlight. The Ringwraiths or Nazgûl were once men who became fell, ghostlike creatures as a function of their service to the Dark Lord, Sauron. Gollum, the pitiful creature who was once a hobbit named Smeagol, provides a vivid example of how a pure being can be transformed into a fell creature, as a result of many years of psychological pain, torture, and corruption through dark magic.[54]

Goblins exist in Rowling's wizarding world as well, though they are not quite as evil as they are in Middle Earth. For Tolkien, goblins represented the dark side of progress, the lust for and subsequent reliance on advanced technology, which is ultimately self-defeating and self-destructive to the human soul. For Rowling, goblins represent a dark side of human nature as well — greed and possessiveness — but in this they are partners to the wizards, serving as bankers for their hordes of gold. Perhaps this difference in the view of the goblins is a reflection of contemporary changes in the real world, which of course is always mirrored in the fantasy world. Tolkien's day was the era of world wars and increasingly industrial warfare, culminating with the atom bomb, global industry, and its evil application to human destruction. For Tolkien, progress was seen as the dark insidious power lurking in the shadows, befouling the beauty of the earth. In Rowling's day, this dark insidious power is held not so much in the war machines and the ones who wield them, but in the all-powerful multi-conglomerate global corporations and international banks, who not only build the machines, but through the power of money, wield the economic and political influence to turn man against man. In *The Sorcerer's Stone*, the engraving above the inner door of the goblin-operated Gringott's Bank reads:

> "Enter stranger, but take heed
> Of what awaits the sin of greed
> For those who take, but do not earn,
> Must pay most dearly in their turn.
> So if you seek beneath our floors
> A treasure that was never yours
> Thief, you have been warned, beware
> Of finding more than treasure there."[55]

Dragons

Frazer believed that the genesis of the dragon archetype, at least in European legend, can be traced back to primitive sacrificial rituals, in which maidens were sacrificed to water spirits. The dragon, which in form is similar to a lake or sea serpent, is an offspring or literary descendant of these ancient serpentine monster-gods.[56] The Greek myth of Andromeda, the virgin princess who was offered as a sacrifice to Poseidon's sea-monster, only to be rescued by the hero, Perseus, serves as a template for subsequent dragons in European folktales. The legend of St. George is probably the most influential and widespread dragon-slaying tale in post-classical European tradition. The basic plot of a king sacrificing his virgin daughter to appease a rapacious water serpent is recast in the St. George legend as a Christian morality tale. The hero uses the power of Christianity, the Sign of the Cross, to wound the dragon. Then, in an interesting twist, he calls to the virgin to toss her girdle round the dragon's neck. Upon being leashed by the virgin's girdle, the once irrepressible dragon is tamed. It follows the princess like a meek puppy-dog. St. George and the princess lead the dragon back to the village where it terrifies the townspeople. St. George promises to slay the beast, but only if the townspeople convert to Christianity, which they quickly do.

The legend of St. George and the dragon is a metaphor for the ascendance of Christianity over the pre–Christian pagan religions. The central male figure in the ancient rite, the father-king who selflessly sacrifices his beloved princess-daughter in order to ensure the fecundity of his community, is replaced in significance by the hero-son, representative of the new religion and its supplanting myth. The hero-son (George) slays the old retrograde god (dragon) and in the process demonstrates both his own supremacy and the impotence of the old father-king. As a consequence, the new Christian hero attains the virgin princess, an appropriate reward for his impressive display of virility, and as a corollary he usurps the royal throne as well. As such, this simple tale of bravery at once symbolizes the conquest of the ego (hero) over the libidinous forces of the id (dragon), the conquest of the oedipal son over the dominating forces of the father-king and his castrating demon (dragon), and the mythical ascendance of the new hero-worshipping spiritual order (Christianity) over the old nature worshipping order (paganism). The water, which was once the domain of the terrifying water god, is now used to baptize the townspeople, its magical power now under the control of the Church. The once pagan king builds a church on the spot where George slew the dragon, dedicating it to the Virgin Mary. The Virgin Mother is clearly linked to the king's own virgin daughter, who was nearly sacrificed to the water god. And as an enduring legacy of the power of the water god that was subdued by the Christian saint, a spring arises as a fountain at the altar of the church. The water from this fountain has the power to cure all diseases.

The virgin princess plays a duel role in the legend. To the hero, who symbolizes the mature ego, she represents an appropriate and desirable love object. To the father-king, who personifies the spirit of Holdfast[57] — the ruling tyrant who refuses to step down despite his obsolescence — the virgin whom he sacrifices represents the lack of his own virility. As a consequence of his impotence he is supplanted by the more virile hero. And to the dragon, which embodies the rapacious and taboo desires of the id, the virgin is a mother figure. She tames the libidinous monster with her girdle, the symbol of her chaste temperament, which in turn envelopes the tremendous sexual power wielded by the eternal feminine. While the hero's cross/sword, (a phallic symbol), can wound the libidinous beast, only the all-powerful mother can repress him.

In terms of character, the dragon represents rapacious greed. Dragons steal and horde two things — gold and maidens — items that the dragon has no personal use for, but commodities that are valued very highly among mortal men. Tolkien wrote of Smaug, the villainous dragon in *The Hobbit:*

> "Dragons steal gold and jewels, you know, from men and elves and dwarves, wherever they can find them; and they guard their plunder as long as they live (which is practically forever, unless they are killed), and never enjoy a brass ring of it."[58]

Dragons in the medieval European tradition are seen as leeches upon society, parasites that suck communities dry by absconding with their most valuable possessions:

> "...he [Smaug] took all their wealth for himself ... for that is the dragons' way, he has piled it all up in a great heap far inside, and sleeps on it for a bed. Later he used to crawl out of the great gate and come by night to Dale, and carry away people, especially maidens ... until Dale was ruined, and all the people dead or gone."[59]

The "dragon's way" is the way of wanton destructiveness, unrepressed desire, and unabashed greed. The dragon himself has no use for gold and even less need of maidens. He simply wants them because men crave these things and value them above all else. He therefore becomes a symbol of man's desire and greed, as well his penchant for destructiveness when these desires are thwarted or repressed. In the Harry Potter books, dragons guard the inner vaults of the goblin-run Gringott's bank, protecting the most valuable treasures from the greedy hands of potential robbers and looters. It is illegal for wizards to own or breed dragons, because of their destructive and tempestuous nature.

Serpents

Evolutionary psychology suggests that an adaptive instinctual fear response to certain environmental threats that existed in the environment of evolutionary adaptation may have developed in the human mind in response to recurring animal threats such as snakes and spiders. The legacy of this adaptive fear response lives on today in the very common object-related phobias of arachnophobia (fear of spiders) and ophidiophobia (fear of snakes).[60] A fear response associated with a pre-wired mental template of serpents and spiders goes beyond the traditional notion of archetypes, which are generally understood to be collective images and ideas passed down from one generation to another through ritual and cultural exchanges. The instinctual fear response towards snakes and spiders, however, goes much deeper, as it may be an inherited neurological disposition — a physiological trait that triggers an instinctive emotional reaction to anything that resembles the preexistent image of a spider or snake in the brain.[61]

Serpents as archetypes elicit associations that may be even more powerful than the instinctual fear response. Serpents were revered in pre–Christian traditions as potent symbols of rebirth (because they shed their skin), and virility (because of their potent venom and phallic shape). The ancient Ouroborus symbol, depicting a circular snake devouring its own tail, was extremely widespread throughout the ancient world, and had many meanings, among them: eternity, unity, rebirth, and eternal reoccurrence. Since it was associated with ancient pagan rituals and deities, the serpent as an archetype was cast in the Judeo-Christian tradition as an instigator of evil, a pawn of the Devil or the Devil himself, a symbol of sexual desire and temptation. The serpent's role in temptation and the subsequent Fall of Adam and Eve is exemplary of the serpent's part in the myths, fairytales, and fantasy stories of post–Classical Western culture.

The ancient associations between snakes and supernatural powers can be seen in some fairytales, such as the Grimms' "The Three Snake Leaves," in which snakes have the power of resurrecting the dead. In "The White Snake," another tale from the Grimms, a young man eats a bite of the magic snake, which gives him the power to understand the language of animals. This power is related directly to the tale of Adam and Eve, who, according to Judeo-Christian mythology, could speak to animals in the Garden of Eden. In "The White Snake," the hero is bestowed a golden apple from the Tree of Life at the end of the tale, which wins him the hand and heart of a nubile princess. Snakes, of course, are ubiquitous in fantasy stories, and are invariably evil. In the Harry Potter books, snakes and snake-like creatures such as basilisks are always related to the wicked Slytherin House of Hogwarts, and are therefore seen as servants of the Dark Lord, Voldemort, who has a distinctly serpent-like semblance himself.

Giant Spiders

Spiders in Faërie are usually female, whereas snakes are usually male. Snakes resemble the male phallus, creating the association with masculinity. Since female spiders are much larger and much more powerful than their male counterparts, and since spiders conspicuously engage in such "feminine" behaviors as weaving (webs) and nesting (egg sacs), the spider takes on a feminine persona. While there are positive spider archetypes, (i.e. the "Grandmother Spider," as in *Charlotte's Web*, and the character of Anansi, the storytelling spider of African folklore), when the spider is larger than normal, it becomes a hideous monster. The maternal association with the spider archetype makes the monster even more terrifying, as it elicits primordial fears of being devoured by a giant, ogre-like, cannibalistic, filicidal mother.

> According to Freud, the capacity of the sight of a spider to precipitate a crisis of neurotic anxiety — whether in the nursery rhyme of Miss Muffett or in the labyrinths of modern life — derives from an unconscious association of the spider with the image of the phallic mother...[62]

Giant monstrous spiders are particularly noticeable in Middle Earth. Ungoliant is a principal villainous monster in *The Silmarillion*. She, along with the evil god, Melkor, destroys the heavenly realm of the Valinor, and at one point is even more powerful than the great Melkor himself. After her downfall, Ungoliant lived in hiding, mating only to devour her mates and most of her own offspring. Nevertheless, she is the mother of all giant spiders in Middle Earth. In *The Hobbit*, the dwarves are captured and enmeshed in webs by a colony of giant spiders in Mirkwood forest. (Fortunately, they are rescued by Bilbo Baggins.) These giant spiders are the brood of Shelob, who appears in *The Lord of the Rings*. Shelob attacks and stings Frodo Baggins, wrapping him in a web for eventual eating. (Fortunately, Frodo is rescued by Sam Gangee.) There are giant spiders in the Harry Potter books as well. They live in the Forbidden Forest outside of the grounds of Hogwarts, and their chief is Aragog, who can speak English.

Ghosts and the Undead

While dread of contact with the dead, according to Freud, is a universal taboo, fantasy stories often dwell on the human interrelationships with both the un-human and the dead or undead, thus providing a safe vicarious experience with the deceased. The undead, according to Freud, are "uncanny," as they are familiar yet alien at once. Ghosts haunt their former dwellings because, rather than accepting their own deaths, they cling hopelessly to their old lives, envying the living. In this way, though they are dead, they are all too human. As we age and get closer to death, our proclivity is to dwell on our pasts, to haunt the memories of our youth, to regret the things we never did, and to begrudge those who did them. As we linger upon the time of youth, the lost age when we felt most alive, we become the ghosts of our own selves, loitering longingly in the houses of the living, losing our present as we pine for the past. In Faërie, there is often a distinct kingdom that is known as "the land of the dead." Mordor, for instance, in Middle Earth, is a dead landscape, replete with shadows and ghosts and other Fell creatures. It is ruled by Sauron, the Dark Lord, who was referred to in *The Hobbit* as the "Necromancer," a sorcerer who summons the dead. To enter Mordor one must pass through the Dead Marshes, a swamp filled with the corpses and haunted spirits of soldiers who died in a war fought ages ago. In Prydain, Annuvin is the land of the dead, ruled over by Arawn, the Dark Lord.

There are also ghosts and undead entities in Middle Earth and Prydain. Sauron's most powerful servants, the Ringwraiths, are essentially ghosts, as are the Dead Men of Dunharrow, ghost soldiers who save the day for the good guys in *The Return of the King*. The cauldron born are zombies created by the servants of Arawn in *The Black Cauldron*. The Harry Potter books, as well, have no shortage of ghosts and undead beings. Ghosts, for the most part, are harmless spirits in the wizarding world. Dementors, on the other hand, are wraithlike entities that embody the visage of death, much like the Grim Reaper, and feed off the spirits of the living. "The Dementor latches its mouth onto a victim's lips and sucks out the person's soul."[63]

There are many other magical creatures in the realm of Faërie — unicorns, phoenixes, mermaids, etc. — but to analyze them all would be to go way beyond the scope and purpose of this chapter. Suffice it to say that the creatures of Faërie — whether human, half-human, or humanlike — all represent different aspects of humanity, from fair to dark, and from magical to mundane. Though they come from all manner of starting points and take manifest forms, they are judged not just by their appearance, but by the quality of their actions. In the end, the function of the beast in Faërie is to remind us that there is beauty in even the most savage beast, and that the most vicious and savage beast of all is Man.

EIGHT

Magic

"Even fairy-stories as a whole have three faces: the Mystical towards the Supernatural; the Magical towards Nature; and the Mirror of scorn and pity towards Man. The essential face of Faërie is the middle one, the Magical."[1]

The ubiquity of magic in myth, fairy tales, folk tales, and fantasy stories could be explained in various ways. From a psychoanalytic perspective, the ability to perform magic, to consort with magical creatures, and to wield magical weapons or instruments, is interpreted as a wish fulfillment fantasy. Contrastingly, being afflicted by black magic (curses, spells), or being attacked by fearsome magical creatures (dragons, monsters), or by black magicians (witches, sorcerers), is interpreted as anxiety or neurotic conflict — whether oedipal in nature (castration anxiety), or more broadly archetypal (fear of the Shadow).[2] From a Jungian perspective, the archetypal theme of magic and archetypal magical figures induces a mindset reminiscent of primitive or prehistoric societies, the symbols of which are retained in the unconscious, thus preserving the powerful psychological resonance that they once evoked in primordial times:

> For in our daily experience, we need to state things as accurately as possible, and we have learned to discard the trimmings of fantasy both in our language and in our thoughts — thus losing a quality that is still characteristic of the primitive mind. Most of us have consigned to the unconscious all the fantastic psychic associations that every object or idea possesses. The primitive, on the other hand, is still aware of these psychic properties; he endows animals, plants, or stones with powers that we find strange and unacceptable.[3]

From an anthropological perspective, magic in stories and legends is related to the primitive rituals in which the first beliefs in magic were immersed. Just as Piaget asserted that the tendency to believe in magic was

part of a universal stage of cognitive development in children (i.e. the "Preoperational Stage"), Frazer asserts that belief in magic is a universal stage of
intellectual/religious development in human societies (i.e. the "Age of Magic"):

> But if in the most backward state of human society now known to us we find
> magic thus conspicuously present and religion conspicuously absent, may we not
> reasonably conjecture that the civilized races of the world have also at some
> period of their history passed through a similar intellectual phase, that they
> attempted to force the great powers of nature to do their pleasure before they
> thought of courting their favor by offerings and prayer — in short that, just as on
> the material side of human culture there has everywhere been an Age of Stone,
> so on the intellectual side there has everywhere been an Age of Magic? There are
> reasons for answering this question in the affirmative.[4]

Frazer explains that the natural intellectual development from magical belief
systems to religious belief systems follows a natural progression in logical
thinking about the natural universe, just as Piaget assumed that the thinking
of a child will gradually become more logical, and that he will naturally
progress from a stage of magical or preoperational thinking, to a stage in
which thinking is more logical, yet still constrained by limits in the ability to
comprehend abstract concepts (i.e. the "Concrete Operational" stage). This
transitory stage, according to Frazer, is the "Age of Religion."

> The movement of the higher thought, so far as we can trace it, has on the whole
> been from magic through religion to science. In magic man depends on his own
> strength to meet the difficulties and dangers that beset him on every side. He
> believes in a certain established order of nature on which he can surely count,
> and which he can manipulate for his own ends. When he discovers his mistake,
> when he recognizes sadly that both the order of nature which he had assumed
> and the control which he had believed himself to exercise over it were purely
> imaginary, he ceases to rely on his own intelligence and his own unaided efforts,
> and throws himself humbly on the mercy of certain great invisible beings behind
> the veil of nature, to whom he now ascribes all those far-reaching powers which
> he once arrogated to himself. Thus in the acuter minds magic is gradually super-
> seded by religion, which explains the succession of natural phenomena as regu-
> lated by the will, the passion, or the caprice of spiritual beings like man in kind,
> though vastly superior to him in power.[5]

The final stage of cognitive development according to Piaget is the Formal
Operational stage, when the child's thinking is governed by logical thinking,
and his beliefs about the nature of the universe are more abstract, but also
based on his empirical observations, which are then qualified by the logical
process of hypothetical-deductive reasoning. Similarly, for Frazer, the natural
intellectual development of the human species is a progression from religious
belief to a more logical system, dictated by empirical, deductive, and rational
thought.

As time goes on this explanation in its turn proves to be unsatisfactory. For it assumes that the succession of natural events is not determined by immutable laws, but is to some extent variable and irregular, and this assumption is not borne out by closer observation. On the contrary, the more we scrutinize that succession the more we are struck by the rigid uniformity, the punctual precision with which, wherever we can follow them, the operations of nature are carried on. Every great advance in knowledge has extended the sphere of order and correspondingly restricted the sphere of apparent disorder in the world, till now we are ready to anticipate that even in regions where chance and confusion appear still to reign, a fuller knowledge would everywhere reduce the seeming chaos to cosmos. Thus the keener minds, still pressing forward to a deeper solution of the mysteries of the universe, come to reject the religious theory of nature as inadequate, and to revert in a measure to the older standpoint of magic by postulating explicitly, what in magic had only been implicitly assumed, to wit, an inflexible regularity in the order of natural events, which, if carefully observed, enables us to foresee their course with certainty and to act accordingly. In short, religion, regarded as an explanation of nature, is displaced by science.

Science and magic are similar belief systems, as they both assume an ordered and structured form to the natural universe, and they both presume that humans can assert a certain measure of personal control over Nature, by means of understanding and manipulating the elements around him. As Tolkien noted:

> Magic produces, or pretends to produce, an alteration in the Primary World. It does not matter by whom it is said to be practiced, fay or mortal, it remains distinct from the other two; it is not an art but a technique; its desire is *power* in this world, domination of things and wills.[6]

Tolkien also explains why Magic, as an element of wish fulfillment, provides a more potent discharge of power than Science:

> Faërie itself may perhaps most nearly be translated by Magic — but it is magic of a peculiar mood and power, at the furthest pole from the vulgar devices of the laborious, scientific, magician.... The magic of Faërie is not an end in itself, its virtue is in its operations: among these are the satisfaction of certain primordial desires. One of these desires is to survey the depths of space and time. Another is ... to hold communion with other living things.[7]

So, in Fantasy, humans can repossess the power they once had as primitive magicians — the power over natural forces that had been stripped of them and given to the gods. In Science Fiction, a subgenre of Fantasy, the power of magic is transliterated into the power of science, and so the wizard becomes a mad scientist, the hero's wand or magic sword becomes a remote control or a light saber, zombies become cyborgs, man-beasts become androids, etc. The archetypes remain the same, only their semblances change. In Fantasy, the opportunity to reuse magic once again is a cathartic homecoming to the sense of empowerment over Nature that our primordial forebears experienced while in the throes of their primitive rituals. So, to understand the role of magic in Faërie, we must understand the role of magic in the primitive ritual, as the magical act in fantasy can be seen as a psychological recapitulation of the magical act in the "primitive" ritual.

Frazer delineated the modes of the use of magic in primitive ritual by distinguishing them from the notions of miracles, divine intervention, or supernatural aid, that are associated with less "primitive" religious beliefs. Frazer's four distinctions could be summarized as follows:

1. No special class of persons is set apart for the performance of the rites...
2. No special places are set apart for the performance of the rites...
3. Spirits, not gods, are recognized...
4. The rites are magical rather than propitiatory.[8]

Magic in the primitive ritual is practiced without priests, temples, gods, or prayer. Any person who acquires the secret wisdom or instruments is able to perform the magical rite. In the primitive world as well as in the fantasy world, magic is free to anyone at any time and in any place. The hero or wizard need only accomplish the task of discovering the key to this magic, and then the spirits of land, water, air, and fire are at his command, without the need to beg or bow to some distant deity. Nature is controlled by magic, which is controlled by humans; as opposed to the less primitive view, in which Nature is controlled by the gods, and humans must supplicate and propitiate these gods in order to appease or provoke their will.

The early chapters of the Old Testament reflect a time in Semitic history when religion was more primitive. It was a time when a vast number of people in the Middle East were nomadic shepherds, traveling from region to region, free-grazing their herds of goats and sheep. For these people, there were no temples. Altars were made, usually on a hilltop or a "high place," anytime they saw fit. Early altars were made of earth, wood, and whatever large rocks were on hand. There were no priests, though in the cities, certain kings did maintain that they were living deities, and had priests serving them. Most people, whether they were masters or slaves, urban or rural, or farmer or shepherd, believed that spirits or gods could be embodied within a totem, talisman, or idol, and that offerings or prayers could be made directly to this magical object. Idol worship was the principal form of worship in these cultures, and it assumed a much closer relationship with the spiritual powers than in less primitive religions. Idols were owned by their worshippers, and in this way the worshippers retained mastership of their own belief systems. The worshippers were their own priests, and they paid no tributes to priestly classes, because they offered their own sacrifices to their own gods. There were no communal temples to build, though in cities their appeared to be communal idols, which usually took the form of large stone sculptures. The lurid exploits of the Sodomites and Gemorites are generally attributed to the sexual practices involved in their supplicatory rites to their god, who was probably a fertility divinity much like Dionysus, the benefactor of their rich volcanic soil.

The nature of magic and how it is effected is variable. At its source is the basic concept of "mana" or essence, a mystical force within nature that exists everywhere and can be tapped into via some ritualistic practice or device.[9] Sometimes mana exists in magical objects such as enchanted seeds, beans, weapons, armor, wands, rings, crystal balls, etc. This form of magic is available to anyone holding the object. Magical rituals, typically involving the concoction of potions and/or the recitation of spells, can conjure mana. This form of magic is only available to those who are well versed, willing to learn, or able to discover the secret ways of magic. Magicians in the traditional sense are those beings who have an innate connection with the forces of mana around them, or with the spirits that control the mana. Magic in this mode is only available to certain people, who may or may not be considered human. Witches, wizards, warlocks, shamans ... these are the people who can perform magic, either by manipulating the mana around them, or by acting as a medium or conduit to the magical spirits. Magical people are humans who have mana within them. Divine priest-kings, demigods, semi-divine heroes ... these people can perform magic of their own accord, without calling upon some external force. And finally, there are the supernatural magical beings — fairies, elves, gods, etc.—who are living incarnations of mana. In Susannah Clarke's classic fantasy epic, *Jonathan Strange & Mr. Norrel,* a strict demarcation is made between the type of magic performed by a magician and the type achieved through agency with the hidden kingdom of fairies. The latter type of magic is exponentially more powerful than the former, as it derives from the true wellspring of magical power, the Realm of Faërie, which is akin to the primeval spirit world of the primitive animists.

The practice of magic by individuals who do not posses magical objects and who are not magical themselves is largely relegated to what Frazer referred to as "Sympathetic Magic." This form of "common magic" is based on the principle that forces in nature can be controlled through items that correspond to these forces, or behaviors that imitate the forces in some way. Sympathetic Magic can be organized according to two basic principles: "The Law of Similarity" and "The Law of Contagion." The former law constitutes the basis of "Homeopathic Magic," while the latter law is the basis for "Contagious Magic." Homeopathic Magic is derived from the simplistic notion that "like produces like." For example, if one were to fashion a "voodoo doll" in the image of an enemy, and then stab that doll with a pin, this magical act would produce an injury or pain in the body of one's enemy. Like produces like. Contagious Magic is derived from the equally simplistic notion that things which have once been connected will remain connected, even if they are no longer together. For example, if you desired another person to fall in love with you, you can purloin a lock of their hair, chop it up, brew it into a "love potion," and drink it. According to the Law of Contagion, the person you desire will now long for you, because a part of themselves in now inside of you, and they are still magically connected to that part of themselves which is now in you. Much of the magic to be discussed in this chapter is related, in one way or another, to Frazer's principles of Sympathetic Magic.

Magic Words

The human capacity for complex, sophisticated, symbolic language is a primary distinguishing characteristic between humans and beasts. In our innate ability to express eloquently in words the abstract concepts that cross our mind, we go beyond the physical realm of the ordinary animal and enter the world of the sublime. Though at times we may look and act like beasts, we speak and write like gods. Hence it is in the substance of language itself— not necessarily the content of speech, but the actual process of speaking and reciting — that we find the essence of magic. It is this trait that elevates us from the lowly kingdom of animals, engendering us with the power of the Creator, who modeled the very first magic when he uttered the words — "Let there be light" — and so conjured the very first illusion.[10]

Piaget used the term "nominal realism" to refer to the belief that an individual's true name is linked to his spiritual essence or soul.[11] According to the principles of Sympathetic Magic, the name of a person or spirit is magically connected with the person or spirit. Uttering the name conjures the spirit. "He who gains possession of the name and knows how to make use of it has gained power over the object itself; he has made it his own with all its energies."[12] The saying — "Speak of the devil...." — uttered when you happen to be speaking about someone who coincidentally appears on the scene, is a relic of the much older proverb "Speak of the devil and he will appear."[13] The modern saying fails to capture the true meaning of the original proverb, which expressed the notion that it is the magical power of uttering the name itself— the act of speech, or the spell — which actually conjures the spirit. The old proverb was a cautionary saying, warning us to be careful of what we speak, because words have power.

The reverence and awe in which language is held is integral to Jewish mythology, mysticism, and folklore. The Third of the Ten Commandments forbids the misuse of God's holy name. In terms of order, the prohibition against using the Lord's name in vain takes precedence over the prohibitions against murder, theft, and adultery. Many of the mystical texts of the Kabbalah have to do with the magical incantations, reorganizations, and illustrations of the Tetragrammaton, the ineffable four-letter name of God, "Yehovah", as well as other "unknown" names of God, and the names of angels and demons. Magic in the Kabbalah is performed in a singular way — via the ritual repetition or inscription of holy or spiritual names.

> One may not say that the invocation of God's Name obliges Him to do the will of the invoker, that God himself is coerced by the recital of His Name; but the Name itself is invested with the power to fulfill the desire of the man who utters it.[14]

The most famous magical creature in Jewish mythology, the Golem, was given life by Rabbi Loew of Prague when he wrote the Hebrew word Emet (Truth) on the clay figure's forehead. Life was taken away from the Golem when the first letter of the word Emet was erased from his forehead, leaving the word Met (Dead). Jewish tradition holds:

> A man's name is the essence of his being ... his name is his soul. But the desire to bless a child with a richly endowed name was balanced by the fear that the soul of its previous owner would be transported into the body of the infant — a fear which stood in the way of naming children after living parents or after any living persons, and thus robbing them of their soul and their life.[15]

Because names are so critically linked to the soul and therefore so potentially dangerous, many societies have customs designed to safeguard private names.

> To know a name is to be privy to the secret of its owner's being and master of his fate. The members of many primitive tribes have two names, one for public use, the other jealously concealed, known only to the man who bears it. Even the immediate members of the family never learn what it is; if an enemy should discover it, its bearer's life is forfeit.[16]

In the Earthsea fantasy novels, Duny is a young boy on Gont, one of the larger islands which dot Earthsea. His mother is dead. During the rite of passage into adulthood, Duny is given his "true name," Ged. In this world, a magician who knows someone's true name has control over that person, so one's true name is revealed only to those whom one trusts implicitly. Normally, a person is referred to by his or her "use name." Ged is Duny's "true" name. Sparrowhawk becomes his "use name." Much of the magic in Earthsea revolves around the discovery and use of people's "true" names

> for magic consists in this, the true naming of a thing.... Magic, true magic, is worked only by those beings who speak ... the Old Speech.[17]

There is always a "coefficient of weirdness"[18] in magical incantations.

> A characteristic feature of the evolution of magic has been its easy passage from the invocation of celestial beings to the manipulation of mere names, or words ... nominalism of this sort made room for the magic word ... the more barbaric the word the more potent it is likely to be.[19]

The words in the magical spell are archaic, esoteric, cryptic, and arcane. The words often come from dead languages or possibly from languages that no mortal ever spoke. All of this mystery adds to the paranormal quality of the magic, fostering the mindset of the primitive ritual, in which the more secret and unfathomable the method was, the more likely it was to be true and effective.

Nominalism is apparent in fairytales as well as in most fantasy stories that feature a Dark Lord character. The well known character of Rumpelstiltskin in the fairytale named after him is incredibly powerful, yet one only needs to discover his true name and repeat it three times in order to vanquish him. In the *The Lightning Thief*, one cannot utter the name of a god or goddess without evoking their wrath, so the young heroes have to be very careful in their speech. The name of Sauron is rarely mentioned in *The Lord of the Rings* for fear of drawing his attention or summoning his spirit. Sauron is referred to as "He whom we do not name..."[20] Similarly, the wizards in the Harry Potter books are loath to utter the name Voldemort, preferring to refer to him as "He-Who-Must-Not-Be-Named" or, more informally, as "You-Know-Who." Dumbledore, however, advised Harry to take a more logical and less magical approach to the matter:

> Call him Voldemort, Harry. Always use the proper name for things. Fear of a name increases fear of the thing itself.[21]

In the Harry Potter books, names, spells, and curses are usually cast in variants of Latin, the archaic predecessor of the modern European languages, which hearkens back to the pagan lords of the ancient world, who believed so adamantly in the animistic forces. The most reviled curse in the wizarding world, one of the three forbidden "Unforgivable Curses," is "Avada Kedavra." It is a killing curse. The etymology of the curse is certainly related to the most famous of all magic words, "Abracadabra," which has its roots in both ancient Hebrew and Aramaic. It is of interest that Rowling took a magic word used in ancient times as a curative spell and turned it into a killing curse by playing upon the Latin word for corpse, "cadaver."

Horcruxes

The "Holographic principle"—following the principle of contagious magic—is the magical belief that the mana within an object separated from its source will carry all of the essential qualities of its source.[22] Much of the recorded practice of "sympathetic magic" or folk magic is based on the holographic principle. A common belief among primitive peoples is that their soul, at one point, is transported out of their own bodies and stored as a "bush soul" in the vessel of an animal or tree. Hence, if something happens to the animal or tree which houses your bush soul, you will suffer or perish. Similarly, if you drink the blood or eat the heart of a totem animal such as a lion, you will inherit its spiritual power and essence, and thus will become fiercer, stronger, or more courageous. We see the same basic principle in modern Catholicism. In the Communion ritual, the priest recites the words of Jesus: "Drink of the wine, it is my blood.... Eat of the bread, it is my body...." It is then believed that the nominal force of the prayer transubstantiates the wine and bread into blood and flesh, and that the devouring of these objects instills the spiritual essence of the deity into the body of the practitioner.

In fantasy, we see the archetypal theme of an enchanter detaching his life essence, spirit, or soul and placing it into an external object. In doing this, the enchanter instills spiritual/magical power into the detached object, while also separating himself from his spiritual core, and thereby becoming un-human or immortal. Rowling referred to this sort of magical object as a "Horcrux." Horcruxes become central to the plot in the latter Harry Potter novels, as Voldemort had stored parts of his soul in seven different objects, thus requiring the heroes to discover and destroy all seven horcruxes. In *Taran Wanderer*, the fourth of the Prydain Chronicles, a dark wizard named Morda stored his soul in one of his detached fingers. While stabbing Morda through the heart doesn't harm him in the least, when Taran finds the finger bone and snaps it in two, Morda is destroyed. Similarly, in *The Lord of the Rings*, Sauron's power and life-force is wrapped up in the One Ring of Power. When the ring is destroyed, so is Sauron.

Swords

Raglan stated definitively of the hero's weapon:

we find that the hero, whether of myth, saga, or fairytale, cannot injure the monster without the magic weapons: and that nobody else can use the magic weapons to injure the monster. Against the hero with the magic weapons the monster is powerless; he falls at the first blow. That is because the hero is a ritual personage using ritual weapons to deliver a ritual blow.[23]

The sword with which St. George slew the dragon was called Ascalon, a name recalling the city of Ashkelon in Israel. The sword, in this sense, was magically imbued with the spiritual power of the Judeo-Christian Holy Land, and this is what gave George the power to slay the archetypal symbol of paganism. King Arthur's legendary sword, Excalibur, was similarly imbued with magic, as it was delivered to him by a goddess, The Lady of the Lake. In fantasy stories, most heroes have a similar form of magic weapon. Taran and Gwydion, the heroes in the Prydain Chronicles, both at different points wield Drynwyn, the enchanted sword of kings. The sword gets its name from the legendary "White-Hilt," the sword of Drynwyn, which, according to Anglo-Saxon mythology, burst into flames when drawn by a man of noble spirit. The same legend may have been the inspiration for the light saber in the *Star Wars* films, the light saber being a science fiction take on the magic sword motif. In the *Chronicles of Narnia*, Peter is given a magic sword, Rhindon, by Father Christmas. In *The Lord of the Rings*, the broken sword of the last great king, Isildur, is re-forged from its shards and wielded by Islidur's heir, Aragorn — symbolizing the fulfillment of the prophecy, that one day Isildur's heir would reclaim the throne of Gondor, bearing his fore-father's sword. In Tolkien's short story "Farmer Giles of Ham," the hero acquires a magic sword, "Caudimorax, the famous sword that in popular romances is more vulgarly called Tailbiter."[24] In this story, the hero is more or less a normal man, it is the magic sword that has the power to slay the dragon, it needs only a willing hand to wield it, as the parson of Ham informs the hero: "This sword ... will not stay sheathed, if a dragon is within five miles."[25]

Wands

Magic wands are a staple of fairytale and fantasy literature. Fairy god-mothers and witches alike are known to wield powerful wands. In *The Wonderful Wizard of Oz*, Glinda the Good Witch of the South and the Wicked Witch of the West both conjure their magic with a wave of their magic wands. In the *Chronicles of Narnia*, Jadis the White Witch wields a wand which can turn people into stone. Wands, of course, play a central role in the Harry Potter books, and are the principal objects used to conjure magic in the wizarding world. The mana or magic in the wand comes from its core, which is always an element from a magical creature, i.e. a unicorn tail hair, a phoenix tail feather, a dragon heartstring, etc.

Metals

The metal iron is held by many traditions to have anti-demonic qualities. There are various theories behind this superstition, but the most sensible is the notion that since "metals are the products of civilization" they are ipso facto, "antipathetic to the spirit masters of primitive pre-metal societies."[26] Hence, an iron cross can be used to dispel demons and vampires. In Michael Scott's *The Alchemyst*, the race of Elders represent the primeval spirits, gods, and demons of archaic societies. While they are all-powerful, they are extremely vulnerable to iron, as the end of the "Golden Age" of the antediluvian gods and demons was heralded by the forging of metals in the beginning of the Iron Age. Similarly, in Tolkien's Middle Earth, the hobbits wield magical eleven swords, assumingly made of iron, that glow in the proximity of Fell creatures such as goblins and orcs. In the first book of the Chronicles of Narnia, the witch-queen Jadis uses an archaic stone dagger to slaughter Aslan in a ritual sacrifice. The stone dagger and altar represent the primeval demonic forces that were worshipped in the Stone Age, while the Christian Peter wields an iron sword given to him by Father Christmas, representing the more wholesome forces of the succeeding ages.

Some imaginative writers believe that meteorites must have been revered by ancient peoples, as they appeared to be gifts from the celestial gods. Since meteorites are most often made of iron, a form of iron that was purer than most primitive peoples could create themselves, then the first iron daggers and swords could have been forged from meteoric iron, giving these swords the quality of magic, not only because they were superior in strength to any other existent weapon, but because the metal itself was seen as being a gift from the gods. Though the idea is a provocative one, there is, however, no real evidence at all that this theory is true in any way.

In certain fairy-tales and fantasy stories, witches and werewolves are vulnerable to silver, especially silver bullets. The anti-demonic power of silver probably has a similar origin to the superstitious beliefs about iron. Gold has a magical aura about it, if even just as a projection of man's boundless materialism and greed. Medieval alchemists (Nicholas Flamel, in particular) were purported to have the ability to transform lead into gold by employing the legendary "Philosopher's Stone," which is a central plot point in the first of the Harry Potter books, as well as in *The Alchemyst*. In the Grimms' fairytale, the magical dwarf Rumpelstiltskin could spin straw into gold.

Mirrors, Fountains, and Crystal Balls

Humans, who are prisoners of time, often dream that we could see into the future so that we can change our fate, or at least be aware of it beforehand. Sometimes, as we are also prisoners of space, the wish is that we could see what is happening in some other corner of our world, so we could be better prepared for the challenges to come. The desire to unleash ourselves of these temporal and spatial restrictions, to gaze beyond the bounds of time and space, is fulfilled in fantasy with the magical aid of clairvoyant objects. However, these objects are almost always symbols of intra-psychic revelation. We are deceived by the illusion of looking outwardly into the crystal ball or magic mirror, while what we are actually seeing is ourselves in reflection, our inner selves, replete with the intuitive wisdom that is inside of us all along.

> True, whoever looks into the mirror of the water will see first of all his own face. Whoever goes to himself risks a confrontation with himself. The mirror does not flatter, it faithfully shows whatever looks into it; namely, the face we never show to the world because we cover it with the *persona*, the mask of the actor. But the mirror lies behind the mask and shows the true face.[27]

The crystal ball in the 1939 film version of *The Wonderful Wizard of Oz* depicts an excellent portrayal of how the magic mirror provides intuitive psychological insight in the guise of paranormal prophecy. In the first act of the film, Dorothy encounters Professor Marvel after she runs away from home. The trickster magician pretends to gaze into the crystal ball with Dorothy, but instead he peaks into her purse and finds a picture of Aunt Em.

> This — this is the same genuine, magic, authentic crystal used by the priests of Isis and Osiris in the days of the Pharaohs of Egypt, in which Cleopatra first saw the approach of Julius Caesar and Mark Antony — and so on and so on. Now, you'd better close your eyes, my child, for a moment — in order to be better in tune with the infinite. We can't do these things without reaching out into the infinite. Yes, that's right. Now you can open them. We'll gaze into the crystal. Ah, what's this I see? A house with a picket fence and a barn with a weather vane of a running horse.... There's a woman. She's wearing a polka-dot dress. Her face is careworn.... Why, she's crying.... Someone has hurt her. Someone has just about broken her heart.... It's someone she loves very much; someone she's been very kind to; someone she's taken care of in sickness.... Why, she's putting her hand on her heart! She's dropping down on the bed.... Well, that's all. The crystal's gone dark.[28]

Dorothy is tricked into believing the crystal ball's revelation — that by running away, she has broken her aunt's heart. But in truth, Professor Marcel simply revealed to her what she already knew in her own heart; she was just not consciously aware of that truth at the moment. Later on in the film, in Oz (in Dorothy's dream), she encounters another crystal ball. In the third act, Dorothy is trapped in the witch's tower. She gazes into the witch's crystal ball, and this time she sees Aunt Em herself, because what she is searching for in her heart is a nurturing mother figure to protect her from the wicked witch.

A similar theme can be found in *Harry Potter and the Sorcerer's Stone*. On the magical Mirror of Erised, the following words are inscribed: "erised stra ehru oyt ube cafru oyt on wohsi." When seen in the reflection of a mirror, the passage reads: "I show not your face but your heart's desire." So we see that the Mirror of Erised is the Mirror of Desire, and like any magic mirror, such as Dorothy's crystal ball, it shows not our outward reflection but our inner reflection, our heart's deepest desire. When Harry gazes into the mirror, he sees the living image of his dead parents. In *The Lord of the Rings*, the Palantír or "seeing stones" are similar to crystal balls in shape and function. When one gazes into one Palantír, he can see into the mind's eye of anyone gazing into the other Palantír. However, since the Palantír only offers glimpses of the truth, they are usually deceptive. Also in *The Lord of the Rings*, the Elf Queen Galadriel's mirror, which is actually a basin filled with water, provides glimpses of things that have happened in the past, things that are happening far away, and things that will come to pass. A similar mirror is found in Narnia. The Hermit of the Southern March, a wizard, has a clear reflective pool of water. When he gazes into it, he could see what is going on in other parts of Narnia. Eilony, the princess-enchantress in the Prydain Chronicles, owns a magic bauble called the Golden Pelydryn, which lights up darkness and shadows, and reveals hidden things that cannot be illuminated by ordinary light.

Gems and Stones

Precious and rare gemstones have enthralled humans since archaic times. This hypnotic quality lends itself well to the leitmotif in myth, fairytale, and fantasy of the existence of gemstones with magical powers. The Urim and Thummim, in the Old Testament, were a dozen magical gemstones engraved with the names of the Israelite tribes. They were worn by the High Priest on a breastplate and would light up in reply to specific questions regarding judicial decisions in a way that would indicate a verdict. As magical objects mentioned by name in the Bible, the Urim and Thummim are quite exceptional, and have therefore become popular objects of fascination in both Judeo-Christian mythology, the mythology of the Church of Latter Day Saints (Mormons), and fantasy literature.

In *The Hobbit*, a legendary gemstone is the primary article sought by the dwarves on their epic quest through Middle Earth:

> But fairest of all was the great white gem, which the dwarves had found beneath the roots of the Mountain, the Heart of the Mountain, the Arkenstone of Thrain.... It was like a globe with a thousand facets; it shone like silver in the firelight, like water in the sun, like snow under the stars, like rain upon the Moon![29]

In addition to gemstones, regular stones often have a magical quality to them as well. In particular, the motif of a person being turned to stone via sorcery is ubiquitous in Faërie.

As Bettelheim noted:

> As in many other fairy stories, this does not symbolize death; rather it stands for a lack of true humanity, an inability to respond to higher values, so that the person, being dead to what life is all about in the best sense, might as well be made of stone.[30]

In Genesis, Lot's wife was punished by God by being turned into a pillar of stone, just retribution for her insensitivity of gazing upon the fate of the doomed Sodomites and Gemorrites. Medusa the Gorgon, in Greek Mythology, has so horrifying a face that just a glance at her visage turns mortal men into stone. In *The Lion, the Witch, and the Wardrobe*, Jadis the White Witch turns Tumnus the faun into stone, a fitting punishment for the faun who so selfishly tricked and betrayed little Lucy. And the trolls in *The Hobbit* are turned into stone by the sunlight, as they prepare to cook and eat their captive dwarves.

Invisibility Talismans

Invisibility Cloaks abound in myth, fairytale, and fantasy. A cloak, in and of itself, is a thing that is used to hide and make oneself unseen. Thus, a magic cloak just exponentially intensifies the intrinsic function of the object, making the wearer completely invisible. The Grimm Brothers' tales "The Raven" and "The Worn-out Dancing Shoes" feature invisibility cloaks. In Tolkien's *The Silmarilliion,* Tuor, son of Hurin, is given an invisibility cloak by Ulmo, Lord of the Waters. And in Rowling's *Harry Potter* series, Harry's oft used invisibility cloak is inherited from his father. In Greek Mythology, the Helm of Hades, or Helm of Darkness, is used by numerous gods and heroes, such as Athena, Hermes, and Perseus. The cap creates a magical cloud or mist that surrounds its wearer, thus making him or her undetectable. In *The Lightning Thief,* Annabeth, a daughter of Athena, owns a Yankees cap that makes her invisible. An equally common trope is the invisibility ring. In Arthurian legends, Maiden Lilith gives an invisibility ring to Owyatt. In Roman myth, Discordia, Goddess of Strife, owns an invisibility ring. Plato cites the fable of "The Ring of Gyges" in his *Republic.* In the story, the bearer of the invisibility ring is seduced by the corruptive power of the ring. The hero, a poor shepherd, abuses the magic of the ring to amass power and wealth. A similar theme, of course, can be seen in *The Lord of the Rings,* especially in the character of Gollum, and to a lesser extent, in the characters of Bilbo, Frodo, and Sam — all of whom were small, weak hobbits who were tempted, in various degrees, to abuse the power of the ring. "Invisibility sometimes suggests that a person is overlooked or disregarded."[31] Hence, invisibility as a magical force that engenders strength and power, in a literary sense, creates perfect irony when the ring is borne by a character who is small and weak, and therefore craves power.

Horns

The horns of animal totems such as rams and bulls have been used in ritual and warfare since primordial times. Possibly the most ancient non-percussive musical instrument and the most ancient tool of communication over long distances, the ram's horn was used like a bugle in battle, to signal charge or retreat, or as a call for reinforcements. The Shofar, a ram's horn used in Jewish rituals, is said to have magical powers. At the famous biblical battle of Jericho, it was the power of the Shofar calls that sent the walls of Jericho tumbling down. The Kabbalah teaches that the sound of the Shofar dispels evil spirits, which is why it is blown on the Jewish New Year. In the *Chronicles of Narnia,* Susan's horn, given to her by Father Christmas, when blown, would bring help, no matter how far away assistance may be. A similar horn is given to Taran in the Prydain Chronicles. When blown, the horn will summon help from the "Fair Folk," the magical little people of Prydain. In *The Lord of the Rings,* Boromir's horn has a similar magical quality,

> a great horn of the wild ox of the East, bound with silver, and written with ancient characters. That horn the eldest son of our house has borne for many generations; and it is said that if it be blown at need anywhere within the bounds of Gondor, as the realm was of old, its voice will not pass unheeded.[32]

Music

In *The Silmarillion*, Middle Earth and the universe it exists in were created through the singing of mystical music by Ilúvatar, the Creator, and his offspring, the Ainur. In *The Magician's Nephew*, the world of Narnia is similarly created through the harmonic vibrations of a mystical music. The belief in the magical and creative power of music is ancient, especially in reference to its ability to sooth and heal. David, in the Bible, was known for playing the harp, which soothed the heavy head of King Saul. Angels are also known for playing the harp, the source of the heavenly music that soothes the soul. Orpheus, in Greek mythology, played such lovely music on his lyre that he could charm the beasts of the field as well as the birds of the air and the fish of the sea. He could even charm the rocks and trees to dance to his tunes, and once charmed Hades himself, when he descended to the Underworld with his lyre to fetch his beloved, Eurydice.

> "Musick has Charms to sooth a savage Breast,
> To soften Rocks, or bend a knotted Oak.
> I've read, that things inanimate have mov'd,
> And, as with living Souls, have been inform'd
> By Magick Numbers and persuasive Sound."[33]

The first line of William Congreve's famous 17th century poem, *The Mourning Bride*, has oft been quoted in reference to the magical qualities of music. Unfortunately, it is also often misquoted as follows: "Music has charms to sooth a savage *beast*." It is this frequent misquotation which may have led to the common motif of heroes in fantasy stories using music to quell a savage beast and thus escape from harm, or even tame the beast and enlist it as an ally. In the third Prydain Chronicle, *The Castle of Llyr*, Ffleuder Fflam the bard uses his harp to sooth Llyan, a giant cat who is ferocious until tamed by Ffleuder's tune. In the first Harry Potter book, Fluffy is a massive, ferocious, three-headed dog who, like Cerberus in Hades, guards the entrance to a secret chamber. Harry and his pals use music from a flute to lull Fluffy to sleep so they can gain access to the chamber.

Magic Numbers

Numbers have always held a place of fascination in the psyche, and the belief in the magical quality of certain numbers is widespread. Most people have a specific "lucky number," and even casual gamblers who play the lottery or "the numbers" will recurrently bet the same lucky numbers again and again.

Numerology is the study of the mystical or magical qualities of numbers, and it remains common in mystical and superstitious traditions around the world. An area of Kabbalistic study called Gematria involves the assignment of a numerical value to each Hebrew letter, through which secret coded messages can be found throughout the scriptures. There is a common and ancient superstition that there is "luck in odd numbers," because even numbers or "pairs" could, inscrutably, "invite demon attack."[34] In any case, we do observe in fairytale and fantasy the association of luck or magic with odd numbers, especially with three and seven, but also, to a lesser degree, with nine and eleven, as seen in the verse which permeates the entirety of Tolkien's epic.

> "Three Rings for the Elven-kings under the sky,
>   Seven for the Dwarf-lords in their halls of stone,
> Nine for mortal men doomed to die,
>   One for the Dark Lord on his dark throne
> In the Land of Mordor where the Shadows lie.
>   One Ring to rule them all, One Ring to find them,
> One Ring to bring them all and in the darkness bind them
>   In the Land of Mordor where the Shadows lie."[35]

One

There is obvious mystical significance in "the unit," as it represents both unity and singularity. In *The Lord of the Rings*, the one ring of power is the unifying magical object that Sauron needs in order to control all of the inhabitants of Middle Earth. Myths and fantasies often focus on a hero figure who is referred to as "the one true king" or "the destined one." In this sense, the hero figure, like Jesus and Arthur, represents the unity between the physical and spiritual realms, as well as the unity between humankind and Nature, and the unity between mortal humans and immortal gods. The hero figure is also a singularity, a one-of-a-kind marvel who is like no other man, and who represents the singular or special qualities within each individual man. The Abrahamic (monotheistic) religions all posit the existence of *one* true god.

Three

Three is the "magic number," and thus has innate power and is often used in the repetition of spells and curses. The phrase, "third time's the charm," probably originated from the ancient belief that a spell or magical charm, in order to be effective, must be repeated thrice. As a ubiquitous theme in terms of the number of times things happen in a story, three is the standard trope. When wishes are granted by a genie or fairy, it is usually in the amount of three. There were Three Little Pigs, Three Blind Mice, Three Bears in the house that Goldilocks invaded, where she tried three things — the porridge, the chairs, and the beds — and so and so on. It is often noted that "good things happen in threes," while it is also said that "bad things happen in threes" as well. "Three is the favored mystical number of all times — the first odd number after the unit; "anything that is repeated three times is magical" was a frequently quoted rule."[36] When something is tripled, it is made especially important. Thirteen, on the other hand, is infamously unlucky or even evil. Since pairs have a demonic quality, the number six, a tripled pair, is believed to be powerfully evil. The number 666, the "Number of the Beast" in the New Testament, is a triple digit representation of the tripled pair.

As the elves are the most magical folk in Middle Earth, they are given three rings, as the number three signifies magic. In religions, three is associated with divinity because of the following trinities: past/present/future, earth/underworld/heaven, father/mother/son (or in the Christian doctrine, father/son/holy ghost). For Jung, the Holy Trinity was defined by the archetypal union of the sexual opposites, the Hieros Gamos or sacred marriage, in which anima and animus copulate, resulting in the birth of a third figure, the divine child. Bettelheim noted a psychosexual significance to the number three:

> Three is a mystical and often a holy number, and was so long before the Christian doctrine of the Holy Trinity. It is the threesome of snake, Eve, and Adam which, according to the Bible, makes for carnal knowledge. In the unconscious, the number three stands for sex, because each sex has three visible sex characteristics: penis and the two testes in the male; vagina and the two breasts in the female.[37]

Four

Four is a sacred number in many traditions. "Four is a ritual number in American Indian lore, referring to the four directions of the universe."[38] Four is particularly significant in Buddhist tradition, as there are Four Heavenly Kings, corresponding to the four cardinal directions, Four Great Elements (earth, wind, water, fire), Four Noble Truths, Four Stages of Enlightenment, and many more mystical groupings of four. In Jewish mysticism, the Tetragrammaton, the four-letter ineffable name of God, is the source of all magic and wisdom. Four is often seen as a number significant for mortal men in the natural world, as there are four corners of the Earth, four cardinal directions, four seasons, four classical elements, four sides to a square, etc. A "quaternity," in Jungian psychology, is a symbol of the self related to the number four, which he related to a symbol found in alchemical texts known as the quad-ratura circuli, "squaring the circle," which represents a return to wholeness from a state of disunity or chaos.[39]

Seven

While three is the magic number, seven is often considered the lucky number. A Jewish mystic sage once wrote, "All sevens are beloved."[40] According-ing to the Kabbalah, this is the 7th Earth, as the previous six creations were destroyed by God. Hence, seven is a particularly relevant number for people living on Earth, while the number six is associated with the underworld. Another aspect of the significance of seven is that God created this Earth in six days, resting on the seventh, so the seventh day is consecrated as the Sabbath in the Jewish, Christian, and Islamic religions. Seven rings were given to the dwarf-lords of Middle Earth, a decision possibly made from an association with the seven dwarves in the fairytale, *Snow White*. Bettelheim noted that, since dwarves are generally associated with the earth and with hard work (since they labor ceaselessly in the mines), then seven could be associated with the seven days of the week that dwarves work (whereas humans only work 5 or 6 days, and then rest on the 6th and/or 7th).

Nine

The number nine is often associated with mortality and death, especially in German folklore.[41] As nine is three squared, its magic may therefore be considered exponentially stronger, hence nine holds the power over life and death. In *The Lord of the Rings*, nine rings were given to "mortal men doomed to die." In Tolkien's novels, the Ringwraiths are often referred to as simply "the Nine." Since the nine human ringbearers all fell under the power of Sauron and became Ringwraiths — undead specters — the association between the Nine and death is intensified. Cats are said to have nine lives, and since cats, especially black ones, are often thought of as harbingers of death and bad luck, (such as when a black cat crosses your path), then the number nine associated with cats could also be interpreted as a deathly omen. It was believed that witches took the form of cats when they wished to travel incognito.

In Dante's *Divine Comedy*, there are nine circles of Hell. Pluto, the ninth planet (before it was recently deposed as a "non-planet"), is the Roman name for Hades, the god of the Underworld. In Jewish tradition, the ninth day of the month of Av is "the saddest day in Jewish history," as both Holy Temples were coincidentally destroyed on that day. Therefore, the number nine is considered unlucky. The day commemorating the destructions, Tisha B'Av (the ninth of Av), is a day of fasting and mourning. The Tisha HaYamim, the first nine days of Av, are nine days of ritual mourning leading up to Tisha B'Av. In the Islamic tradition, Ramadan, the month of fasting and prayer, is the ninth month in the Islamic calendar. And finally, September, the ninth month in the Julian and Gregorian calendars, in modern times has become associated with terrorism. The PLO terrorist group, Black September, has committed a number of atrocities, including the murder of eleven Israeli athletes during the 1972 Olympic Games in Munich, during the month of September. Most recently, the terrorist attacks on America on September 11, 2001, have reinforced the association between September and terrorism, causing the 9th month to be designated as "National Preparedness Month."

The Bicameral Mind and Its Influence on Myth, Fairytale and Fantasy

"As the stag pants after the waterbrooks,
So pants my mind after you, O gods!
My mind thirsts thirsts for gods! For living gods!
When shall I come face to face with gods?"

–Psalm 42[1]

In 1976, Julian Jaynes published an extremely thought provoking and controversial book, *The Origin of Consciousness in the Breakdown of the Bicameral Mind*. At the time, Jaynes' theory was quite popular, and the book was received well by readers and critics alike, becoming a bestseller and a nominee for the National Book Award in 1978. However, Jaynes' theory was not widely accepted in academic circles, mainly because the central hypothesis was a bit far reaching; and since it explored notions of how ancient peoples may have thought in prehistoric times, it could not be supported by empirical evidence. Nevertheless, the hypothesis that ancient humans were not conscious (in the way that Jaynes defined consciousness), and that their decisions and judgments were based primarily on unconscious ("bicameral") functions, that were experienced by individuals as hallucinations, is vastly intriguing — and in my opinion, extremely relevant to the subject of this book — as it provides an interesting and unique explanation for the emergence of the archetypal symbols that reappear continuously in the literature of Faërie.

Jaynesian Consciousness

Although the focus of this chapter is on bicameral themes in myth, fairytale, and fantasy, and not on consciousness, because Jaynes' theory is, in essence, a theory of the origin of consciousness, it is necessary to review Jaynes' definition of consciousness before proceeding, as his definition is quite specific and also divergent from other definitions of consciousness. Following Jaynes' logic in approaching the topic, I will start with excluding the cognitive functions that Jaynes considered to be not indicative of consciousness, and also provide one of the same examples that he used in his book.[2]

Imagine that you are driving a car. While driving, you are thinking about something (say, for example, you are thinking about the definition of consciousness). You may even be so immersed in your thinking that you can even hear the sound of your own voice in your head, pronouncing your thoughts as you conceive of them. This phenomenon is referred to as internal speech, internal monologue, or inner voice. It is considered to be a universal phenomenon in humans, though it is doubtful that nonhumans experience it, as its existence is dependent on the acquisition of formal language. I will use the term "inner monologue" to refer to this phenomenon. So, while driving and thinking, your body and mind are also engaged in numerous functions that you are not "consciously" aware of. For example, your feet are operating the gas and brakes and your hands are operating the steering wheel and gearshift. They complete the necessary operations without you having to focus on them at all, and you are unconscious of these operations, unless something calls your attention to them, such as an obstacle in the road, which will elicit the need to decelerate and swerve. You may remember that when you were first learning to drive, it was difficult to coordinate these functions, and you had to focus deliberately on them, which required concentration and effort. However, as an experienced driver, these operations are now so habitual that they have become automatic, and require no effort or concentration at all. You are unconscious of the operations of your hands and feet, except for those moments in which you must focus and concentrate, such as when the obstacle appears. To generalize this phenomenon, the majority of the physical operations we engage in all day long — driving, walking, eating, moving, etc.— are for the most part executed without consciousness. Jaynes referred to these activities as "preoptive."[3]

While you are driving, your eyes are observing and perceiving many things simultaneously, such as the distance between your car and the cars in front of you, behind you, and on either side of you, as well as the curvature of the road ahead, the physical state of the road itself, the velocity of your car, etc. While you perceive all of these bits of sensory information and are aware of them, you do not have to focus on them or think about them, unless something happens, such as the appearance of an obstacle on the road. In the absence of an obstacle, you drive on, focusing only on the thoughts in your head, expressed as an internal monologue. Thus, consciousness is not sensory perception and awareness. This assertion is accentuated by the fact that you can close your eyes and cover your ears, yet you can still focus on your own thoughts — you are still conscious — despite the lack of sensory experience.

As you drive, you pass miles and miles of scenery. You do not focus on anything passing by unless it calls your attention to it, such as a policeman's vehicle or an accident, at which time consciousness is directed towards that unusual, threatening, or interesting stimulus. Let's say that at the end of your journey, someone asks you if you noticed the blossoming dogwood trees along a certain stretch of the highway. Though you did not focus on the dogwoods as you drove by them, and you did not think of them at all, when the person asks you about them, you can visualize the image of the blossoming trees by recalling the memory of them. (This memory is not necessarily a picture of the actual trees, but a conscious reconstruction of what the trees must have looked liked, compiled by your memories of dogwood blossoms and the highway.) In any case, your "memory" of the trees was registered in your mind without any conscious awareness or intention. Thus, memory is not consciousness.

Now, try to remember the experience of learning to drive. The initial experience was probably frustrating, because it was difficult to focus on so many things at the same time. However, once the basic operations were coordinated on a basic level, learning to drive was really just a matter of practice and repetition. The more you drove, the less you had to focus on the operations involved in driving. The less conscious driving became, the easier it was, until the point when driving became an almost completely unconscious activity, leaving your mind free to ponder thoughts unrelated to driving. Except for the very initial stage of learning, the process of learning and mastery did not require much focus or concentration. This point is perhaps better made in the case of a less complex activity, such as walking. Babies can walk, and so can most animals, but while we assume that babies and animals can learn, we generally do not attribute consciousness to them. Thus, the learning of many physical activities is for the most part not consciousness.

So what is consciousness?

When we exclude from the driving experience all preoptive operations, sensory perception, awareness, memory, and learning, we are left with only one thing ... the thoughts that are occupying our mind at any given moment — the internal monologue. This phenomenon, in Jaynes' definition, is consciousness.

What are the qualities of "Jaynesian consciousness"?

1. Consciousness is "introspectable."[4] We are aware when we are conscious. We can locate the thoughts as coming from within our own minds ("introspectable mind space").[5] We "own" our own thoughts, and understand them as products of our own minds (though influenced by sensory perceptions, memories, and numerous other factors).

2. Consciousness is abstract. Our conscious thoughts are "analogs"[6] or cognitive models of the real world, which we create in order to understand it. Because consciousness is abstract, we can create hypothetical scenarios that exist only in our mind, and we can imagine things that never existed and can never exist, and we can think in terms of metaphors and symbols, which represent the world figuratively rather than literally.

3. Consciousness is "intimately bound with volition and decision."[7] We consciously decide to do things. Although some decisions are made automatically or unconsciously, we still consciously ponder and cogitate upon decisions, especially the more important ones. We often act upon our decisions (volition), but sometimes we do not. Oftentimes our volition is not directed by consciousness, as when we are sleepwalking, and sometimes our volition defies our conscious decisions, as when we act impulsively or instinctively.

There are other aspects of Jaynesian consciousness that I will mention just briefly, as I hasten to get to the point. Consciousness involves "narratization," we think of ourselves and our world in the form of a chronological order or story, in which one thing leads to another. Consciousness involves "concentration," the ability to focus on stimuli that are either external (sense perception) or internal (analog thoughts). Consciousness also involves "suppression," intentionally not concentrating on specific thoughts, "excerption," concentrating on one specific stimulus to the exclusion of the surrounding or associated stimuli, and "consilience," assimilating stimuli into existing cognitive schemas so that they make sense to us.[8]

The Bicameral Hypothesis

Now that we know what Jaynesian consciousness is and is not, we can proceed to the core of the bicameral model, which can be delineated into three main points:

1. At one point in human evolution, humans did not have consciousness, at least not in the form that it exists in modern times. This point is easy enough to accept, if we assume that most other animals do not have consciousness, and that humans evolved from lower forms of animal life. Also,

since Jaynes' definition of consciousness is dependent on an inner monologue, which in turn is dependent upon formal language, Jaynesian consciousness cannot exist prior to the acquisition of formal (grammatical) language in the human species. In the original (1976) version of his theory, Jaynes postulated that formal language did not develop in humans in the Near East until the Neolithic Age (approximately 10,000 — 5,000 B.C.); but in his later (1986) explanation, he places the evolution of language at around 200,000 B.C., in the Paleolithic Age.

2. Prior to consciousness, in the Paleolithic Age or possibly earlier, ancient humans (hominids) lived in small nomadic groups of hunters and gatherers, not so dissimilar to other non-human primates. All of the decisions and judgments and activities required for survival were achieved through cognitive functions described previously as functions that do not require consciousness. Humans, like other animals, were creatures of habit and instinct. However, as the ancient human brain developed the ability to think in terms of formal language, a new dimension of cognition became available to them, the ability to think abstractly. This ability requires "analogical" thinking — thinking in terms of symbols and metaphors. For, as Jaynes asserted, what is language, if not the cognitive understanding of specific words as symbolic representatives or analogs for something else, such as an object, place, or action. Language is metaphor. Metaphors are symbols. Symbols are abstract. Thus, the ability to think abstractly was a vast adaptive benefit to ancient humans. Instead of simply reacting to dangers, challenges, or obstacles in their environments, they could now cogitate upon different hypothetical scenarios and arrive at a decision based on thinking and reasoning, rather than instinct or impulse.

3. There was a period of time in which ancient humans had both language and abstract cognition, but the two functions were not yet coordinated into the form of consciousness that we refer to as the "internal monologue," which is the essence of Jaynesian consciousness. Before the internal monologue, before consciousness, the ancient human brain processed information unconsciously and arrived at decisions unconsciously. It then projected this decision to the part of the mind that directed volition, which resulted in a decision based action (as opposed to an instinctive or impulsive reaction). Since the ancient human brain had no internal monologue, the decision that was projected by the decision-making part of the brain was experienced as an external stimulus — a hallucination. This phenomenon is referred to by Jaynes as "bicameralism," because it posits two distinct aspects of the preconscious human mentality: 1. the decision-making part (i.e. abstract cognition), and 2. the follower part (volition). The period of time in which ancient humans

had abstract cognition but no internal monologue or consciousness can be referred to as the "bicameral period" or "bicameral age."

Obviously, there is a lot more to Jaynes' theory than is sketched out in the simple outline presented above, but for the purposes of this chapter, and in the continued interest of hastening to the point, the brief outline will have to due. I encourage readers who find the theory of interest but would like more explanation to read Jaynes' original 1976 book; or, for a succinct but accurate summary, Jaynes' 1986 lecture/article, *Consciousness and the Voices of the Mind.*[9]

Bicameral Dreams

As a point of transition from the brief outline of the bicameral theory to the topic of archetypes and symbols, it is helpful to discuss the nature of dreams, and its relation to bicameralism. Jaynes did not cover the topic of dreams in his 1976 book or his 1986 article; yet, he did outline a chapter on dreams for the original manuscript of his book. This chapter was not included in the book, but was set aside for inclusion in a second volume on bicameralism, *The Consequences of Consciousness,* which was never completed.[10] As Jaynes' chapter on dreams was never published, we do not know his thoughts on the subject. However, I believe that dreams are an extremely important aspect of bicameralism, especially in relation to symbols and archetypes.

Freud surmised that the pictorial language of symbols preceded verbal language in both speech and cognition.[11] To quote Erich Fromm: "Indeed, the language of the universal symbol is the one common tongue developed by the human race, a language which it forgot before it succeeded in developing a universal conventional language."[12] The picture language of dreams is a symbolic language. Dreams are abstract. They express themselves in the form of symbols and metaphor, and project hypothetical (nonexistent) situations. Dreaming is also an unconscious process. It is not introspectable, (we are not aware that we are dreaming while experiencing the dream), and it is also not bound to decision and volition.[13] Hence, dreams possess qualities of both consciousness and unconsciousness. In this sense, the dream state is somewhat similar to the mentality of ancient bicameral humans, who had the capacity for abstract thought, but were not consciously aware of this capacity. Secondly, the images and sounds of the dreamscape are experienced as sensory stimulation, though the stimulation is in response to an internal rather than an external stimulus. Thus, dreams are akin to hallucinations, the only difference being that dreams are intra-psychic sensory stimuli experienced while unconscious (asleep), while hallucinations are intra-psychic sensory stimuli experienced while conscious (awake). This is why dreams have so often been referred to by psychologists as "hallucinatory images."[14]

Dreams are a puzzle to modern humans because they are cognitions that are not products of the conscious mind. If we choose not to ignore them, then they must be interpreted consciously. It is clear from both the written records we have of ancient beliefs (Myth) and the anthropological records of preliterate ("primitive") peoples in modern times, that dreams were and are not such a puzzlement to those who believe that dreams are an extrasensory experience rather than an intra-psychic one. Both ancient peoples and modern preliterate peoples believe that dreams come from the gods or the spirit world, and that their function is to provide symbols that offer wisdom, guidance, warning, or consolation. In this sense, the function of the dream is *exactly* the same as the function of the bicameral hallucination. It is a visual and/or auditory message from a part of the mind enabled with abstract cognition, expressed through symbols, that provides some form of guidance. In the mentality of ancient bicameral peoples, dreams were essential for decision-making and judgments. In the mentality of modern conscious peoples, dreams are more-or-less unnecessary and superfluous, as we use our conscious minds to make decisions and judgments.[15]

It could be that Jaynes' theory of bicameralism was simply this: preconscious humans who did not posses the internal monologue and were therefore unaware of their own cognitive abilities to think in the abstract, often had dreams that expressed abstract ideas or hypothetical situations in symbolic form. These "hallucinatory images" were assumed to come from external sources, because the dreamer had no "analogic I"—no sense that they themselves could think in such abstract terms. The dreams themselves were not interpreted, because the dreamer did not possess the cognitive ability to explain abstract metaphorical symbols in terms of objective phenomena. Instead, bicameral peoples simply accepted the visions and voices they encountered in dreams as messages from some external power, and obeyed the messages as best they could. It is also possible that, since the preconscious humans made no attempt to consciously understand or interpret their dreams on a logical level, the dream symbols were processed and understood intuitively rather than deliberately. Because the dream was accepted completely and unquestioningly by the dreamer as a message from the external (spirit) world, it was experienced as a moment of spiritual insight, understood via intuition rather than through cognition. Bicameralism, understood in this sense, would be a much less controversial, though much less intriguing, theory. The part of

Jaynes' theory that raises eyebrows is the part that presumes that ancient peoples regularly had the dreamlike experience described above, but in the wakeful state.

To return, briefly, to the topic of "What is and What is Not Consciousness," Jaynes asserted that consciousness is, somewhat paradoxically, not necessary for *thinking*. To put it simply, we often come up with our best ideas when we are not consciously focusing on anything at all. Many great thinkers reported that their breakthrough ideas came to them in a dream, or while daydreaming. Jaynes wrote: "During World War II, British physicists used to say that they no longer made their discoveries in the laboratory; they had their three B's where their discoveries were made — the bath, the bed, and the bus."[16] This is not to say that great leaps of thought are always made unconsciously, only that thinking can and does happen on an unconscious level, and that dreaming is a lucid example of how we think abstractly about things while in an unconscious state. The ideas that come to us in dreams are not conscious cognitions, they are more akin to moments of inspiration or intuition, which are also examples of how abstract thinking occurs independently, on an unconscious level. Carl Jung placed much more value in the thought processes of the unconscious than in the cognitive functions of the conscious mind: "Man is never helped by what he thinks for himself but by revelations of wisdom greater that his own."[17]

An important facet of Jaynes' theory is that in the bicameral period, unconscious messages, whether experienced as a dream or a hallucination, were accepted readily as communications from gods or spirits. The voices and/or visions were sacred, purveyed complete authority, and were obeyed without question. Psychoanalysts who study dreams report that dreams of encountering a figure of ultimate power and authority — often represented by just a voice — are common, especially among people suffering from intense neurosis. Below is a psychoanalytic study of a dream series, reported by a man described by Carl Jung as "a scientist of today."

> The voice is a frequent occurrence in this dream series. It always pronounces an authoritative declaration or command, either of astonishing common sense and truth, or of profound philosophic allusion. It is nearly always a definite statement, usually coming toward the end of a dream, and it is, as a rule, so clear and convincing that the dreamer finds no argument against it. It has, indeed, so much the character of indisputable truth that it often appears as the final and absolutely valid summing up of a long unconscious deliberation and weighing of arguments. Frequently the voice issues from an authoritative figure, as from a military commander, or the captain of a ship, or an old physician. Sometimes, as for instance in this case, there is simply a voice coming apparently from nowhere. It was of considerable interest to see how this very intellectual and

skeptical man accepted the voice; often it did not suit him at all, yet he accepted it unquestioningly, and even humbly. Thus the voice revealed itself during the course of many hundred carefully recorded dreams as an important and even decisive representation of the unconscious. In as much as this patient is by no means the only case under my observation that has exhibited the phenomenon of the voice in dreams and in other peculiar conditions of consciousness, I have to admit the fact that the unconscious mind is capable at times of assuming an intelligence and purposiveness which are superior to actual conscious insight. There is hardly any doubt that this fact is a basic religious phenomenon, which is observed here in a case whose conscious mental make-up was certainly most unlikely to produce religious phenomena. I have not infrequently made similar observations in other cases and I must confess that I am unable to formulate the data in any other way. I have often met with the objection that the thoughts which the voice represents are no more that the thoughts of the individual himself....[18]

These types of dreams, which Jung heard from his patients (and himself) time and time again, entail all of the aspects of bicameral hallucinations. They resonate with authority and illicit both intuitive understanding and unquestioning acquiescence. The messages of the dreams reflect deep thinking on an abstract yet unconscious level. And there is a spiritual quality to the voice in the dreams, which adds to the aura of power and authority that it conveys. It is also important to note that Jung's patients also reported hearing similar voices "in other peculiar conditions of consciousness," which can mean only one thing — auditory hallucinations. Jung goes on to discuss the sensation that the voice in the dream or hallucination is coming from an external source.

Someone may object that the so-called unconscious mind is merely my own mind and that, therefore, such a differentiation is superfluous. As a matter of fact the concept of the unconscious mind is a mere assumption for the sake of convenience. In reality I am totally unconscious of— in other words, I do not know at all — where the voice originates. I am not only incapable of producing the phenomenon at will but I am also unable to anticipate the mental contents of the voice. Under such conditions it would be presumptuous to call the factor which produces the voice *my* mind. This would not be accurate.... There is only one condition under which you might legitimately call the voice your own, namely, when you assume your conscious personality to be a part of a whole or to be a smaller circle contained in a bigger one.... We may assume that human personality consists of two things: first, of consciousness and whatever this covers, and second, of an indefinitely large hinterland of unconscious psyche.... Since the contents of our minds are only conscious and perceivable in so far as they are associated with an ego, the phenomenon of the voice, having a strongly personal character, may also issue from a center — one, however, which is not identical with that of our conscious ego....

My psychological experience has shown time and again that certain contents issue from a psyche more complete than consciousness. They often contain a superior analysis or insight or knowledge which consciousness has not been able to produce. We have a suitable word for such occurrences — intuition. In pronouncing it, most people have an agreeable feeling as if something had been settled. But they never take into account the fact that you do not make an intuition. On the contrary it always comes to you; you have a hunch, it has produced itself and you only catch it if you are clever or quick enough.... Consequently, I explain the voice, in the dream of the sacred house, as a product of the more complete personality to which the dreamer's conscious self belongs as a part, and I hold that this is the reason why the voice shows an intelligence and a clarity superior to the dreamer's actual consciousness. This superiority is the reason for the unconditioned authority of the voice.[19]

Jung believed, ultimately, in the existence of external spiritual forces that communicate to humans through the esoteric mind-space of the collective unconscious. "The superior wisdom of the dream voice," he explained, "is a basic religious phenomenon and that the voice which speaks in our dreams is not our own but comes from a source transcending us."[20] Jaynes' theory, however, explains both the experience of external voices and visions and the reason for a universal belief in them through bicameralism. If, as Jaynes contended, ancient peoples regularly experienced encounters with spirits as auditory and/or visual hallucinations, and the experience of these encounters was processed on an unconscious, intuitive level — because bicameral people did not have a true conscious mentality to process the experience — then the wakeful mental life of these ancient peoples was similar, in some ways, to the sleeping life of modern humans. To put it in a more fanciful way, "life was just a dream...."

The spiritual quality of dreaming was noted by Fromm, when referring to the feeling one has upon awakening within a dream: "It is as if friendly, or unfriendly, spirits had visited us and at the break of day had suddenly disappeared; we hardly remember that they had been there and how intensely we had been occupied with them."[21] So, in dreams we find a link between both ancient and modern beliefs in spirits and deities, and the ancient and modern desire to commune with spirits and deities, which in the bicameral age was experienced while sleeping but also, quite frequently, while awake; but in modern humans, with the exception of schizophrenics and shamans, is experienced only while asleep. The dream, in essence, offers not only a glimpse, but a re-experience of the unconscious mental state of preliterate humans in primordial times:

The dream is a little hidden door in the innermost and most secret recesses of the soul, opening into that cosmic night which was psyche long before there was any ego consciousness, and which will remain psyche no matter how far our ego consciousness extends.... All consciousness separates; but in dreams we put on the likeness of that more universal, truer, more eternal man dwelling in the darkness of primordial night. There he is still the whole, and the whole is in him, indistinguishable from nature and bare of all egohood. It is from these all-uniting depths that the dream arises, be it ever so childish, grotesque, and immoral.[22]

Dream Archetypes in Ritual, Religion and Myth

The psychological link between myth symbology and dream symbology has been a major theme in this book. To summarize, in the words of Erich Fromm:

At any rate, whether ignored, despised, or respected, myths are felt to belong to a world completely alien to our own thinking. Yet the fact remains that many of our dreams are, in both style and content, similar to myths, and we who find them strange and remote when we are awake have the ability to create these mythlike productions when we are asleep ... all myths and all dreams have one thing in common, they are all "written" in the same language, *symbolic language.*[23]

Dreams present the sensory experience appropriate to myth. In both scenarios, there is a gap in the laws of reason and nature. Time doesn't work as it does in the conscious state, neither do the physical laws of the universe. If the people of the bicameral period experienced their waking existence in a way that is similar to the way that modern people experience dreams, it was because their perception of the world was filtered through the lens of the unconscious mind rather than the conscious mind. Hence, a perception that would seem illogical or unreal to us — for instance, a centaur gazing at the stars — would seem to bicameral people to be a perfectly normal and realistic occurrence. The conscious mind functions according to empirical logic, in which the observable world must conform to certain standards of logic, reason, and realism. For the conscious mind, "seeing is believing." The unconscious mind is not beholding to logic or reason. In dream logic, it would be perfectly normal for a man to literally transform into a centaur. Similarly, within the context of the orgiastic throes of a primordial ritual, the physical transformation of a costumed shaman into an actual centaur would also be a normal experience, as the sensory perception constructed by the bicameral person's mind would support the belief system that he was faithful too. (Please recall that sensory perception is not "recorded" but constructed, our mind decides what we see and hear, and this perception is only indirectly related to the actual auditory and visual stimuli existing in the "real" world. Furthermore, it is important to note that perception is not a conscious process, a fact that makes possible not only dreams and hallucinations, but other phenomenon as well, such as optical illusions and the experience of unreal stimuli elicited by posthypnotic suggestion.)

Since a bicameral person's perceptions are filtered through the unconscious mind, what he sees is open to suggestion, and not governed by the logic and realism of the conscious mind. His perception is malleable, as his beliefs can manipulate his perceptions by way of hallucinatory sensory experience, which can add to, subtract from, change, or otherwise transform any perception of the external world. So, while the conscious mind functions according to the maxim "to see is to believe," the unconscious mind functions according to the reverse logic, "to believe is to see." Hence, while the modern conscious mind cannot allow the delusion or hallucination of the centaur to take hold, as the perception would be illogical and inconsistent with the observable stimuli; the ancient unconscious mind actually sees the costumed man transfigure into a centaur, as the bicameral person's belief in the transfiguration evokes a hallucinatory manipulation of the stimuli in the visual field. In a sense, two people from different eras observing the same scene would see two different things. The bicameral person sees a man become a centaur, while the modern conscious person sees a shaman dressed in a ceremonial costume pretending to be a centaur as part of a ritual.

Freud and Jung both believed that dream logic functions according to association. For instance, I have a dream in which I'm eating ice cream, and then my daughter suddenly appears to have ice cream with me, and then the scene suddenly changes to a playground, and then instead of an adult I'm a child, and then my daughter becomes my sister, etc. Looking at this dream through the lens of consciousness, it seems like a bunch of illogical nonsense. However, if we keep in mind that dream logic functions according to associations, as opposed to real world logic, which functions according to reason, then the dream makes perfect sense. My daughter suddenly appears because I associate her with ice cream, which she loves. The scene becomes a playground because I associate a playground with time spent with my daughter. I become a child again because being in the playground reminds me of my childhood. My daughter then becomes my sister because I associate being a child in a playground with my youth, in which my sister was my playmate. Applying conscious logic to the dream is pointless, because in the real world, people don't suddenly appear and disappear, people don't go back in time or morph into other people, places don't suddenly change into other places, etc. Perception in the dream world is not logical, it is analogical — it reasons according to analogy, association, and metaphor. While the language of the conscious mind is the literal language of words, the language of the unconscious mind is the analogical or metaphorical language of symbols.

The logical conscious mind is interactively connected with the analogical unconscious mind. The interconnectivity is so great that it is impossible to tell where the conscious mind ends and the unconscious mind begins. It is one mind, interconnected, with complementary and supplementary functions running concurrently. This interconnected mind allows us to introspect about ourselves while also perceiving the external world, allowing us to "dream" up stories about what might happen to us and what might happen to the world in ways that are fanciful and imaginative and metaphorical, while also being controlled by the logical function of consciousness. Daydreaming is the conscious mind allowing itself to dip into the domain of unconscious thinking, while still maintaining control of the thought process. Nighttime dreaming, when the conscious is turned off, is not subdued by logical realism. The unconscious mind is given free reign over the thought process, and without the harsh rule of logic, anything that could be imagined is immediately perceived. Nighttime dreaming has the added benefit of not having to process external sensory perception, because the eyes are closed and the senses are, for the most part, deprived of overt stimulation. In dreams, perception is left entirely to the devices of the unconscious mind, which paints its pictures based on imagination, symbol, analogy, association, and metaphor. If the wakeful life of bicameral people was something like a daydream, or like dreaming with one's eyes open, it was because the canvas of the perceptual field was based on the sensory perceptions of actual external stimuli, while the interpretation of the perceptual field, the painting of the picture, was highly influenced by symbolic or analogical thinking. The palette of imagination and belief, in turn, prompted the hallucinatory function of the bicameral mind to adjust or add to the perceptual field in order to make the perception of what was seen fall in line with the cognitive interpretation of the meaning of what was seen. In other words, "believing was seeing."

It is this state of mind that may have given rise to the archetypes of the collective unconscious. A beloved father who dies is physically gone, but his comforting presence can be retained and experienced on a daily basis, simply by projecting his image or the sound of his voice into the perceptual field. In dreams, Freud called this "wish fulfillment"—the experience of a desired stimulus in the dream state. For bicameral persons, this type of wish fulfillment can be experienced in the wakeful state, when the unconscious mind projects the image or voice of the desired personage in the form of a hallucination. The fact that the image or voice of the deceased father provides valuable guidance as well as consolation only adds to the psychological impact of the voice or vision. And, perhaps it is this primordial experience — the hearing and/or seeing of the deceased loved one — which gave birth to the universal idea that there is such a thing as a spirit or soul. For what better explanation could there be for the experience of seeing or hearing the image or voice of a dead person, other than the notion that there is something that exists within a person that is not physical and which does not die when the physical being dies? The soul or spirit lives on and even communicates with the living through dreams, voices, and visions. This basic idea, educed by bicameral hallucinations, is the seminal germ of all religious thought.

As Jaynes draws out his theory of bicameralism, he sees its consequences in the origin and development of religious beliefs. As humans are inherently social beings, it is natural for them to share not only resources, but also beliefs. Therefore, an individual's belief that he can see and hear the spirit of his dead father could be shared with others in the same clan, thus the origin of the Wise Old Man archetype. The same could be said of the origin of the maternal archetype, the Goddess. A deceased hero, shaman, or tribal leader can also be re-experienced as a spiritual voice or vision. This spirit, replete with power and authority, could even utter commandments and decrees, demand supplication, sacrifice, or worship, and claim vast influence over the forces of nature and creation, thus giving rise to the notion of a god. Jaynes posited that just such a communal deity was the root of the divine-king figure in both history and myth, a figure that drew its immense power and authority from the fact that he was actually perceived as a living spiritual entity by many generations of bicameral believers.

The phenomena of animism and totemism (discussed in previous chapters) can be seen in a whole new light through the lens of the bicameral theory. Animism, the belief that spirit exists within everything, would be a natural byproduct of bicameralism. According to Jaynes, bicameral people experienced hallucinations whenever they needed to make a critical decision. He posited that environmental stress was the neurological mechanism that evoked hallucinations, just as stress evokes psychotic (i.e. hallucinatory) experiences in schizophrenics. (When experienced in tremendous amounts, stress can evoke psychosis in non-schizophrenics as well.) Jaynes also believed that the experience of auditory hallucinations in the form of "voices" was most likely the standard form of hallucination, just as the hearing of voices is the most frequent psychotic symptom in schizophrenics. This may be because the auditory mode of perception is subdominant to the visual mode in humans, and is therefore more subject to unconscious persuasion. Also, since the experience of the internal monologue is typically heard as an actual voice inside one's head, the human brain, subsequent to the advent of language, may be "hardwired" to experience an "inner voice" that is not the product of external stimulation. So a bicameral person, enabled with a mentality that readily hallucinates a voice at any moment in which a critical decision must be made, would quite likely identify an animal or a tree or a bush as the source of a voice offering guidance or warning. If the voice in question is identified as the disembodied spiritual voice of a deceased ancestor or tribal leader, then the animal or object identified as the source of the voice would become, de facto, an object of reverence or devotion. Hence, animism and totemism, the reverence of the spiritual quality within specific animals, both emerge during the bicameral period, as primitive understandings of bicameral hallucinations.

Totemism, specifically, arose when groups of humans created communal associations with particular animals. It is interesting to note that totem animals tended to be dangerous carnivores, such as cave bears and saber tooth tigers. This would be no coincidence, with regard to bicameral theory, as the encounter with a vicious tiger would certainly meet the threshold level of stress necessary to evoke a sudden auditory hallucination, which would then be ascribed to the animal itself. Thus, the archetypal figure of the talking beast is formed. The spiritual designations of certain trees (see the biblical Garden of Eden story), or bushes (see the biblical Burning Bush story), or rocks (see the biblical Well-Stone of Miriam story), could also be explained through bicameralism, as sites where bicameral peoples experienced particularly intense hallucinations, due either to stress or as the result of mere suggestion.

The origin of the archetype of the anthropomorphic figure, the "man-beast," can also explained through bicameralism. The figure of the man-beast is seen widely throughout the mythologies of the world, and is one of the most ancient identifiable archetypes, as it can be seen in many of the prehistoric cave paintings in Southern France and Spain, dating back to 50,000 years B.C. The man-beast is typically interpreted as a symbol of the duality of the human being, who is half civilized and half wild. In the bicameral interpretation, the man-beast arises as a consequence of primordial encounters with beasts that elicited auditory hallucinations. The bicameral mind, experiencing a beast who can speak, would project the hallucinatory mask of humanlike qualities onto the mystical talking beast. Having experienced this, the individual tells his tale to his cohort, thus creating the seed of the man-beast archetype. As tribes and clans invest communal reverence into the archetype, it becomes integrated into the peoples' rituals, and so we have the image of the dancing shaman garbed in the ceremonial costume of the man-beast, who, in the suggestible "mind's eye" of his bicameral tribesmen, actually becomes half-man, half-beast. And so the legend of the man-beast, as the ages pass, is remembered in story and song, immortalized in paintings and figurines, and even worshipped, in some cultures, as gods.

Jaynes described a somewhat similar explanation for the creation of idols, which appear to have been ubiquitous in ancient Near Eastern cultures. Idols, he believed, provided a visual counterpart to auditory hallucinations, serving as the source of the spirit voice(s). Thus an idol, when properly sanctified and worshipped according to the appropriate rites and offerings, becomes the vessel of the disembodied spirit to be worshipped, the new "body" for a deceased mom or dad — or in the case of larger idols, the communal object of veneration, the earthly home of the heavenly deity, not unlike the biblical Golden Calf, the bronze statues of the dark god, Moloch, or even the Holy Ark of the Covenant itself.

Campbell's archetypal hero can also be interpreted through the lens of bicameralism. In this case, the mythical hero arises in the post-bicameral age, which for Jaynes emerged at around the time of the collapse of the Bronze Age empires in the Near East, during the 2nd millennium B.C. It was at this time, due to the confluence of a number of critical factors — among them being overpopulation, a wave of natural catastrophes resulting in mass migrations, and the emergence of writing — that bicameralism was replaced by modern consciousness. At this time in history, we see a recurrent theme in the religious texts of cultures throughout the ancient Near East, which could be summed up and epitomized in the following passage from a Babylonian scripture:

> My god has forsaken me and disappeared,
> My goddess has failed me and keeps at a distance.
> The good angel who walked beside me has departed.[24]

The theme of the departed god, the god who has forsaken his people, is born at this time. As a corollary to the wailing of the peoples for their lost deities, there is born the prophecy of the messiah, the return of the departed divine-king, the savior who is still spiritually connected with the gods, who will redeem his people by reuniting the gods with their forsaken mortal believers. This is the legend of the hero. He is the man who can still hear the voice of God, unlike his mortal brethren, who have only its pitiful replacement, the conscious voice of the internal monologue. Yet, unlike the elder generations, forgotten in the foggy mists of time, who merely heard and obeyed the voices of gods, like so many zombie-minded slaves, the hero is conscious as well. He has a mind of his own, and he can use that mind to consciously challenge the new order of evil empires, who keep the people enslaved, despite their lack of divine qualifications.

The Call to Adventure for the bicameral hero is a spiritual voice, a voice unheard among the people for many generations. Yet the voice has a queer strain to it, as it can be heard only by the hero and nobody else. Hence the Refusal of the Call, as the hero doubts the veracity of the voice, and doesn't understand why he and he alone is privy to its call. Supernatural Aid arises as a talisman that confirms the veracity of the call and provides a physical and spiritual connection between the hero and the source of the voice. (In keeping with the intra-psychic theme of Campbell's theory, the connection between external spirit [voice] and the hero is actually internal, as the voice ultimately comes from within.) The Meeting with the Goddess occurs when the hero consults an oracle. The collapse of the Bronze Age, as Jaynes explains, marks the emergence of throngs of prophets, oracles, sooth-sayers, astrologers, witches, mediums, and all others who still hear the bicameral voices, but are conscious as well—thus making them walking anachronisms in their own time. In a sense, the hero is one of these anachronisms as well, as the heroes of the Abrahamic religions were all prophets and god-sent messiahs. (In the Middle Ages, the hearers of bicameral voices were perceived as the demonically possessed. In the modern age, the same atavistic traits are diagnosed as symptoms of psychosis, disassociation, or hallucinogenic substance abuse.)

The stage of Atonement with the Father occurs with the hero's realization that the Voice is internal, resulting in the stage of Apotheosis, an epiphany. "If the Voice is in me, then I am God," reasons the hero. The Ultimate Boon is the fulfillment of the hero's task, which is the establishment of a physical link between the spiritual and physical realms, i.e. the Ten Commandments, the Holy Grail, the sacred Quran, etc. As Master of the Two Worlds, the hero is both the master of conscious thought and unconscious (bicameral) inspiration. He transcends the unidirectional path of primitive bicameralism to realize that the voice of divinity comes from his own mind. Since he is self-conscious of his own thoughts, and thus can lead others, he is a divine king—a conscious god among unconscious follow-ers. And Freedom to Live, ultimately, is the freedom from mind-controlling command voices. Whether they emerge from communal deities or divine-kings, true freedom arises from within. Freedom of the mind, self-directed consciousness as the basis of independently minded existence, is the hard-won prize of modern conscious humanity. The hero is the symbol of autonomous judgment, independent conscious thought, though his message has typically been misused and misunderstood by theocratic zealots, who value blind faith and mindless obedience over self-reflective conscious thought.

Bicameralism in the Bible

Jaynes supported the premise of his theory with a meticulous study and interpretation of the ancient Greek epics, *The Iliad* and *The Odyssey*. By comparing and contrasting the two epics, Jaynes demonstrated that the older epic, *The Iliad*, is typical of a bicameral mentality, while the younger epic, *The Odyssey*, depicts humans who are conscious. Jaynes also studied the Old Testament, remarking of the ancient Hebrew scripture: "This magnificent collection of history and harangue, of song, sermon, and story is in its grand overall contour the description of the loss of the bicameral mind, and its replacement by subjectivity over the first millennium B.C."[25] The Bible, in this sense, is a chronicle of the last generation of bicameral thinkers, the tales of distant forefathers who actually heard the real voice of the one true God.

The development of religious belief over the past three millennia, and the advent of monotheism in particular, could be seen as both a product and a cause of the shift from bicameral to conscious thinking. Bicameralism is best suited to a belief system in which there are many deities, i.e. animism, totemism, or polytheism, because bicameral peoples communicated directly with their own personal gods. Monotheism is not amenable to bicameralism, as the average monotheist was not expected to hear the voice of the one true God — this being the exclusive privilege of the high priests, prophets, messiah, or divine king. Monotheistic theocratic regimes, in fact, have a long history of persecuting individuals who claimed to speak with or hear the voices of deities. These people were tortured, burned, and hung as witches, heretics, false prophets, and the demonically possessed, starting from the end of the bicameral period in the 2nd millennium B.C., and continuing on till this day. The Bible also reports that the non-monotheistic, idol worshipping natives of the "Promised Land" were categorically persecuted and in some instances exterminated, along with their altars, temples, and idols, by the fundamentalist monotheistic regimes of the early Israelite conquerors. For example, the prophet Zechariah declared:

> On that day, I will banish the names of the idols from the land, and they will be remembered no more," declares the Lord Almighty. "I will remove both the prophets and the spirit of impurity from the land. And if anyone still prophesies, their father and mother, to whom they were born, will say to them, 'You must die, because you have told lies in the Lord's name.' Then their own parents will stab the one who prophesies. "On that day every prophet will be ashamed of their prophetic vision...[26]

The history of religious thought demonstrates a more or less steady development from animism (gods and spirits are everywhere), to totemism (gods and spirits are associated with specific people, places, and things), to polytheism (gods and spirits are plentiful but typically separated from the physical plane and hidden from the world of humans), to monotheism (there is only one God, who is never seen and was once, long ago, heard by a few people, but is now never heard by anyone). These transitions show a gradual but steady distancing of the gods from the world of humans, a distancing that would coincide with the gradual decline in the frequency of bicameral hallucinations, that Jaynes theorized would have occurred in the three millennia before the birth of Jesus, as the advent of formal language and writing drove the dominance of conscious thinking and the repression of bicameral cognitions. It is also clear that as religious thought progressed, gods became increasingly more integral as shared symbols that unified communities. In the animistic stage, every individual saw spirits wherever his unconscious mind saw fit. Visions and voices of spirits, probably the disembodied souls of deceased ancestors and loved ones, were experienced personally and directly. In the totemistic stage, spirits were communalized into collective deities — each clan or tribe had its own totem animal — and individual experiences of the totem were not just personal spiritual encounters, but rather, they were encounters with a communal spirit that had relevance to the entire community. In the polytheistic stage, when cultures like ancient Sumer had become quite large and sophisticated, localized deities became cultural gods, which were then classified according to rank and importance, creating a pantheon of gods for an entire nation to worship.

The foundational stories of Genesis deliver a different, singular, monotheistic message: blind faith, unquestioning obedience in Jehovah, is the only acceptable form of worship. The lesson of the first story in the Bible that includes people, the story of Adam and Eve, is that the voices of the gods must be obeyed unerringly and without question. (Jaynes notes that the biblical God in Genesis is usually referred to as "Elohim," which in Hebrew is a plural-masculine term that literally means "gods." Jehovah, as a singular-masculine identity, seems to emerge in the Bible as the most dominant of the Elohim, and eventually rises as the last of the many Elohim.) When the voices of the Elohim are disobeyed, Adam and Eve are disconnected from the gods' graces and cast out of the garden. Yet, at the same time, the story tells us that once Adam and Eve ate from the Tree of Knowledge — i.e. once they acquired consciousness — they became like gods themselves, which is to say, they now had their own internal voices to direct their decisions, so the voices of the gods were no longer necessary.

The Hebrew God speaks only to a few people in the Pentateuch, (the

Five Books of Moses), most notably: Adam, Eve, Cain, Noah, Abraham, Jacob (Israel), and Moses. Of all of these "prophets," Moses is the closest to God, as the Scriptures declare:

> Then the LORD came down in a pillar of cloud; he stood at the entrance to the tent and summoned Aaron and Miriam. When the two of them stepped forward, he said, "Listen to my words: "When there is a prophet among you, I, the LORD, reveal myself to them in visions, I speak to them in dreams. But this is not true of my servant Moses; he is faithful in all my house. With him I speak face to face, clearly and not in riddles; he sees the form of the Lord... [Numbers 12: 5–8].

Note that Jehovah himself explains that his typical mode of communication is through dreams and visions, and even in these indirect expressions, his message is delivered in riddles that must be consciously construed. This is indicative of the end of the bicameral period, when conscious thinking is becoming dominant, blocking the unconscious bicameral messages, and relegating them to the mental nether regions of dreams and the occasional, sporadic hallucinatory vision. Moses, the greatest hero of Hebrew scriptures, was the exception. He was also the last person to have a truly bicameral connection with Jehovah, in which communication occurred regularly and in direct ways. At the end of the Pentateuch, after Moses departs from this world, the Scriptures state:

> And there has not arisen a prophet since in Israel like unto Moses, whom the Lord knew face to face... [Deuteronomy 34: 10].

After Moses, we see a succession of lesser leaders, judges, and prophets, who receive their communiqués from Jehovah in such a sporadic and irregular fashion, in messages so unclear and unverifiable, that the entire tradition of prophecy becomes obsolete, and the bicameral period is finally ended. What's left is a tradition of prayer and sacrifice that is completely unidirectional — prayers and offerings go up, but replies never come down — and so we are left feeling abandoned and forsaken by the gods who once knew all of us in a personal, "face to face" relationship. The psychological term for this feeling, though usually associated with a parent, is "separation anxiety." Jaynes noted that nearly all of the Psalms in the Old Testament resound with the same sentiment, the intense feeling of separation anxiety from the heavenly father, and the yearning for even a brief moment of reconnection, for even the faintest whisper of his divine voice:

> But the mind is still haunted with its old unconscious ways; it broods on lost authorities; and the yearning, the deep and hollow yearning for divine volition and service is with us still."[27]

Bicameral Themes in Fairytales

In previous chapters, it was argued that the body of literature referred to as "fairytales" contain archetypal figures and themes that originated in the animistic and polytheistic traditions that preceded the monotheistic traditions in Europe and the Near East. As such, in accord with Jaynes' theory, many of these archetypes are reflective of bicameral mentalities. The archetype of the fairy godmother, for instance, denotes the notion that anyone can have a personal spirit or god, who will provide comfort, protection, or guidance, and will appear at the moment of one's greatest need, in the form of a voice or vision, or perhaps in the guise of an animal such as a bird. Talking animals, which abound in fairytales, recall the totemistic belief systems, in which specific animals have humanlike qualities, such as the ability to think, reason, and speak. Talking mirrors, such as the one in *Snow White*, as well as other magical reflectors, such as crystal balls and mystical fountains, represent the tendency for the internal unconscious voice to be externalized and projected onto another person, even when that person is merely a reflection of one's self. Ghosts, disembodied spirits of the dead, also abound in fairytales — but this archetype will be dealt with separately, as a subtype of fantasy tales ... 'ghost stories.'

Certain fairytales and folktales provide insight into the superstitious mentality, which can be perceived as retaining atavistic traits, such as partial bicameralism. *The Golem* is an ancient figure in Jewish folklore. The most famous rendition of the "Golem" tale features the famous Rabbi Loew, the chief rabbi of Prague in the 16th Century, as the golem's creator. The creature itself is made out of clay and brought to life through a magical spell in which the Hebrew word "Emet" — "Truth" — is written on his forehead. The golem is incapable of independent thought. It has a "zombie mind" that is controlled externally by Rabbi Loew, who commands the golem either by direct verbal orders or by written orders fed into his mouth. In a sense, the golem is like a man at the very earliest stage of the bicameral period. He has no independent conscious voice of his own, and is merely a follower to the commands of the bicameral voice, which come from a seemingly external source. The word that animates the golem, "Emet" or "Truth," has a religious connotation. "The voice that comes to your mind," Mr. Golem, "is the word of God, as Rabbi Loew is unto you like a god, as Jehovah is unto Rabbi Loew like a god. The voice that you hear is the unmitigated truth, you must never doubt it. To hear the voice is to obey." Eventually, the golem is destroyed by its creator, who rubs out the first letter of the word on his forehead, leaving the Hebrew word "Met" — which means "Dead."

Bicameral Themes in Fantasy Literature

Ghost stories are perhaps the oldest form of folktale. Previously in this chapter, I suggested that the "seeing" of ghosts by ancient peoples, or the "hearing" of their spectral voices in the wind, may have been the germ of the ancient belief in the existence of a spirit, which grew and multiplied into all religious belief. The ghost story is still very much alive today in every aspect of literature and entertainment, but the popularity of ghost stories arguably reached its peak in its literary form in the 19th century. It is interesting to note that the typical features of the "gothic" horror story, such as Henry James' *The Turn of the Screw* (1898) or Edgar Allan Poe's *The Fall of the House of Usher* (1839), very much resembles the psychotic break of a schizophrenic. If we assume a bicameral origin to the supernatural, in which ghosts are a combination of delusions and hallucinations, then the ghost story tells a tale of a person who experiences both visual and auditory hallucinations of increasing frequency and emotional intensity, until finally, the person reaches a state of complete psychosis, losing completely his or her hold on reality.

The typical gothic horror story usually begins with a person entering a new environment, such as a mansion or country house, in which there is some kind of emotional stressor, such as isolation or loneliness. Stress, as usual, is the environmental stimulus that evokes an initial hallucination. Like the schizophrenic experiencing his first psychotic break, the initial hallucination evokes a much more acute form of stress — paranoia. Living in a world where all sensory experience must have an external, objective, and empirical origin, the person experiencing sensory stimulation from an internal, subjective source is forced to doubt his own senses. As the paranoia and stress increase, so do the hallucinations. The person is a prisoner of his own sensory experience, and the inability to rationally explain his sensory experiences results in the realization of only two possibilities: 1. the voices and visions have a supernatural origin or 2. The voices and visions have an internal origin.

The first solution is terrifying, resulting in more stress and more hallucinations. As the person is rarely believed by his cohorts, it is usually assumed by the others that the person is mad, that the voices and visions are delusions and hallucinations, thus increasing the sense of paranoia in the person, who feels that others may be conspiring against him, or even creating the voices and visions to purposefully manipulate him or drive him mad (delusions of persecution). The Second possible solution is even more terrifying. The realization that one may be going mad is similar to the realization that the world as you know it no longer exists, and that your own mind has turned against you. (Make note that most of the positive symptoms of schizophrenia, which are apparent both in the gothic ghost story and also in the onset of psychosis, are not necessarily caused by the psychiatric "illness" — rather, they are caused by the individual's inability to consciously process the sensory stimuli, because the experience of intra-psychic sensory perception is deemed unacceptable by modern society and the conscious mind. While the initial "symptoms," hallucinations, occur organically, usually evoked by environmental stress, the succeeding "symptoms" are evoked by the individual's inability to rationalize these perceptions. The subsequent positive symptoms of schizophrenia — paranoia and delusions of persecution — come about as a result of the individual not being able to consciously understand his sensory experiences, resulting in self-doubt, fear, and the suspicion that others may be manipulating his senses.)

If the same hallucinations, however, occurred in the bicameral period, the psychological reaction would have been much different. The initial visions and voices would not be assumed to be intra-psychic, they would be accepted as extrasensory spiritual encounters, which in the bicameral period were deemed not only socially acceptable, but were greatly desired. We could assume that the voices and visions were, in many cases, positive experiences — just as many modern schizophrenics enjoy the presence of their hallucinations, despite the fact that such experiences marginalize their status in society. (Note, in contemporary preliterate societies in which shamans and mystical mediums are still respected, the ability to see or hear "spiritual" visions and voices remains a very highly prized and esteemed facility.) However, even when the voices and visions were negative experiences, such as when they were perceived as demons or evil spirits, they were still less harrowing, as the hallucinations were not likely to be accompanied by paranoia or delusions of persecution, since the experiences themselves were socially acceptable, and the seeing or hearing of demons did not brand one as "mad," nor did it cause damage to one's social status.

And finally, of course, ghosts and other spirits are common in modern fantasy stories. There are many ghosts in the Harry Potter books, but what is more interesting, from the perspective of bicameral theory, is the existences of patronuses. A patronus, much like a fairy godmother or godfather, is a projection of an individual's private emotions, usually involving his feelings of attachment towards his parent, hence the "paternal" root of the name. In times of distress, any wizard or witch can summon his or her own patronus by invoking a charm, "Expecto Patronum." The patronus appears, not in the form of the parent, but in the form of an animal that represents the spirit of the parent. In this way, the patronus is much like a totem, who provides guidance, protection, or comfort in times of need, can be summoned at will, and is psychologically/spiritually linked with a deceased parent. How psychologically beneficial would this have been for ancient bicameral peoples? The ability to summon your own personal god in the form of a spirit animal — enveloping the soul of a deceased mother or father — who could offer solace and company whenever one felt sad or alone.

The Lord of the Rings books are also filled with ghosts and spirits, such as the Ringwraiths. Sauron, the Dark Lord, is, like Jehovah, never seen directly and never described physically. He is experienced by the Ringbearers as an all-seeing eye, which can look into the soul of whoever bears the Ring and manipulate his thoughts, feelings, and dreams. As such, Sauron and the Ring represent an external locus of power, controlling the mind of the ringbearer, in the same way that a bicameral person would be controlled by the bicameral voices of his own unconscious, which seemingly emanated from an external source.

In the Narnia books, only children can experience the magical people and places in the mystical fantasy world. As such, the Narnia encounters can be compared to the "imaginary friend" experiences of early childhood, in which children imagine playmates that are invisible and inaudible to anybody but themselves. Imaginary friends are quite common at this stage of development. (Snuffleupagus, Big Bird's imaginary friend on Sesame Street, who could only be seen and heard by Big Bird, is a prime example.) A good deal of research suggests that many children actually see and hear these playmates, which would constitute them as hallucinations.[28] We must take these reports with a grain of salt, as small children are not particularly good at differentiating between fantasy and reality, but this overlap between intra-psychic perception (fantasy) and external sensory perception (reality), which is the norm in early childhood, is precisely the point I am trying to make. In early childhood, during the stage of cognitive development that Piaget labeled "Preoperational," children tend towards magical and animistic thinking. They see and hear what they believe, and since their beliefs are guided by preoperational (illogical) thinking, they believe in all sorts of things that can only really exist in early childhood, for once their thinking becomes operational and dominated by logic, magical beings can no longer exist — they are exiled from conscious thought and blocked from re-entry forever — just as Adam and Eve, after tasting from the fruit of the Tree of Knowledge, were exiled from Eden and blocked from re-entry by the mystical sword that turns in every direction.

The mind of the child has been the subject of much conjecture in this book, as the archetypes of Faërie are often particularly resonant for children, who are more apt to believe in them as "real." If consciousness in modern humans is thought to be acquired rather than congenital, a function that

develops in the formative years of early childhood, then the premise of recapitulation theory could apply for consciousness as well — just as very young
preliterate humans can be considered preconscious, so too may have our
ancient, preliterate ancestors been preconscious. Jaynes considered the existence of imaginary friends in early childhood to be a "vestige of the bicameral
mind."[29] In his book *The God Delusion* (2006), Richard Dawkins suggested
that this phenomenon may have been the paedomorphic antecedent of the
notion of gods in the human psyche.[30] (Paedomorphosis is defined as the
retention of childish characteristics and beliefs into adulthood.) But whether
we speak of gods or fairies, revelations or hallucinations, dreams or fantasies,
the essence of the universal symbols found in myth, fairytale, and fantasy, is
the internal psychological need to believe in something outside of ourselves,
the need to feel protected by a wise old man even when our father is gone,
the need to feel nurtured by a loving goddess even in the absence of our
mother, the need to feel connected with nature and wildlife even when our
world has alienated nature from our everyday existence, and the need to believe
that there is more to our existence than what can be consciously understood
on the physical plane. Simply put, because reality cannot fulfill our deepest
needs, fantasy and Faërie *must* exist.

Conclusion

"The loneliness of mythlessness is the deepest and least assuageable of all."[1]

Nietzsche was possibly the first to point out in writing the dangerous position modern society is placing itself in, when it allows itself to become bereft of myth:

> Here we have our present age ... bent on the extermination of myth. Man today, stripped of myth, stands famished among all his pasts and must dig frantically for roots, be it among the most remote antiquities.[2]

Humankind's psychological roots are found in Myth, which both nourishes its soul and grounds its feet in the natural world, so that its limbs can reach up towards the heavens. But modern society, since the time of Nietzsche, has been going about the business of pruning these roots, detaching itself from the soil of Myth, so rich in the nutrients of archetypes, symbols, and existential meaning. Campbell, referencing Nietzsche himself as one of these reckless landscapers of the garden of Myth, describes the plight of modern society as the plight of an individual who cannot make meaningful connections, either with others around him, or even within himself, as the symbols that fostered these connections are no longer an elemental part of his psychological lexicon:

> The democratic ideal of the self-determining individual, the invention of the power-driven machine, and the development of the scientific method of research have so transformed human life that the long-inherited, timeless universe of symbols has collapsed. In the fateful, epoch-announcing words of Nietzsche's Zarathustra: "Dead are all the gods." One knows the tale; it has been told a thousand ways. It is the hero-cycle of the modern age, the wonder story of mankind's coming to maturity. The spell of the past, the bondage of tradition, was shattered with sure and mighty strokes. The dream-web of myth fell away;

the mind opened to full waking consciousness; and modern man emerged from ancient ignorance, like a butterfly from its cocoon, or like the sun at dawn from the womb of mother night.... The problem of mankind today, therefore, is precisely the opposite to that of men in the comparatively stable periods of those great coordinating mythologies which now are known as lies. Then all meaning was in the group, in the great anonymous forms, none in the self-expressive individual; today no meaning is in the group—none in the world: all is in the individual. But there the meaning is absolutely unconscious. One does not know toward what one moves. One does not know by what one is propelled. The lines of communication between the conscious and the unconscious zones of the human psyche have all been cut, and we have been split in two.[3]

Rollo May explains that it is not just the myths that guided us, but the rituals associated with the myths that cast a light on the meaning of our existence, our place in society, and the part we played in the ongoing myths of our people. Without either the myths or the associated rituals, we are cut off from others and from our true selves:

Many people in our day, separated from tradition and often cast out by society, are alone with no myths to guide them, no unquestioned rites to welcome them into community, no sacraments to initiate them into the holy—and so there is rarely anything holy.... Unrelated to the past, unconnected with the future, we hang as if in mid-air. We are like the shades Odysseus meets in the underworld, crying for news about the people up in the world but unable themselves to see anything.[4]

And so, from varying viewpoints, we find ourselves, modern humanity: "famished," "split in two," "cast out," hanging "in mid-air," and "crying" out for Myth. With nowhere else to turn, we at last look inwardly, only to find more of nothing. "When the prevailing myths fail to fit the varieties of man's plight, frustration expresses itself first in mythoclasm and then in the lonely search for internal identity."[5] This is a pitiable state to be sure, but the great sages foreseeing doom often fail to see salvation right in front of them. The myths have not died, nor did the symbols fade away into nothingness. Mythoclasm (the death of myth), has been assuaged and diverted by Mythopoeia (the creation of myth), in the genre of fantasy. Tolkien, the greatest of the mythopoeic fantasists, referred to the human being as "Sub-creator." His art is sub-creation, in that the "Primary World," the "real world," is the Creation of God — the Creator — who, in his beneficence, granted his consummate creature with the gift of sub-creation, which is revealed in his ability to create secondary worlds of infinite complexity and grace.[6]

When speaking of sub-creation in the mode of mythmaking and/or storytelling, Tolkien uses the term "higher mythology" in reference to tales that express a wish to explain or understand the Primary World, i.e. nature-myths, creation stories, and even — to a certain extent — the Old and New Testaments; while the "lower mythology" refers to tales that exist completely within the realm of sub-creation, i.e. fairy-tales and fantasy. But whether a tale is part of a lower or higher mythology, it is still primarily the same act of sub-creation. "In God's kingdom," Tolkien insists, "the presence of the greatest does not depress the small.... There is no fundamental difference between the higher and lower mythologies. Their peoples live, if they live at all, by the same life, just as in the mortal world do kings and peasants."[7] Hence, fantasy writing is a godlike endeavor, as Human Being, the sub-creator, uses his God-given gift to act in a way that emulates and aspires to the acts of the Primary Creator. As for the name of this gift, Tolkien refers to it simply as "Imagination."

The "successful sub-creator" makes a Secondary World which your mind can enter into. Inside this world, all that is "true" is anything that is in accord with the laws of that world. "You therefore believe it, while you are, as it were, inside. The moment disbelief arises, the spell is broken; the magic, or rather art, has failed."[8] The Secondary World, therefore, is real, as it retains "the inner consistency of reality."[9] It is in humankind's nature to create these worlds, because he was created in the image of his Creator, thus the worlds-within-the-world are an inherent part of the original design of the Primary World, and so the parts of the whole are as real as the whole itself.[10] As Tolkien explains, "Fantasy, the making or glimpsing of Other-worlds, was the heart of the desire of Faërie."[11]

Tolkien's short story "Leaf by Niggle" is perhaps the best explanation of his principle of sub-creationism. In the story, Niggle is a simple man, an artist, who is obsessed with painting a portrait of a landscape, which includes as a centerpiece a magnificent tree. But due to his many mundane obligations and chores, Niggle never completes the painting, even until the day he dies. However, in his afterlife, Niggle enters the world in which his beloved tree actually exists, and it is far more beautiful and intricate than he ever could have recreated in his own painting. "It's a gift!" Niggle exclaims, referring to the miraculous Tree; but he is also referring to his own gift, his ability to imagine the tree during his mortal life, and his further ability to create the image of the tree with his paints and brushes. His ability and drive to create (or, more precisely, to "sub-create") is the true gift. It is the same gift that links every sub-creator with the divine and immortal. This gift inside of us, in fact, is the only part of us that is divine and immortal. "When we have shuffled off this mortal coil," it is only this gift, and the things created with this gift, that remain. Though at many times during Niggle's life, and Tolkien's as well, the burden of his dreams seemed to him more like a curse, the final realization is that it is a gift, and therefore must be accepted without question, and shouldered through thick and through thin. Tolkien's letter to an acquaintance explains the inspiration behind his decision to dedicate so many years of his life to the singular purpose of creating a myth of his own, complete with its own world, creatures, languages, and histories. No rationale, reason, or justification is offered, because none are necessary:

> To many, Fantasy, this sub-creative art which plays strange tricks with the world and all that is in it, combining nouns and redistributing adjectives, has seemed suspect, if not illegitimate. To some it has seemed at least a childish folly, a thing only for peoples or for persons in their youth. As for its legitimacy I will say no more than to quote a brief passage from a letter I once wrote to a man who described myth and fairy-story as "lies": though to do him justice he was kind enough and confused enough to call fairy-story-making "Breathing lie through Silver.
>
> > "Dear Sir," I said — "Although now long estranged,
> > Man is not wholly lost nor wholly changed.
> > Dis-graced he may be, yet is not de-throned,
> > and keeps the rags of lordship once he owned:
> > Man, Sub-creator, the refracted Light
> > through whom is splintered from a single White
> > to many hues, and endlessly combined
> > in living shapes that move from mind to mind.
> > Though all the crannies of the world we filled
> > with Elves and Goblins, though we dared to build
> > Gods and their houses out of dark and light,
> > and sowed the seed of dragons–'twas our right
> > (used or misused). That right has not decayed:
> > we make still by the law in which we're made."[12]

The Realm of Faërie, as we have seen, is not just a depository of fanciful creatures, tales, and themes. Rather, it is a reflection of our deepest beliefs and our most profound anxieties. It offers meaningful triumphs in a world inherently devoid of meaning, and it provides answers in a world filled only with questions.

Chapter Notes

Preface

1. von Franz, p. 103.
2. Bettelheim, p. 88.

Introduction

1. Jung, *Collected Works,* p. 495.
2. Bettelheim, p. 69.
3. May, chap. 1.
4. Bettelheim, p. 62.
5. von Franz, pp. 158–159. "The one-side spiritualization of Christianity had brought about in certain classes an estrangement from the instinct. As Jung observes in *Psychology and Alchemy,* we are Christianized in the higher levels of the psyche, but down below we are still completely pagan. While fairy tales are for the most part entirely pagan, some of them ... contain symbols which one can understand only as being an attempt of the unconscious to unite again the sunken pagan tradition with the Christian field of consciousness."
6. May, p. 203.
7. Campbell, *The Hero with a Thousand Faces,* p. 57.
8. Freud, *Totem and Taboo,* chaps. 3 and 4.
9. Campbell, *The Hero with a Thousand Faces,* p. 336.
10. Tolkien, *Tree and Leaf,* p. 32.
11. Frazer, p. 43.
12. Jaynes, *The Origin of Consciousness in the Breakdown of the Bicameral Mind.*
13. Bruner, p. 285.
14. Tolkien, *Tree and Leaf,* p. 71.

Chapter One

1. Campbell, *The Hero with a Thousand Faces,* p. 19.
2. Bulfinch, p. 278.
3. Fromm, p. 12. "Symbolic language is language in which the world outside is a symbol of the world inside, a symbol for our souls and our minds."
4. May, pp. 30–31.
5. Ibid.
6. Ibid., p. 20.

7. Ibid., pp. 30–31.
8. Ibid., p. 54.
9. Ibid., pp. 30–31.
10. Jung, *The Portable Jung*, p. 321.
11. Tolkien, *Tree and Leaf*, p. 28.
12. Ibid., pp. 26–27.
13. Bettelheim, p. 25.
14. Ibid., p. 26. "It is unfortunate that both the English and French names for these stories emphasize the role of fairies in them — because in most, no fairies appear. Myths and fairy tales alike attain a definite form only when they are committed to writing and are no longer subject to continuous change. Before being written down, these stories were either condensed or vastly elaborated in the retelling over the centuries; some stories merged with others. All became modified by what the teller thought was of greatest interest to his listeners, by what his concerns of the moment or the special problems of his era were. Some fairy and folk stories evolved out of myths; others were incorporated into them. Both forms embodied the cumulative experience of a society as men wished to recall past wisdom for themselves and transmit it to future generations."
15. May, p. 196.
16. Tolkien, *Tree and Leaf*, p. 24.
17. Ibid., p. 25.
18. Ibid., p. 46.
19. Ibid., p. 66.
20. Ibid., p. 67.
21. Ibid., p. 57.
22. Ibid., p. 58.
23. William Wordsworth, *Poems, In Two Volumes* (1807).
24. Tolkien, *Tree and Leaf*, p. 68.
25. Bettelheim, p. 37. "The myth is pessimistic, while the fairy story is optimistic, no matter how terrifyingly serious some features of the story may be. It is this decisive difference which sets the fairy tale apart from other stories in which equally fantastic events occur, whether the happy outcome is due to the virtues of the hero, chance, or the interference of supernatural figures."
26. Campbell, *The Hero with a Thousand Faces*, p. 330. "Mythology has been interpreted by the modern intellect as a primitive, fumbling effort to explain the world of nature (Frazer); as a production of poetical fantasy from prehistoric times, misunderstood by succeeding ages (Müller); as a repository of allegorical instruction, to shape the individual to his group (Durkheim); as a group dream, symptomatic of archetypal urges within the depths of the human psyche (Jung); as the traditional vehicle of man's profoundest metaphysical insights (Coomaraswamy); and as God's Revelation to His children (the Church). Mythology is all of these. The various judgments are determined by the viewpoints of the judges. For when scrutinized in terms not of what it is but of how it functions, of how it has served mankind in the past, of how it may serve today, mythology shows itself to be as amenable as life itself to the obsessions and requirements of the individual, the race, the age."
27. Ibid., p. 21. "It is the business of mythology proper, and of the fairy-tale, to reveal the specific dangers and techniques of the dark interior way from tragedy to comedy. Hence the incidents are fantastic and 'unreal': they represent psychological, not physical, triumphs."
28. Ibid., p. 219.
29. Le Guin, p. 57.
30. Campbell, *The Hero with a Thousand Faces*, p. 111.
31. Raglan, chap. 3.

32. May, p. 290.
33. Raglan, p. 148.
34. Campbell, *The Hero with a Thousand Faces,* p. 331.
35. Ibid., pp. 7–8. "It has always been the prime function of mythology and rite to supply the symbols that carry the human spirit forward, in counteraction to those constant human fantasies that tend to tie it back. In fact, it may well be that the very high incidence of neuroticism among ourselves follows from the decline among us of such effective spiritual aid. We remain fixated to the unexercised images of our infancy, and hence disinclined to the necessary passages of our adulthood.... The psychoanalyst has to come along, at last, to assert again the tried wisdom of the older, forward-looking teachings of the masked medicine dancers and the witch-doctor-circumcisers; whereupon we find, as in the dream of the serpent bite, that the ageless initiation symbolism is produced spontaneously by the patient himself at the moment of the release. Apparently, there is something in these initiatory images so necessary to the psyche that if they are not supplied from without, through myth and ritual, they will have to be announced again, through dream, from within— lest our energies should remain locked in a banal, long-outmoded toy-room, at the bottom of the sea."
36. Bettelheim, p. 278.
37. Ibid., p. 35. Mircea Eliade, for one, describes these stories as "models for human behavior [that,] by that very fact, give meaning and value to life." Drawing on anthropological parallels, he and others suggest that myths and fairy tales were derived from, or give symbolic expression to, initiation rites or other *rites de passage*— such as metaphoric death of an old, inadequate self in order to be reborn on a higher plane of existence. He feels that this is why these tales meet a strongly felt need and are carriers of such deep meaning.
38. Campbell, *The Hero with a Thousand Faces,* p. 335. "The universal triumph of the secular state has thrown all religious organizations into such a definitely secondary, and finally ineffectual, position that religious pantomime is hardly more today than a sanctimonious exercise for Sunday morning."
39. May, p. 196.

Chapter Two

1. Dickerson and O'Hara, p. 16.
2. Joseph Campbell in *The Complete Grimms' Fairy Tales* (Campbell's entry in the "Folklorist Commentary" section"), p. 864. "If ever there was an art on which the whole community of mankind has worked— seasoned with the philosophy of the codger on the wharf and singing with the music of the spheres— it is this of the ageless tale. The folk tale is the primer of the picture-language of the soul."
3. Bettelheim, p. 66. "To the child, and to the adult who, like Socrates, knows that there is still a child in the wisest of us, fairy tales reveal truths about mankind and oneself."
4. Bettelheim, as quoted in Yolen, p. 24.
5. Fromm, p. 7. "But in spite of all these differences, all myths and all dreams have one thing in common, they are all 'written' in the same language, *symbolic language* ... the one universal language the human race has ever developed ... a language one must understand if one is to understand the meaning of myths, fairy tales, and dreams."
6. Tatar, p. 80.
7. Campbell, *The Hero with a Thousand Faces,* p. 220. "But if we are to grasp the full value of the materials, we must note that myths are not exactly comparable to dream. Their figures originate from the same sources— the unconscious wells of fantasy— and their grammar is the same, but they are not the spontaneous products of sleep. On the

contrary, their patterns are consciously controlled. And their understood function is to serve as a powerful picture language for the communication of traditional wisdom."

8. Tatar, p. 80.
9. Yolen, p. 89.
10. Tolkien, *Tree and Leaf,* pp. 31–32. "I do not think I was harmed by the horror *in the fairy tale setting,* out of whatever dark beliefs and practices of the past it may have come. Such stories have now a mythical or total (unanalysable) effect, an effect quite independent of the findings of Comparative Folk-lore, and one which it cannot spoil or explain; they open a door on Other Time, and if we pass through, though only for a moment, we stand outside our own time, outside Time itself, maybe."
11. Bettelheim, p. 62.
12. Campbell, *The Masks of God,* p. 170.
13. Bettelheim, p. 145.
14. Ibid., pp. 145–6.
15. Tatar, p. 190.
16. Tolkien, *The Lord of the Rings,* p. 981.
17. Lewis, *The Chronicles of Narnia,* p. 406.
18. Bettelheim, p. 107.
19. von Franz, p. 71.
20. Bettelheim, pp. 12–13.
21. Betty Comden, Adolph Green, and Jule Styne, lyricists for the 1954 Broadway musical, *Peter Pan.*
22. J. M. Barrie, playwright of the original *Peter Pan,* upon which the 1953 Disney movie was based.
23. Alexander, *The High King,* chap. 21.
24. Lewis, *The Chronicles of Narnia,* pp. 540–1.
25. Piaget, *The Child's Conception of the World.*
26. Bettelheim, pp. 45–6.
27. Piaget, *The Moral Judgment of the Child.*
28. Lewis, *The Chronicles of Narnia,* p. 752.
29. Ibid.
30. Ibid.

Chapter Three

1. Campbell, p. 289.
2. von Franz, p. 62.
3. Bettelheim, p. 41.
4. Raglan, pp. 113–4.
5. Ibid., p. 148.
6. Ibid.
7. Ibid., pp. 162–3.
8. Rank, p. 57.
9. Rank, p. 62.
10. Bettelheim, p. 68.
11. Rank, p. 63.
12. Campbell, *The Hero with a Thousand Faces,* p. 23.
13. Bulfinch, p. 369.
14. Exodus 3:10.
15. Exodus 3:11.
16. Exodus 3:12.
17. Exodus 4:1.

18. Exodus 4:10.
19. Exodus 4:11–12.
20. Exodus 4:13.
21. Rowling, *Harry Potter and the Sorcerer's Stone*, p. 82.
22. Campbell, *The Hero with a Thousand Faces*, p. 90.
23. Bettelheim, p. 183.
24. Tolkien, *The Lord of the Rings*, p. 356.
25. Rowling, *Harry Potter and the Sorcerer's Stone*, p. 294.
26. Steve Kloves, screenwriter for the film *Harry Potter and the Sorcerer's Stone* (2001).
27. Campbell, *The Hero with a Thousand Faces*, p. 130.
28. Ibid., p. 303.
29. Ibid., p. 167.
30. Ibid., p. 170.
31. Ibid., p. 178.
32. Ibid., p. 188.
33. Ibid., p. 289.

Chapter Four

1. Buckley and Gottlieb.
2. Géza Róheim, as quoted by Joseph Campbell in *The Masks of God*, p. 103. "It is a well-known fact that the sight of the bleeding vagina produces castration anxiety in the male."
3. Research and Forecasts, Inc., *The Tampax Report: Summary of Survey Results on a Study of Attitudes Towards Menstruation*. New York: Research and Forecasts, 1981.
4. May, p. 203.
5. Grimm and Grimm, p. 296.
6. Bettelheim, p. 139.
7. Mallet, p. 179.
8. Grimm and Grimm, p. 93.
9. Fromm, p. 240.
10. Bettelheim, p. 173.
11. Ibid., p. 176.
12. *Funk and Wagnall's Dictionary of Folklore* (New York: Harper and Row, 1950).
13. Garry and El-Shamy, p. 238.
14. Bettelheim, p. 265.
15. Garry and El-Shamy, p. 421.
16. Ibid., p. 435.
17. Grimm and Grimm, p. 110.
18. Garry and El-Shamy, p. 432.
19. Grimm and Grimm, p. 172.
20. Bettelheim, pp. 232–3.
21. Grimm and Grimm, p. 172.
22. Ibid., p. 173.
23. May, chap. 11.
24. Yolen, p. 22.
25. Bettelheim, p. 219. "Three is a mystical and often a holy number, and was so long before the Christian doctrine of the Holy Trinity. It is the threesome of snake, Eve, and Adam which, according to the Bible, makes for carnal knowledge. In the unconscious, the number three stands for sex, because each sex has three visible sex characteristics: penis and the two testes in the male; vagina and the two breasts in the female.
26. Ibid., p. 202.
27. Grimm and Grimm, p. 181.

28. Bettelheim, p. 207. "The queen ... thought she had eaten Snow White's lungs and liver. In primitive thought and custom, one acquires the powers or characteristics or what one eats. The queen, jealous of Snow White's beauty, wanted to incorporate Snow White's attractiveness, as symbolized by her internal organs."

29. Grimm and Grimm, p. 155.

30. Ibid.

31. Garry and El-Shamy, p. 119.

32. Grimm and Grimm, p. 156.

33. Ibid.

34. Ibid.

35. Ibid.

36. Ibid. p. 157.

37. Tolkien, *Tree and Leaf*, p. 68. "Even when a prohibition in a fairy-story is guessed to be derived from some taboo once practised long ago, it has probably been preserved in the later stages of the tale's history because of the great mythical significance of prohibition. A sense of that significance may indeed have lain behind some of the taboos themselves. Thou shalt not — or else thou shalt depart beggared into endless regret. The gentlest "nursery-tales" know it. Even Peter Rabbit was forbidden a garden, lost his blue coat, and took sick. The Locked Door stands as an eternal Temptation."

38. Bettelheim, p. 295.

39. Cashdan, p. 192.

40. Tatar, p. 159.

Chapter Five

1. Cashdan, p. 189. "The fantasy of the wicked stepmother not only preserves the good mother intact, it also prevents having to feel guilty about one's angry thoughts and wishes about her — a guilt which would seriously interfere with the good relation to Mother."

2. Bettelheim, p. 94. "The witch ... in her opposite aspects is a reincarnation of the all-good of infancy and the all-bad mother of the oedipal crisis. But she is no longer seen halfway realistically, as a mother who is lovingly all-giving and an opposite stepmother who is rejectingly demanding, but entirely unrealistically, as either superhumanly rewarding or inhumanly destructive. These two aspects of the witch are clearly delineated in fairy tales where the hero, lost in the forest, encounters an irresistibly attractive witch who, at first, satisfies all his desires during their relation. This is the all-giving mother of our infancy, whom we all hope to encounter in our life."

3. Campbell, *The Hero with a Thousand Faces*, p. 110. "The universal goddess makes her appearance to men under a multitude of guises; for the effects of creation are multitudinous, complex, and of mutually contradictory kind when experienced from the viewpoint of the created world. The mother of life is at the same time the mother of death; she is masked in the ugly demonesses of famine and disease."

4. Jung, *The Archetypes and the Collective Unconscious*, p. 82.

5. Bettelheim, p. 69.

6. Campbell, *The Hero with a Thousand Faces*, p. 92.

7. Lewis, *The Chronicles of Narnia*, 147.

8. Campbell, *The Masks of God*, pp. 73–4.

9. Klein, p. 170.

10. Grimm and Grimm, p. 315.

11. Ibid., p. 186.

12. See, for example, the recent media sensation over the Casey Anthony case.

13. Tatar, p. 78.

14. Ibid., p. 140. "The many facets of maternal evil in fairy tales represent the obverse of all the positive qualities associated with mothers. Instead of functioning as nurturers and providers, cannibalistic female villains withhold food and threaten to turn children into their own source of nourishment, reincorporating them into the bodies that gave birth to them. Like the Jungian *magna mater,* they take ferocious possessiveness to an extreme. "Now the children are in my body," one mother-in-law triumphantly declares. These figures work hard to earn the trust of their victims with magnanimous maternal behavior, then reveal their true colors as cannibalistic monsters."
15. Campbell, *The Masks of God,* p. 68.
16. Grimm and Grimm, p. 158.
17. Ibid.
18. Ibid., p. 143.
19. Mallet, p. 83.
20. Ibid., p. 87.

Chapter Six

1. Campbell, *The Hero with a Thousand Faces,* pp. 59–60. "Not infrequently, the supernatural helper is masculine in form. In fairy lore it may be some little fellow of the wood, some wizard, hermit, shepherd, or smith, who appears, to supply the amulets and advice that the hero will require. The higher mythologies develop the role in the great figure of the guide, the teacher, the ferryman, the conductor of souls to the afterworld. In classical myth this is Hermes-Mercury; in Egyptian, usually Thoth (the ibis god, the baboon god); in Christian, the Holy Ghost. Goethe presents the masculine guide in *Faust* as Mephistopheles — and not infrequently the dangerous aspect of the 'mercurial' figure is stressed; for he is the lurer of the innocent soul into realms of trial. In Dante's vision the part is played by Virgil, who yields to Beatrice at the threshold of Paradise."
2. Campbell, *The Hero with a Thousand Faces,* p. 57: "For those who have not refused the call, the first encounter of the hero-journey is with a protective figure (often a little old crone or old man) who provides the adventurer with amulets against the dragon forces he is about to pass."
3. Carter, *Understanding Religious Sacrifice.*
4. Frazer, chap. 3.
5. Campbell, *The Hero with a Thousand Faces,* p. 303.
6. Ibid.
7. Ibid.
8. Ibid., p. 289.
9. Frazer, pp. 309–330.
10. Ibid., p. 324.
11. Judges 11:30–39.
12. Tolkien, *The Lord of the Rings,* pp. 832–835.
13. Lewis, *The Chronicles of Narnia,* p. 182.

Chapter Seven

1. Freud, *The Complete Psychological Works,* p. 808.
2. Ibid., p. 915.
3. Ibid., pp. 915–916.
4. Ibid., pp. 916–918.
5. Ibid., pp. 924–925.
6. Freud, *Totem and Taboo,* chap. 3.
7. Freud, *The Complete Psychological Works,* p. 925.

8. Campbell, *The Power of Myth*, pp. 76–78.
9. Jaffe, pp. 262–3.
10. Ibid., pp. 263–4.
11. Jung, *The Archetypes and the Collective Unconscious*, p. 125.
12. Campbell, *The Hero with a Thousand Faces*, p. 336.
13. Jung, *The Archetypes and the Collective Unconscious*, p. 6.
14. Ibid., p. 252.
15. Rowling, *Harry Potter and the Prisoner of Azkaban*, p. 237.
16. Lewis, *The Chronicles of Narnia*, p. 773.
17. Tatar, p. 177.
18. Bettelheim, p. 297.
19. Ibid., p. 283.
20. Baring-Gould, *The Book of Werewolves*.
21. Ibid.
22. Scott, pp. 132–3.
23. Rowling, *Harry Potter and the Prisoner of Azkaban*.
24. Ibid.
25. Alexander, *The Book of Three*, chap. 13.
26. Lewis, *The Chronicles of Narnia*, pp. 271–273.
27. Tolkien, *The Hobbit*, pp. 188–119.
28. Genesis 3:1–3:5, Numbers 22:28.
29. Tolkien, *Tree and Leaf*, p. 53.
30. Schwartz, p. 434.
31. Jung, *The Archetypes and the Collective Unconscious*, p. 252.
32. Lewis, *The Chronicles of Narnia*, p. 669.
33. Ibid., p. 685.
34. Rowling, *Harry Potter and the Sorcerer's Stone*, p. 192.
35. May, pp. 200–201.
36. Bettelheim, p. 101.
37. Ibid., p. 290.
38. Jones, p. 99.
39. Campbell, *The Hero with a Thousand Faces*, p. 43.
40. von Franz, p. 73.
41. Grimm and Grimm, p. 171.
42. Bettelheim, p. 317.
43. Mallet, p. 180.
44. Orenstein, *Cinderella Ate My Daughter*.
45. Rank, p. 65.
46. Bettelheim, p. 210.
47. Ibid., pp. 27–28.
48. Jones, p. 100.
49. von Franz, p. 122.
50. Ibid., pp. 123–124.
51. Tolkien, *The Tolkien Reader*, "Farmer Giles of Ham," pp. 126–127.
52. Tolkien, *The Silmarillion*, p. 47.
53. Tolkien, *The Hobbit*, p. 70.
54. Tolkien, *The Tolkien Reader*, Preface, p. xvi. "Anyway, all this stuff is mainly concerned with Fall, Mortality, and the Machine. With Fall inevitably.... Mortality ... as it affects art and the creative (or as I should say, sub-creative) desire.... It has various opportunities of 'Fall.' It may become possessive, clinging to the things made as its own, the sub-creator wishes to be the Lord and the God of his private creation. He will rebel against the laws of the Creator — especially against mortality. Both of these (alone or together)

will lead to the desire for Power, for making the will more quickly effective — and so to the Machine (or Magic). By the last I intend all use of external plans or devices (apparatus) instead of developments of the inherent powers or talents — or even the use of these talents with the corrupted motive of dominating: bull-dozing the real world, or coercing others wills. The Machine is our more obvious modern form though more closely related to Magic than is usually recognized."

55. Rowling, *Harry Potter and the Sorcerer's Stone*, p. 72.
56. Frazer, pp. 168–169.
57. Campbell, *The Hero with a Thousand Faces*, p. 337.
58. Tolkien, *The Hobbit*, pp. 35–6.
59. Ibid., pp. 35–6.
60. Nesse, Arne Öhman.
61. Ibid.
62. Campbell, *The Masks of God*, pp. 73–4.
63. Rowling, *Harry Potter and the Prisoner of Azkaban*, p. 69.

Chapter Eight

1. Tolkien, *Tree and Leaf*, p. 33.
2. Freud, *Totem and Taboo*, p. 99.
3. Jung, *Man and His Symbols*, p. 30.
4. Frazer, p. 58.
5. Ibid, p. 59.
6. Tolkien, *Tree and Leaf*, p. 53.
7. Ibid., pp. 10–13.
8. Frazer, pp. 476–477.
9. Campbell, *The Hero with a Thousand Faces*, p. 221. "The universal doctrine teaches that all the visible structures of the world — all things and beings — are the effects of a ubiquitous power out of which they rise, which supports and fills them during the period of their manifestation, and back into which they must ultimately dissolve. This is the power known to science as energy, to the Melanesians as *mana*, to the Sioux Indians as *wakonda*, the Hindus as Sakti, and the Christians as the power of God. Its manifestation in the psyche is termed, by the psychoanalysts, *libido*."
10. Dickerson and O'Hara, pp. 235–242. "The first view toward magical power sees it as inherent in the magician or wizard himself or herself.... Tolkien's wizard Gandalf and Le Guin's mage Ged both are full of native power. They learn certain spells and words of power, but these act more to release their own powers than to conjure up some external force.... Yet another type of magic is the magic of words. Spells work because words have power. We see this throughout Rowling's books. And it is a teaching not only consistent with, but *fundamental* to Christian scripture. God created the world, we are told in Genesis 1, through language. He spoke and it happened."
11. Piaget, *The Origins of Intelligence*.
12. Ernst Cassier, as quoted in Garry and El-Shamy, p. 115.
13. Garry and El-Shamy, p. 116.
14. Trachtenberg, p. 83.
15. Ibid., p. 81.
16. Ibid., p. 82.
17. Ursula Le Guin, from *The Wizard of Earthsea*, as quoted in Dickerson and O'Hara, p. 177.
18. Malinowski, "The Language of Magic and Gardening."
19. Trachtenberg, p. 83.
20. Tolkien, *The Lord of the Rings*, p. 656.

21. Rowling, *Harry Potter and the Sorcerer's Stone*, p. 298.
22. Frazer, p. 147.
23. Raglan, p. 111.
24. Tolkien, *The Tolkien Reader*, "Farmer Giles of Ham," p. 147.
25. Ibid.
26. Trachtenberg, p. 162.
27. Jung, *The Archetypes of the Collective Unconscious*, p. 20.
28. *The Wizard of Oz*, the 1939 film, original book by Frank L. Baum, screenplay by Noah Langley.
29. Tolkien, *The Hobbit*, p. 220.
30. Bettelheim, p. 77.
31. Garry and El-Shamy, p. 160.
32. Tolkien, *The Lord of the Rings*, p. 404.
33. William Congreve, *The Mourning Bride* (1697).
34. Trachtenberg, p. 120.
35. Tolkien, *The Lord of the Rings*, p. vii.
36. Trachtenberg, pp. 121–122.
37. Bettelheim, p. 219.
38. Campbell, *Masks of God*, p. 77.
39. Jung, *The Archetypes of the Collective Unconscious*.
40. Trachtenberg, p. 122.
41. Ibid., pp. 122–3.

Chapter Nine

1. As quoted in Jaynes, *The Origin of Consciousness...*, p. 313.
2. Ibid., pp. 84–85.
3. Jaynes, "Consciousness and the Voices of the Mind," p. 3.
4. Ibid, p. 8.
5. Ibid, p. 6.
6. Jaynes, *The Origin of Consciousness...*, p. 62.
7. Jaynes, "Consciousness and the Voices of the Mind," p. 6.
8. Ibid., p. 8.
9. See Bibliography for complete citation.
10. Woodward and Tower, p. 44.
11. Freud, *The Interpretation of Dreams*.
12. Fromm, p. 18.
13. With the exception of those moments in which we wake up while dreaming, at which time we are conscious that we are/were dreaming. Furthermore, the images and experiences revealed to our conscious minds in that moment of conscious intrusion into the dreamscape may, on occasion, offer insight, which can then affect our decision-making and volition.
14. Rollo May, Erich Fromm, Sigmund Freud, and Carl Jung have all used the term "hallucinatory" in reference to dream imagery.
15. With the exception of Psychoanalysis, which posits that dreams offer important insight into unconscious issues, as Freud declared: "Dreams are the royal road to the unconscious."
16. Jaynes, "Consciousness and the Voices of the Mind," p. 6.
17. Jung as quoted in Fromm, p. 97.
18. Jung, *Psychology and Religion*, pp. 45–49.
19. Ibid.
20. Ibid., p. 46.

21. Fromm, pp. 5–6.
22. Jung, as quoted in McGuen, p. 94.
23. Fromm, p. 7.
24. From the *Lubdul Bel Nemequi*, as quoted in Jaynes, "Consciousness and Voices of the Mind," p. 12.
25. Jaynes, "Consciousness and Voices of the Mind," p. 294.
26. Zechariah 13: 2–4.
27. Jaynes, "Consciousness and Voices of the Mind," p. 313.
28. Ibid., pp. 396–397.
29. Ibid., p. 397.
30. Dawkins, *The God Delusion*.

Conclusion

1. May, p. 12.
2. Friedrich Nietzsche, from *The Birth of Tragedy from the Spirit of Music*, as quoted in May, p. 11.
3. Campbell, *The Hero with a Thousand Faces*, pp. 333–334.
4. Ibid.
5. Jerome Bruner, "Myth and Identity," in *Myth and Mythmaking*, ed. Henry A. Murray (New York: George Braziller, 1960), as quoted in May, p. 16.
6. Tolkien, *Tree and Leaf*, p. 23.
7. Ibid., p. 24.
8. Ibid., p. 37.
9. Ibid., p. 72. "But this story is supreme; and it is true. Art has been verified. God is the Lord, of angels, and of men — and of elves. Legend and History have met and fused."
10. Ibid., p. 72. "I would venture to say that approaching the Christian Story from this direction, it has long been my feeling (a joyous feeling) that God redeemed the corrupt making-creatures, men, in a way fitting to this aspect, as to others, of their strange nature. The Gospels contain a fairy-story, or a story of a larger kind which embraces all the essence of fairy-stories. They contain many marvels — peculiarly artistic, beautiful, and moving: 'mythical' in their perfect, self-contained significance; and among the marvels is the greatest and most complete conceivable eucatastrophe.* But this story has entered History and the primary world; the desire and aspiration of sub-creation has been raised to the fulfillment of Creation. The Birth of Christ is the eucatastrophe of Man's history. The Resurrection is the eucatastrophe of the Incarnation. This story begins and ends in joy. It has pre-eminently the 'inner consistency of reality.' There is no tale ever told that men would rather find true, and none which so many skeptical men have accepted as true on its own merits. For the Art of it has the supremely convincing tone of Primary Art, that is, of Creation. To reject it leads either to sadness or death."
11. Ibid., p. 41.
12. Ibid., p. 72. "The Christian has still to work, with mind as well as body, to suffer hope, and die; but he may now, perhaps, fairly dare to guess that in Fantasy he may actually assist in the effoliation and multiple enrichment of creation. All tales may come true; and yet, at the last, redeemed, they may be as like and as unlike the forms that we give them as Man, finally redeemed, will be like and unlike the fallen that we know."

Eucatastrophe is Tolkien's term for the typical ending of a fairytale or fantasy story, when what seems to be an inevitable catastrophe for the heroes is turned around suddenly and completely, becoming a complete victory.

Bibliography

Alexander, Lloyd. *The Black Cauldron*. New York: Bantam Doubleday Dell Books for Young Readers, 1965.

_____. *The Book of Three*. New York: Bantam Doubleday Dell Books for Young Readers, 1964.

_____. *The Castle of Llyr*. New York: Bantam Doubleday Dell Books for Young Readers, 1966.

_____. *The High King*. New York: Bantam Doubleday Dell Books for Young Readers, 1968.

_____. *Taran Wanderer*. New York: Bantam Doubleday Dell Books for Young Readers, 1967.

Baring-Gould, Sabine. *The Book of Werewolves: Being an Account of a Terrible Superstition*, 1865. New York: Causeway Books, 1973.

Beane, W. C., and W. G. Doty. *Myths, Rites, Symbols: A Mircea Eliade Reader*. New York: Harper Colophon, 1976.

Bettelheim, Bruno. *The Uses of Enchantment: The Meaning and Importance of Fairy Tales*. New York: Alfred A. Knopf, 1976.

Bruner, Jerome. "Myth and Identity." In *Myth and Mythmaking*, ed. Henry A. Murray. New York: George Braziller, 1960.

Buckley, T., and A. Gottlieb, eds. *Blood Magic: The Anthropology of Menstruation*. Berkeley: University of California Press, 1988.

Bulfinch, Thomas. *Bulfinch's Mythology*. New York: T.Y. Crowell, 1947.

Campbell, Joseph. *The Hero with a Thousand Faces*. Princeton: Princeton University Press, 1949.

_____. *The Masks of God: Primitive Mythology*. New York: Viking, 1959.

_____. *The Power of Myth, with Bill Moyers*. New York: Doubleday, 1988.

Carter, Jeffrey. *Understanding Religious Sacrifice*. New York: Continuum Books, 2003.

Cashdan, Sheldon. *The Witch Must Die: The Hidden Meaning of Fairy Tales*. New York: Basic Books, 1999.

Dawkins, Richard. *The God Delusion*. New York: Mariner Books, 2008.

Dickerson, Matthew, and David O'Hara. *From Homer to Harry Potter: A Handbook on Myth and Fantasy*. Grand Rapids: Brazos Press, 2006.

Frazer, Sir James George. *The Golden Bough: A Study in Magic and Religion*. New York: Touchstone, 1922.

Freud, Sigmund. *The Complete Psychological Works: Standard Edition*. 24 vols. ed. J. Strachey. London: Hogarth Press, 1956.

_____. *The Interpretation of Dreams*. In *The Complete Psychological Works: Standard Edition*, vols. 4 & 5, 1900.

_____. *The Psychopathology of Everyday Life*. In *The Complete Psychological Works: Standard Edition*, vol. 6, 1901.

_____. *Totem and Taboo: Some Points of Agreement Between the Mental Lives of Savages and Neurotics*. New York: Vintage Books, 1918.

Fromm, Erich. *The Forgotten Language: An Introduction to the Understanding of Dreams, Fairy Tales, and Myths*. New York: Grover Press, 1951.

Garry, Jane, and Hasan El-Shamy, eds. *Archetypes and Motifs in Folklore and Literature: A Handbook*. London: M.E. Sharpe, 2005.

Heuscher, Julius E. *A Psychiatric Study of Fairy Tales: Their Origin, Meaning and Usefulness*. Springfield, IL: Charles C. Thomas, 1963.

Jackson, Rosemary. *Fantasy: The Literature of Subversion*. New York: Routledge, 1981.

Jaffé, Aniela. "Symbolism in the Visual Arts." In *Man and His Symbols*, ed. Carl G. Jung. New York: Dell, 1964.

Jaynes, Julian. "Consciousness and the Voices of the Mind." *Canadian Psychology*, Volume 27. 2 (1986).

_____. *The Origin of Consciousness in the Breakdown of the Bicameral Mind*. Boston: Houghton Mifflin, 1976.

Jones, Ernest. "Psychoanalysis and Folklore." In *The Study of Folklore*, ed. Alan Dundes. Englewood Cliffs, NJ: Prentice Hall, 1965.

Jung, Carl G. *Archetypes and the Collective Unconscious*. In *Collected Works*, Vol. 9, 1936.

_____. *Collected Works*. H. Read, M. Fordham and G. Adler, eds. Princeton: Princeton University Press, 1953.

_____. *The Integration of the Personality*. In *Collected Works*, Vol. 11, 1939.

_____. *Man and His Symbols*. New York: Doubleday, 1964.

_____. *Memories, Dreams and Reflections*. New York: Random House, 1961.

_____. *The Portable Jung*. Ed. Joseph Campbell. New York: Viking Penguin, 1971.

_____. *Psychology and Religion*. New Haven: Yale University Press, 1960.

_____. *Psychological Aspects of the Mother Archetype*. In *Collected Works*, Vol. 9, 1960.

_____. *Synchronicity: An Acausal Connecting Principle*. In *Collected Works*, Vol. 8, 1936.

_____. *Two Essays on Analytical Psychology*. In *Collected Works*, Vol. 7, 1951.

Klein, Melanie. "Early Stages of the Oedipus Conflict." *International Journal of Psycho-Analysis*, 9 (1928), 167–180. Reprinted in *The Writings of Melanie Klein*, vol. 1. New York: Free Press, 1975.

Kuijsten, Marcel. *Reflections on the Dawn of Consciousness: Julian Jaynes's Bicameral Mind Theory Revisited*. New York: Julian Jaynes Society, 2008.

Le Guin, Ursula K. *The Language of the Night: Essays on Fantasy and Science Fiction*. New York: G.P. Putnam's Sons, 1979.

Lewis, C.S. *The Chronicles of Narnia*. New York: HarperCollins, 1982.

_____. *Of Other Worlds: Essays and Stories*. New York: Harcourt, Brace, & World, 1967.

_____. *Studies in Worlds*. London: Cambridge University Press, 1967.

Malinowski, Bronisław. "The Language of Magic and Gardening." In *Coral Gardens and Their Magic*. New York: Dover, 1935.

Mallet, Carl-Heinz. *Fairy Tales and Children: The Psychology of Children Revealed through Four of Grimm's Fairy Tales*. New York: Schocken Books, 1984.

Manlove, C.N. *Modern Fantasy: Five Studies*. London: Cambridge University Press, 1975.

May, Rollo. *The Cry for Myth*. New York: Norton, 1991.

McGuen, William G. *The Bicameral Brain and Human Behavior*. New York: Vantage Press, 1988.

Nesse, Arne Öhman. "Face the Beast and Fear the Face: Animal and Social Fears as Prototypes for Evolutionary Analyses of Emotion." *Psychophysiology, 2*, Issue 3 (March 1986), pp. 123–145.

Orenstein, Peggy. *Cinderella Ate My Daughter: Dispatches from the Front Lines of the New Girlie-Girl Culture.* New York: Harper, 2011.

Piaget, J. *The Child's Conception of the World.* London: Kegan Paul, Trench, Trubner, 1929.

_____. *The Moral Judgment of the Child.* London: Kegan Paul, Trench, Trubner, 1932.

_____. *The Origins of Intelligence in Children.* New York: International University Press, 1952.

Rank, Otto. *The Myth of the Birth of the Hero.* 1914. In *In Quest of the Hero.* Princeton, NJ: Princeton University Press, 1990.

Raglan, Lord. *The Hero: A Study in Tradition, Myth and Drama.* 1956. In *In Quest of the Hero.* Princeton, NJ: Princeton University Press, 1990.

Rowling, J.K. *Harry Potter and the Chamber of Secrets.* New York: Scholastic Press, 1999.

_____. *Harry Potter and the Deathly Hallows.* New York: Scholastic Press, 2007.

_____. *Harry Potter and the Goblet of Fire.* New York: Scholastic Press, 2000.

_____. *Harry Potter and the Half-Blood Prince.* New York: Scholastic Press, 2005.

_____. *Harry Potter and the Order of the Phoenix.* New York: Scholastic Press, 2003.

_____. *Harry Potter and the Prisoner of Azkaban.* New York: Scholastic Press, 1999.

_____. *Harry Potter and the Sorcerer's Stone.* New York: Scholastic Press, 1997.

Schwartz, Howard. *Tree of Souls: The Mythology of Judaism.* New York: Oxford University Press, 2004.

Scott, Michael. *The Alchemyst.* New York: Delacorte Press, 2007.

Tatar, Maria. *The Hard Facts of the Grimms' Fairy Tales.* Princeton, NJ: Princeton University Press, 1987.

Thompson, Stith. *The Folktale.* New York: Holt, Rinehart, & Winston, 1946.

_____, and John Gassner. *Our Heritage of World Literature.* New York: Dryden Press, 1946.

Tolkien, J.R.R. *The Hobbit.* New York: Random House, 1937.

_____. *The Lord of the Rings.* New York: Houghton Mifflin, 1994.

_____. *The Silmarillion.* Ed. Christopher Tolkien. New York: Random House, 1977.

_____. *The Tolkien Reader.* New York: Ballantine Books, 1966.

_____. *Tree and Leaf.* Boston: Houghton Mifflin, 1964.

Trachtenberg, Joshua. *Jewish Magic and Superstition: A Study in Folk Religion.* New York: Forgotten Books, 1939.

von Franz, Marie. *The Interpretation of Fairy Tales.* Boston: Shambala, 1970.

Woodward, W.R., and J.F. Tower. Julian Jaynes: Introducing His Life and Thought. In *Reflections on the Dawn of Consciousness: Julian Jaynes's Bicameral Mind Theory Revisited.* Ed. Marcel Kuijsten, 2008.

Yolen, Jane. *Touch Magic: Fantasy, Faërie & Folklore in the Literature of Childhood.* Little Rock: August House, 2000.

Zipes, Jack, translator. *The Complete Fairy Tales of the Brothers Grimm,* 3rd ed. New York: Bantam Books, 2003.

Index

193